TOUCHING
Cloudbase

The Complete Guide to Paragliding

4th Edition

Ian Currer

Published by :

Air Supplies, Dunvegan Lodge, Main St, Barmby Moor, York, YO42 4EB, UK

www.touching-cloudbase.com

First and second editions published by Leading edge Press and Publishing Ltd ISBN 0-948135-27-1; ISBN 0 948135-41-7

Third edition published by Air Supplies, March 1996 ISBN 0 9528862-0-0

Fourth, revised and updated edition published by Air Supplies, July 2003.

British Library Cataloguing in Publishing Data

A catalogue record for this book is available from te British Library.

ISBN: 0-9528862-1-9

Text: Ian Currer

Illustrations: Kathy Underwood & David Barber

Page design & layout: Neil Cruickshank

Cartoons: Bill Lehan

Printed and bound: Perfils, Spain

Contents

Acknowledgements

I am very grateful for the help and encouragement of many people and companies in producing this book.

In particular:

The late Bernard Kane and Stan Abbot for their encouragement back in 1990 in helping me get the first edition written.

Neil Cruickshank for the help and input and the hard work knocking it into shape.

Sue Larkin for the many hours at the keyboard.

Ian Brown and Martin Storer for their valuable input, and all the staff and instructors at Northern paragliding.

Thanks too to John Silvester, Gary Cook of Sky Systems, Jon Radford of Rad aviation, and Raul Rodriguez of the SAT team for their expert help.

The illustrations, which are so important in this type of book are the work of David Barber and Kathy Underwood. Several are based on original drawings by Rob Cruickshank.

Photo credits are included in the book but special thanks are due to Gus Hurst of f8 Photography, David Wooton of DW photography, Red Bull, FreeX Gmbh Swing Gliders, and Sup-air SARL.

And of course all the readers who have bought and given me feedback on previous editions.

All the mistakes are my own!

Finally thanks to Jackie for putting up with all the hassle.

Ian Currer July '03

Foreword

Welcome to the absorbing world of paragliding. With this new edition of Touching Cloudbase as your guide you will progress with confidence in this wonderful aerial sport. Ian Currer has been right at the front of paragliding training throughout its development, and would appear on any list of the most respected instructors in the business.

The techniques revealed in this book have evolved from Ian's many years of experience as a BHPA Examiner and member of the Safety Panel. Read everything with care. Paragliding is not just another sport to play at. It is real flying and you have to learn to be a *pilot*. Once you have developed the mental outlook that being a safe pilot demands, and have mastered the basic flying techniques under good instruction, the sky really is the limit!

With a good instructor and benign weather, the early stages of learning to handle a paraglider can be very easy. In a few hours you will be able to skim down the training hill and land under control. Those flights will probably be as exhilarating as anything else you have ever done, but they are simply a beginning. It is vital that all the different skills and knowledge essential to piloting are built up steadily, together. Launching and guiding the wing are a very small part of an overall picture which includes terrain, weather, air law, glider choice, site discipline and advanced cross-country flying. Here, Ian leads you expertly through all the steps in an easy and understandable way.

In the twelve years since the first edition of this book appeared, paragliders have developed amazingly in both performance and safety. This new version will enable anyone to be up-to-date with the best-proven practices, drawn from worldwide experience. It is far more than simply a book for novices. I am sure that paraglider pilots in many countries will make Touching Cloudbase an essential source book for guidance through to the highest stages of qualification. I have every confidence in recommending it.

Noel Whittall

Noel has been Chairman of the British Hang Gliding Association, Secretary of the Hang Gliding and Paragliding Commission of the FAI and is author of several books about flying for sport.

Introduction

If you choose or have chosen a course in paragliding, you will quite soon find that your dreams of walking on air and soaring like a bird are starting to be realised.

There are many challenges, and it will take some time and effort and patience to be a competent pilot, but it will be worth it for the rare experience of being one of the few who can enjoy truly free flight.

This handbook is meant as an aid to learning and can be referred to throughout and after your course.

IT IS NOT A "TEACH-YOURSELF" MANUAL

Paragliding is perhaps the simplest and easiest form of aviation. Thousands of people from all walks of life and a variety of age groups enjoy its unique appeal. However, like all adventure sports, paragliding can result in injury or death through error or ignorance, or if practiced in the wrong conditions.

THE ONLY SAFE WAY TO LEARN IS TO BE TRAINED BY A PROFESSIONAL, QUALIFIED INSTRUCTOR.

If you have any questions on any topic in this handbook or anything to do with flying do not hesitate to ask your instructor. There is no substitute for experience and he or she will be happy to help.

Throughout this book, both pilots and instructors are referred to as "he". This is only for the sake of writing style:

paragliding is in many ways an ideal sport for women and is certainly one in which women can participate on equal terms.

Further copies of this book, or a video version of Touching Cloudbase is also available. In that, many of the techniques, subjects and equipment referred to in this book are demonstrated. Copies should be available from wherever you bought this book. Alternatively you can obtain a list of stockists from:

Air Supplies
Dunvegan Lodge
Barmby Moor
York, UK
YO42 4EB

TEL: 44 (0) 1759 304404
FAX: 44 (0) 7092 305173
www.touching-cloudbase.com

A Brief History

Back in the 1940's on the east coast of America, just down the road from the site of the Wright brothers' first successful flights, another aviation pioneer was conducting experiments with kites made of pieces of glazed curtain material. His name was Dr. Francis Rogallo and, after much persuasion, his work was eventually followed up by his employers. NASA

It was 1948 when he filed for a patent for his flexible delta kite. From Dr. Rogallo's work came a whole mountain of research, testing and flexible wing (flex-wing) construction technology.

This resulted in both the Ryan Aircraft Company's bizarre looking aerial cargo-delivery wings - which used a folding "kite" wing - and the steerable recovery parachutes used by the Gemini series in the US space programme.

But by far the most important offshoot of this research (as far as we are concerned), is that the Rogallo wing was utilised by several latterday aviation pioneers as an excellent way of getting off the ground. This occurred either by means of a tow- launch behind a boat or a car, or by foot launching. Some of the earliest exponents of "hang gliding" (so called because, in those days, you literally had to hang on by your armpits), made their wings from bamboo, polythene and sticky tape. Not surprisingly, the golden rule was never to fly higher than you would care to fall.

Very soon, the machines were being made of stronger stuff and, as early as 1961, Tom Purcell Junior was tow launched on a Rogallo wing in the USA. The following year John Dickenson, a water skier, began to fly a Rogallo wing in preference to the flat kites that had sometimes been used. It was he who introduced the idea to two men whose names are recognised by hang glider pilots world wide today - Bill Moyes and Bill Bennett. These two dominated the early development of the sport of hang-gliding as we know it today.

The amazing Ryan aircraft

Left to right; Dr Francis Rogallo, Rick Ware, the author and Mark Dale of the BHPA. This photo was taken in 1985.
(Photo: Northern Paragliding.)

An early standard Rogallo hang-glider circa 1976. (Photo: Nick Goodyear)

How it all began ~ Jan Nielson foot-launches a 9-cell jump chute. (Photo: Vincene Muller)

Meanwhile, in the UK, Walter Neumark was flying new types of parachute designed by Lemoigne and Pioneer, which were capable of far superior performance and control than the existing types. Even back in 1961, Neumark, a sailplane pilot, could envisage a self-inflating parachute being used for soaring flight. Shortly afterwards, he wrote a manual, Operational procedures for ascending parachutes, and training began in what was to become known as parascending.

In 1968 Dan Poynter recorded in an article for Parachutist magazine that canopies were foot launched at Lake Placid in the USA during the annual parachute competition. In 1973 the British Parachute Association withdrew support for the emerging sport of parascending and the British Association of Parascending Clubs was formed. In 1989, the association changed its name to the British Association of Paragliding Clubs, reflecting its interest in a range of related pursuits from over-water towing operations, towed parascending and, most recently, foot launched paragliding. It was not until about 1980 that parachutes were foot launched regularly from hills.

At first it was a small minority of pilots, mostly in the French and Swiss Alps, who began to emulate the hang glider pilots by launching from the steep slopes with their ram-air "rigs", but the sport was to grow with surprising speed. In the UK there was Gerald Williams, a lone hang glider pilot who could be seen drifting to earth beneath his canopy in the Peak District while his fellows shook their heads and muttered that it would never catch on. In the intervening years the sport of hang gliding itself had become firmly established: the brightly coloured wings were to be seen on mountainsides on every continent but Antarctica. Agreements were made with landowners for the use of their hills, training procedures were established and a great deal was learned about the performance and stability of these extraordinary aircraft. Cross-country flights of hundreds of miles were made; even club pilots regularly used thermal and wave lift to gain thousands of feet of altitude.

Gerald Williams, still flying after 20 years!

An early foot-launched paraglider, the Off-Chute Mirage. (Photo: Northern Paragliding)

As the performance of the craft improved, so too did the expense and time required to learn to fly them. Despite the lure of being able to soar like a bird, the sport has always been for the few who had the considerable determination to carry the 70lb craft up the hill time and time again during their training and the courage to attempt what can appear a frightening or dangerous activity (although, of course, with current equipment and training techniques, hang gliding is in reality nowhere near as dangerous as many people might imagine).

In the early 1980's everything was in place for the birth of foot-launch paragliding as we know it today - the expertise and example of the hang gliding fraternity and the high performance ram-air canopies. The canopies being used were initially jump chutes designed to withstand the stress of opening in free-fall. It very soon became apparent that these stresses were not present with the less abrupt inflation of self-launch, and very soon manufacturers sprang up producing wings made from non-porous materials. Such fabrics would probably cause a modern paraglider to explode if it was opened by a free-falling skydiver at terminal velocity, but it offered a major performance advantage. Jump chutes also had to inflate evenly and rapidly and, as competitions often involve a near vertical descent to achieve target accuracy, these design criteria had led to the evolution of square canopies with very large cell entries and docile behaviour in the stall.

The paragliding manufacturers, however, had different criteria. They were looking for a very slow rate of descent and a good gliding performance and, as the wing was inflated before launch, they could afford to be less particular about instant opening. Very soon paragliders diverged totally from their jump 'chute roots. They utilised high-lift airfoils, narrow cell entries and long, slender wings, more akin to the shape of a hang glider.

In terms of aircraft development, the evolution of the hang glider had been remarkable. There had been precious little research done on the behaviour of aerofoils at speeds below 40mph but, even so, every year the designers and manufacturers came up with significant improvements in performance and stability.

There had, of course, been a number of failures, some of them fatal, and the national associations of the major hang gliding nations had introduced test facilities so that each new design could be thoroughly checked before being given a certificate of airworthiness.

If the development of hang gliders had been remarkable, that of paragliders was positively meteoric, with new and improved designs appearing on an almost monthly basis, although there has now been a sharp slowdown in terms of performance gain, mirroring the hang gliders development curve of the 70's and 80's.

Fortunately, because the national association in most countries is the same for both sports, the procedures and equipment for testing were already in place and in virtually all European countries at least, there is a mandatory test programme for new designs.

At the time of writing, the distance record for a paraglider is 421 km, achieved by circling and climbing in thermals and hopping from one cloud to the next, in the same way as hang-gliders and sailplanes have been doing for years. Perhaps more significant than this, though, is the sheer number of people attracted to the sport. In Alpine countries they number tens of thousands, and the activity is still growing in places as diverse as the UK, Australia, North and South America, India and the Far East.

In the UK, the sport was initially administered by the British Association of Parascending (later Paragliding) Clubs. In December 1990 the association voted to allow negotiations to begin to amalgamate with the British Hang- Gliding Association into one body. The following year, after much debate, the BHGA passed a similar motion. In 1992, the two associations amalgamated to form the British Hang-Gliding and Paragliding Association (BHPA).

Similar associations exist in most countries where flying takes place, and whilst this book is based on the practices in the UK, similar procedures (though sometimes less effectively regulated) are common worldwide.

Presently there are good training systems in many countries and the majority of manufacturers are supporting the airworthiness programmes for equipment. The accident rate for pilots is on a reassuringly downward slope, and paragliding is certainly getting cheaper! The sport now has a 15 year track record, and whilst we are still relatively young and are still learning, paragliding has become a well-established activity.

A modern paraglider. (Photo: Airwave gliders)

Health and Safety

Before you embark on a paragliding course, the school will probably ask you to sign a form attesting that you will not be under the influence of alcohol or drugs, and also that you are of reasonably sound body (they seldom enquire after your mind!). Flying itself actually requires very little physical effort in most circumstances. However, to fly well does require reasonable reactions and, certainly during the training period, you do need to be able to climb a fairly steep hill several times.

People of a wide variety of ages and occupations enjoy paragliding, but if you are daunted at the prospect of walking up a steep hill or have a history of epilepsy, heart complaints or other medical conditions, you should consult the school before signing up.

As a general rule the school will, in such instances, ask you to produce a doctor's note certifying that you are fit to fly.

Many schools require a similar note for pupils aged 55 or more.

Recent research has shown that a surprisingly high percentage of women over 40 exhibit signs of osteoporosis (loss of bone density) which may significantly increase the risk of sustaining a fracture in an impact situation. This is an important consideration in a sport like paragliding.

The Air Navigation Order states that you may not be the solo pilot of an aircraft below the age of 16. Those aged 18 or less must have written consent from their parent or guardian. You will also probably find somewhere on your booking conditions that the chief instructor reserves the right to refuse to train anyone he considers unfit or ill-prepared to fly. The reasons are self-evident. The schools primary concern is safety.

Partial deafness is usually no problem, provided the instructor is informed (in one instance a student pilot did not mention the fact that he was deaf in one ear – unfortunately, the radio system being used at the time only had a speaker on that side of the helmet!).

Flying requires good visual awareness, both for setting up a landing at the correct position and altitude, and also for knowing where other pilots are when you are flying: it becomes second nature to keep a kind of visual map of the position of other fliers which is constantly updated by glimpses as you turn, and through your peripheral vision.

If your sight is OK with glasses, that is fine, as you can wear them with no difficulty (though some people use a cord or elastic to make sure they stay in place). Contact lenses are less practical as they could fall out, and a heather covered hillside is not a good place to look for them. Any permanent visual impairment may make you unfit to fly, and again the instructor should ask for a doctor's certificate before accepting your booking.

Schools are sometimes asked by doctors for details of what is involved before issuing such a certificate. The standard reply is that the person must have a sound musculature and skeletal system, and have no problems with balance, coordination or visual perception. He must have a sound heart and respiratory system and be able to exert himself without ill effects. In practice the potential pilot should be able to run 50 metres, jump over a 0.5metre obstacle, be able to walk up a steep hillside, and be capable of falling over from a standing position without ill effect.

If you take up paragliding you are likely to be flying in close proximity to others, and whilst 99% of the time it is all fairly routine, at some point you may have to react very quickly and if you do not respond in a decisive and co-ordinated way you may seriously injure yourself and possibly others. There are a significant number of people who can (say) drive a car in reasonable safety but whose reactions are simply not sufficiently sharp to deal with the kind of situations that can occur in crowded airspace where others may be coming at you from any direction or where you may suddenly lose 50ft of altitude.

If you are not sure that this is the sport for you then it is important to have a frank discussion with your instructor before progressing on to the soaring stage.

Responsibility

There has been an ever-growing trend over the last few years in our society to hold someone responsible for any mishap that occurs. It is of course only proper that a negligent individual or company is called to account for their actions, but unfortunately the reverse of this coin is that there is a tendency (fuelled by the legal profession!) for individuals to abdicate taking responsibility for themselves.

Flying generally and paragliding particularly is very unforgiving of poor judgement; it is reliant on the vagaries of the wind and weather, which are not always predictable.

There have been instances of pupils who expect both to be paraglider pilots and to have their safety absolutely guaranteed. This is not possible. Even when learning you will probably be flying solo; the instructor is powerless to assist you other than by briefings and by advice on a radio. For this reason it is important that every potential pilot understands that he needs to accept the risks and take responsibility for himself. You must feel confident that you can cope with the exercise being attempted, and because the risks of an adventure sport like paragliding cannot be totally eradicated, you must be prepared to accept that risk.

Insurance

The BHPA's insurers cover individual pilots for their 3rd party liability, but it does not have any personal accident element. It is strongly recommended that anyone taking up the sport should ensure (for their own sake and that of their dependants) that they have suitable cover.

This is available from a variety of general insurance companies and for qualified pilots who are BHPA members there is very often no additional loading of premiums, (though there may well be a "no cover" period of weeks or months to minimise short term claims.)

Cover for loss of earnings through injury is also available from other sources, several pilots have policies with a friendly society, these are primarily savings plans

Flying suits are a convenient windproof layer. (Photo: Sup'Air)

with added loss of earnings cover. They are more expensive to maintain, but the beauty of them is that after a few years of contributions you have a lump sum..

For Paragliding only cover it is also possible to get a short term policy (available through your school and the BHPA). Whilst the scope is more limited than a regular permanent health policy it has the advantage of being instant and a "one off" premium and so is very convenient for those attending a course.

Third party cover is also available from most other national associations, but do check your situation if you are flying abroad. For British pilots used to free NHS treatments the cost of medical expenses can be very high in many countries. It is vital you get suitable medical and repatriation travel cover before flying abroad.

The other insurance worth mentioning is the commercial liability cover of schools. Due to a number of claims over the years it is becoming more difficult to obtain suitable commercial cover and the situation may soon exist where none is available. In such a case it is clearly more vital than ever that each student carries suitable personal injury cover.

Clothing

In the summer months or in warm climates it is not unusual to see pilots flying in shorts and T-shirts. However, until you have amassed a good deal of experience it is better to to wear something that offers more protection – it is quite possible that you will be falling over, or even being dragged along the ground. During your course you will be required to roll about on the grass or heather as part of your training, so do not wear anything that is too fragile or expensive! Gloves are invaluable as, even in summer, a good breeze on a hill-top can be cold, and when you are flying your hands are always in the airflow. A good wind-proof jacket is also essential in all but the best weather. If you are flying in winter, wear plenty of layers: it is easy to take things off if you have brought too much, and it can spoil your enjoyment and affect your concentration if you are shivering. If you take the sport up and fly regularly, you will soon find that temperature drops sharply with altitude, and the wind always finds the gaps between jackets and trousers. Many trousers have pockets that are difficult to get at when in a harness, for these reasons most pilots who fly regularly invest in a purpose built flying suit.

These suits have insulation in the front where it is most needed, zips to allow them to be put on and off without removing your boots, and are designed with pockets for radios etc in the right positions. All good flying centres will stock flying suits.

Good boots are essential.
(Photo: Patrick Holmes/UK Airsports)

Footwear

Good footwear is essential: during training you will be walking up hills and a good grip is necessary. If your landings are less than perfect, the ankles are the first set of shock absorbers available so something offering good support is a good idea. Hiking or fell boots are fine. In any event, bring spare shoes, as your flying gear may get wet. If you are serious about taking up the sport then there are some ideal boots that are light, waterproof and have good ankle support and grip, which are made especially for paragliding and most centres stock them.

Introduction to the Equipment

The Canopy

A paraglider is a simple aircraft, but in common with all other aircraft it is in fact the result of complex and painstaking design. Small changes in the line lengths or subtle alteration of the cut of the fabric can make the difference between a sweet responsive wing and one with poor characteristics.

The canopy is constructed of a top and bottom surface joined by a number of (usually) vertical segments. The resulting chambers are called cells. They have an opening at the front - the leading edge. Larger entries generally indicate a slower and more stable aircraft; narrow or valved entries are found on craft on which the aim is to maximise performance. Each cell is separated from its neighbours by an inter-cell wall. These define the shape of the wing section: the more inter-cell walls, the more accurate the

An aircraft that fits in a rucksack!
(Photo: FreeX)

control of the section of the wing, and the better the performance.

These walls feature several holes, or ports, so that air can pass from one cell to the next, helping to keep the internal pressure balanced and the wing evenly inflated. The front part of the cell walls is often reinforced with heavier fabric or mylar to give additional strength and stiffness. This helps the cells stay open for easier inflation and stability.

When it is fully inflated, the cell takes up an aerofoil shape with a flattish lower surface and a curved, or cambered, top surface. The point of maximum thickness usually occurs between 15 and 30

Inside an inflated cell.

per cent of the way back from the leading edge.

The rear of the wing is called the trailing edge. On a typical canopy there may be anything from 30 to 100 cells. Those in the centre will be longer than those at the tips, giving the canopy a tapered or elliptical shape; this shape, when viewed from above, is called the planform. Many

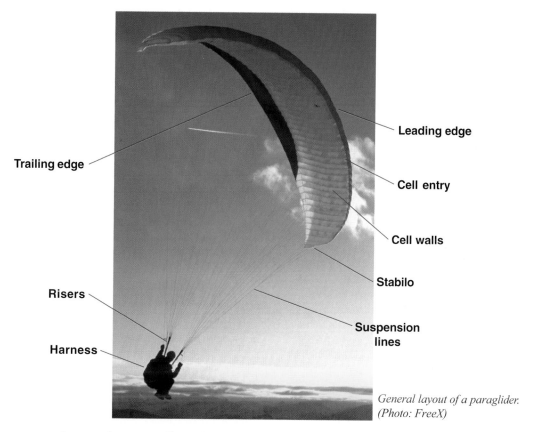

General layout of a paraglider.
(Photo: FreeX)

canopies may have small vertical areas at the tips, known as stabilos or "ears". Their function is to provide stability; stretch the wing as they are forced outwards and reduce induced drag.

On many designs the leading edge is a combination of open and sealed (closed) cells. The sealed cells are reliant on the internal pressure of the wing to remain inflated, and have the advantage of forming a well defined airfoil section. They also resist deflation in the case of a tuck as the air cannot easily escape; however, they can take longer to inflate initially or after a collapse. The designer's skill is in combining the different elements of cell entry shape, sealed or sometimes valved cells and internal airflow, to maximise performance and minimise instability.

Paragliders use non-porous coated fabrics (either nylon or polyester), and some of these may have an additional finishing coat to further protect against ultraviolet degradation.

The lines

The lines are made of very strong materials so that they can be kept thin to minimise drag and weight. There are two main types: Kevlar, which is a polyaramid (carbon fibre) material, usually encased in an outer sheath of Dacron (terylene) or something similar; and polyethylene, usually known as Dyneema or Technora (Spectra in the USA). Polyaramid material is extremely strong and has excellent resistance to stretching or shrinking. It is not temperature

Lines

sensitive. However, it requires regular checking as kinking or knotting around a small radius can easily damage it. This is most commonly used for the major suspension lines where retaining an accurate length is critical.

Polyethylene (dyneema) is also very strong and it is more flexible too, which tends to prolong its life, especially with hard use. Because it much more resistant to being knotted and pulled through pulleys etc, it is commonly used for the brake lines.

However, it is more likely to stretch or shrink and is fairly temperature sensitive, so lines of this material should be protected from high temperatures (being left in a car in full sun for example). Some gliders have used dyneema for main suspension lines, but for the reasons mentioned above this material

proved to have problems in retaining an accurate length. The golden rule with all line material is to check it regularly for stretch, shrinkage and strength.

For more details on the properties of line materials see Chapter 20: Packing & Care of Your Canopy.

In order to minimise drag and make the whole construction less complex, the lines branch into two (or more) about halfway up their length. Lines are referred to by their position on the canopy, A-lines being those at the leading edge and C or D-lines being those at the rear. The control lines are attached to the trailing edge terminating in a handle on the rear riser are often produced in a distinctive colour to make them easy to locate.

The risers

The risers connect the canopy to the harness. Usually made of one inch or 25mm webbing, they transfer the loads from the harness through the lines. There is usually one attachment point on each side of the harness to which the bottom of the risers are connected with a maillion or

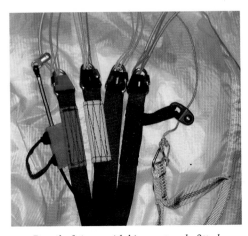

Detail of risers with big-ear toggle fitted.

carabiner. The tops of the risers (there may be three or four per side) terminate in small steel maillions or links to which the lines are attached. The risers give the pilot a convenient point to hold when launching and make it simple to swap one harness with another.

The rear risers also feature small rings or pulleys, known as keepers, through which the control lines pass. These, as the name suggests, prevent the control lines flying away out of reach in the wind. The control handles themselves, attached to these lines, are usually fastened to the riser by some easy release system such as a magnetic clasp or a popper. Virtually all modern canopies have an accelerator system attached, operated by a foot

Detail of magnetic popper for brake attachment.

stirrup. (These are discussed in more detail in Chapter 22)

The front (A) riser is frequently divided into two, or has a smaller branch attached. The outer portion supports just one or two lines. The reason for this is to make the "big ears"manoeuvre easier to perform and it also helps with certain aspects of ground handling.

A few models also feature trimmers so that the length of the rear riser can be adjusted in flight. These are most commonly found on tandem wings (where a foot operated accelerator is not practical) or on some high performance wings whose pilots are likely to require trim alterations in flight.

A modern harness with back protection.

The harness

Paragliding harnesses follow the same basic pattern - a solid seat plate, usually made of plywood, fibreglass, or a carbon composite, a webbing structure that includes the leg and waist straps and which also continues around the pilot's back and under the seat, and a fabric shell. The fabric is primarily for comfort, for providing storage space and a reserve parachute compartment, and to house any protective padding. There are a host of other features that may be included, such as attachments for accelerator systems, foot stirrups, compartments for radios or ballast, and various passive protection systems.

All harnesses include adjusters so you can refine the size and adjust the shape and flying position. There are a great variety of harnesses to choose from, varying from superlight versions for mountaineering (some without seat plates), those with sophisticated protection systems and racing harnesses designed for minimum drag. These types are covered in greater detail in Chapter 19.

Helmets

In a training environment you will probably be using an open face or adjustable helmet. It is important that your hearing is not impaired, as judging your airspeed is very much a function of hearing the airflow moving past your ears; and of course your instructor may be giving you commands by radio.

The lightweight adjustable types are good for walking up the hill- something you will be doing quite a bit of for the first few days, but when you come to purchase your first helmet there are a number of other factors to consider. Primarily you need protection - there is a CE certification standard for airsports helmets - fit, warmth, and of course, style!

Helmets are covered in more detail in Chapter 19.

Adjustable climbing-type helmet, often used in schools because of its versatility.

Full-face helmet. (Photo: f8 Photography)

How a Paraglider Flies

When any object is dropped, it will fall towards the surface of the earth. We cannot prevent this happening, but we can use a couple of techniques (and the atmosphere) to minimise the impact! One technique is to make the drag of the object very large in relation to its weight, so that it will fall slowly. And the second is to deflect or vector the force of gravity, so that we fall off to one side rather than straight down. Paragliders use a combination of both approaches. Clearly they are relatively large, and we can use the air to help us vector the force of gravity by using an aerofoil; which is essentially a shape that will slide sideways through the air in a stable and efficient way.

When a paraglider is fully inflated, it forms a solid wing with an aerofoil section that creates lift in the same way as that of a conventional aircraft. In order to fly, it must create enough lift to carry its own weight and that of its pilot, and it achieves this with gliding flight. The wing is constantly flying forwards and downwards through the air and in doing so causes the airflow over the wing section.

So how does an aerofoil work? Look at *Fig 5.1*. As the wing glides forwards and down, the molecules of air that hit the leading edge are divided into two streams, -those over and those under the canopy. Those below it are contacting the lower surface at a shallow angle and creating a high-pressure area. About one third of the aerofoils' lift is derived from this "push" or deflection. The molecules that pass over the top surface, however, are obliged to follow a longer path as they are forced upwards over the cambered top surface. As the curve continues, the flow is deflected further upwards, while at the same time the air above the aerofoil is doing its level best to remain undisturbed and not alter its position (or alter course if it is moving). This process is strengthened by the natural tendency of the air to try and drift away from the curved surface, rather like a car going around a bend at speed. The result of this is that the air flowing over the top of the section is squeezed between the physical barrier of the wing below it and the inertia of the "normal" air above it.

It behaves exactly like water being squeezed through a narrow space (like the end of a hosepipe) by accelerating, so the air is travelling more quickly over the top surface. At this point the physics becomes a little more complex, but the result of this acceleration is that the pressure reduces (Bernoulli's theorem). This

Fig 5.1: Airflow around a wing section.

low-pressure area generates a pulling force and contributes about two thirds of the lifting force of the wing.

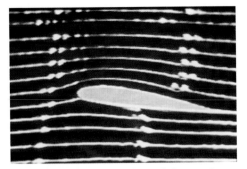

Photograph taken in a wind-tunnel showing the airflow over an aerofoil section. (Photo: Shell UK)

So far, we have established two forces acting on the canopy, gravity, which is acting to pull us down, and lift, acting upwards and slightly forwards. There is a third force as well; drag. This acts opposite to our direction of travel and reduces the speed and efficiency on the wing. The lift and drag combined are

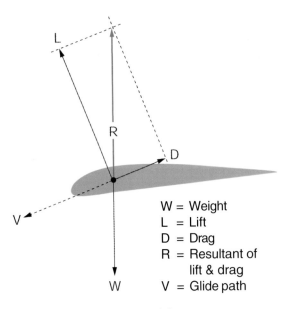

W = Weight
L = Lift
D = Drag
R = Resultant of lift & drag
V = Glide path

Fig 5.2: Forces on an aerofoil

shown in *Fig 5.2* as R-the resultant. (Drag is mentioned in more detail in chapter 5,Terms). When all these forces are in equilibrium, the wing will glide at a specific rate. This glide path is the actual direction of travel through the air. (V) - See *Fig 5.2*. Providing the canopy is flying with sufficient speed and at a suitable angle of attack, it will continue to glide correctly. But what happens if we disturb this equilibrium?

Firstly, let us suppose that the angle of attack is too low. This is not readily achievable in normal flight as, at high speeds, the drag created becomes too great to permit any further acceleration. However, if too low an angle is achieved, the soft aerofoil ceases to inflate properly and begins to deform, internal pressure drops, and as the cell entries cannot work and the load is removed from the front lines, the wing will collapse at the front. This is known as a "tuck" and is quite easy to bring about if the pilot is stationary on the ground. In the air, the pilot tends automatically to swing under the canopy to the correct position, but a tuck can happen in flight if the pilot has induced a low angle of attack in recovering from a stall for example, or in turbulent air.

A paraglider is generally fixed in its angle relative to the pilot (unless trim devices are fitted), but we can alter the angle of attack by use of the controls. There is a ratio between the lift and the drag generated, and by adding more drag (by braking) we can alter that ratio. This means that the wing is now moving forwards less rapidly and the airflow is at a higher angle of attack. (If you look up as you add brake, you can see the leading edge of the canopy move back slightly as

Fig 5.3: A stalled wing section caused by too high an angle of attack (A)

A

it takes up a more rearward position).

The initial result of this is an increase in the amount of lift - the greater the pressure difference between the top and bottom surfaces, the greater the lift. The point of maximum lift is known as the minimum sink rate. However, if the angle is increased too much, the air is unable to flow smoothly over the curve, and at the point at which the airflow breaks away (which in normal flight is next to the trailing edge), rushes forwards across the aerofoil until almost all the top surface is covered in a turbulent airflow. The low- pressure area is broken up and the wing ceases to work. This situation is a stall - see *Fig 5.3.*

Some canopies in certain circumstances will find a point of equilibrium even with

an angle of attack that is too high. The wing remains at least partially inflated but, because it has little or no forward speed, it is unable to generate sufficient lift and sinks very rapidly. This state is known as a "deep" or "parachutal" stall. If forward motion is lost altogether, by a sharp application of maximum brake for example, the internal pressure will drop and the cells will deflate. The aerofoil section is then lost. This is a "dynamic" or a "full" stall. Both deep and dynamic stalls can be recovered from easily, though this may involve considerable altitude loss - see Chapter 28, Instability & Recovery. For this reason, a paraglider - like an aircraft - should be flown at slightly above the absolute minimum speed to ensure a margin for error.

The controls and how they work

Paragliders can be steered by "weight" shift and most models have accelerator stirrups to add extra speed, but all of them rely principally upon the control lines. The term "controls" is used rather than the common name of brakes because, in addition to their function in controlling speed, they are also used for steering and to stabilise the canopy in

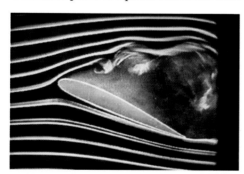

Photograph taken in a wind-tunnel showing the airflow over a stalled aerofoil section.
(Photo: Shell UK)

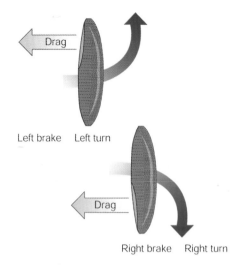

Fig 5.4: The mechanics of inducing a turn.

the event of a collapse. Each control is a single line, usually colour coded to prevent confusion with the suspension lines. Unlike them, it is not attached to the riser directly but runs through a ring or "keeper" attached to the rear riser, and ends in a handle. The top of the control line is divided into a "cascade" or "fan" of smaller lines which attach to the trailing edge at several points.

When a pilot pulls down one of the controls, the trailing edge of the canopy on that side is deflected downwards into the airflow. (See photo opposite). This has two effects - the first is to increase the angle of attack of that side of the canopy slightly and to increase the lift generated. The second effect is to massively increase the drag and reduce the airspeed of that side. These two effects work against each other, one trying to turn the canopy one way and one the other. On most conventional aircraft this creates the problem known as adverse yaw, which is usually overcome with the addition of a rudder. But, on a canopy, the drag created in this way is far more effective than any oppos-

ing effect of lift and the craft will always turn towards the deflected side. If both controls are applied at the same time, the wing will slow down uniformly and may also create slightly more lift. The further the controls are depressed the more drag is created and the slower the wing will fly until, eventually, the canopy will have such a high angle of attack that the wing will stall.

Obviously, if the canopy is being flown slowly and one control is raised, this will also produce a turn. The steepest turns are achieved by simultaneously raising one side and depressing the other. CAUTION - it is possible to stall one half of the wing in this way and enter a spin.

The controls also have three other uses: the first is on the ground during ground handling or a reverse launch where they can be used to manipulate the wing to change the height and position of the "wall". The second is to collapse the canopy after landing or if you are being dragged (see Chapter 16, Landing). The third use is to aid recovery from various unstable situations - tucks etc. - see chapter 28, Instability & Recovery.

The controls are the equivalent of brakes and steering wheel on a car combined.

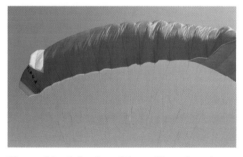

Photo of the deflection of the trailing edge when a large amount of brake is applied.

It is vital that they are in good order and free of hitches or wear. They are also the easiest part of the canopy to get into a tangle - always use the poppers or magnets provided to attach the controls to the riser after every landing.

View from below, clearly showing the deflection of the trailing edge during a right turn.

Terms

In many specialised areas of knowledge and activities people use technical language or jargon to describe a thing or concept. Paragliding is no different, and the language around pilots and in the training school is sometimes not all that clear to the newcomer. Paragliding uses regular aviation terms and of course quite a few of our own.

Below is a guide to the more commonly used and useful terms and what they mean.

Centre of pressure

Different areas of the aerofoil and the span of the canopy produce varying amounts of lift. For the purpose of showing this force, the term "centre of pressure" is often used. More accurately this is the centre of pressure difference, a theoretical balance point through which the lift can be said to act. This point does move back and forth as the angle of attack is altered. This knowledge is not relevant to the pilot in normal flight, but during the design and development phase the behaviour of the centre of pressure is critical, as it determines the recovery characteristics of the wing.

Drag

The term has already been mentioned a couple of times. What is drag? This is the thing that holds us back! It is the resistance of the air to anything passing through it, and it can be divided into two major categories.

Parasitic drag

Friction caused by any surface or obstruction (pilot, lines etc.) The faster you travel through the air the more parasitic drag you create. Doubling your speed quadruples the parasitic drag. Parasitic drag can be sub-divided again into components such as skin friction, form drag and profile drag. (The latter relates to the turbulence caused, for example, by moving any non-lifting surface through the air).

Induced drag

The action of an aerofoil disturbs the air as it passes through and this creates induced drag. There is always a little drag induced at the trailing edge where the airflow from above and below the aerofoil meet again at slightly different speeds. The majority of the induced drag, however, is normally created at the wing tips. The area of low pressure above the wing is "attractive" to the air at a higher pressure below the wing. But at the wingtips, it is easier for the air to flow around the end of the wing, and this is what happens. The result is a vortex at each tip - see *Fig 6.1* and photo below.

Photograph taken in a wind-tunnel illustrating the formation of wing-tip vortices.
(Photo: Shell UK)

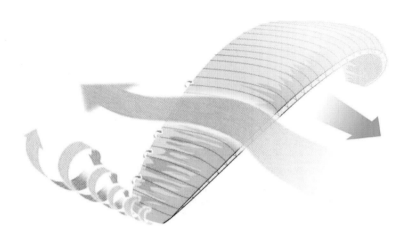

Fig 6.1: Wing tip vortices; at the tips, the pressure difference between the upper and lower surfaces is equalised by the air flowing up and around the end of the wing. As the canopy moves forwards it leaves a trail of rotating air behind each tip. This is the prime cause of induced drag. (And the cause of "wake turbulence" often encountered downwind of an aircraft.)

Some designs feature "stabilos" or "ears" at the tips and one of their intended functions is to try and minimise this problem. The high aspect ratio (long slim) wings that are becoming more common reduce this problem in the same way as hang-gliders, sailplanes and albatrosses - simply by having a relatively smaller area of wing tip.

As can be seen on the graph (*Fig 6.2*), induced drag reduces with speed, and parasitic drag increases with speed, so there is a certain point at which parasitic and induced drag combined give a minimum total figure. This is the speed at which the "lift/ drag ratio" is best. Note that the graph lines stop at about 13kph; at this airspeed the angle of attack is usually so high that the craft stalls. When this occurs the whole drag profile changes dramatically; the airfoil no longer works and the drag is now simply a huge parasitic force operating vertically. At speeds over about 60kph the parasitic drag becomes too great for the weight to overcome and the wing cannot achieve any higher airspeed.

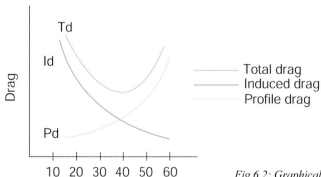

Total drag
Induced drag
Profile drag

Fig 6.2: Graphical illustration of the effect of drag.

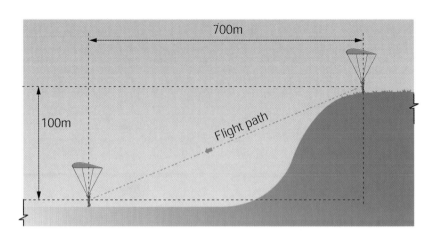

Fig 6.3: Lift to drag ratio and glide angle. The pilot launches in still air and flies 700m horizontally for a total height loss of 100m. His glide ratio, or lift to drag ratio in this case is 7:1.

Lift/Drag Ratio (glide angle)

L = lift and D = total drag, so the L/D ratio measures the gliding efficiency of the wing. The best L/D ratio occurs when the lift is greatest relative to the drag. See *Fig 6.2*. (The effect of speed on drag).

In practice this is when the canopy is flown at the speed where it will cover the most distance from a given height. For example, if a paraglider has an L/D ratio that allows it to glide 700 metres along for every100 metres of altitude lost, this is referred to as glide angle of 7:1 (see *Fig 6.3*) This figure can only really be used as a comparative guide to the performance of the canopy. When you are actually in the air, any wind or any lifting or sinking air will distort the performance by several hundred percent in either direction.

Sink rate

If you read manufacturers' information sheets, another figure you may see quoted is minimum sink rate. This refers to the slowest rate at which the canopy will descend through still air. If your minimum sink rate is, say, 1.2 metres per second, then the canopy will always be descending through the air at at least that rate. To soar,i.e to maintain or gain height the trick is to find some air that is rising faster than you are sinking.

The minimum sink rate is frequently rather poorly identified by inexperienced pilots. Because adding some brake increases the angle of attack, it slows the wing down and the wing briefly generates more lift. The pilot feels the resulting climb, and a variometer may even chirp briefly to register this as a better sink rate.

Very soon the pilot "learns" that adding a bit of brake seems to reduce the sink rate, and thereafter always flies with some brake in order to sink as slowly as possible.

However the "surge" that is felt is often the conversion of stored energy into a short-lived climb (such as on launch), or a small defined patch of lifting air.

In fact a paraglider's brakes add so much drag that the increased lift caused by the altered angle of attack is invariably cancelled out by the added drag, and performance is actually reduced. Many new pilots fly too slowly as a result, and cannot understand why their sink rate is not as good as someone else's.

In consistently smooth air (including lift) the best sink rate is generally found at the glider's trim (hands off) speed. We are talking here about the actual aerodynamic sink rate which is not necessarily your most efficient speed to fly. In practice there may be very valid reasons for flying a bit more slowly. If you are going though a lifting patch of air, for example, a less efficient but slower airspeed may keep you in the lift longer and so, on balance, you win. Or if it is rough, keeping some brake applied helps to stabilise the wing and reduce the chance of a collapse.

While we are on the subject, there is a way of increasing the angle of attack whilst avoiding much of the drag penalty of brakes, and that is by using trim devices, which tilt the whole wing. These are much more efficient, but because they fix the wing at a different angle of attack, they can unfortunately make managing and recovering from unstable situations like stalls and collapses more demanding. For this reason, trimmers are usually found only on high-performance or tandem wings.

Aspect ratio

The aspect ratio is a measure of the canopy's shape. When a paraglider is laid out flat, the planform (the shape viewed from above) can give us clues about the characteristics and likely performance of the wing. A high aspect ratio wing is long and slim, which probably means high performance and lower stability, though

A high aspect ratio wing.

A low aspect ratio wing. (Photo: Airwave)

of course all manufacturers are struggling to improve the first without compromising the second. An albatross or a sailplane will have a very high aspect ratio, whereas a paraglider or a songbird will have a low one.

Aspect ratio is calculated by dividing the square of the span by the area of fabric. For example, a canopy with a span of 10.5 metres and an area of 25 square metres would work out as 10.5 x 10.5 = 110.25 divided by 25 = an aspect ratio of 4.41. This is a mid-range wing, and is likely to have average performance and good stability.

There are two different aspect ratio figures that you may come across; one is the "flat" aspect ratio as described above. The other is the projected aspect ratio. This is always slightly lower, as it is calculated not by the "actual" area of the wing but by the projected area i.e the area of the shadow of the wing when the wing is inflated and in flight. Because the canopy takes up a curved shape, the projected area is always lower.

This figure is given because different designs have different degrees of curvature and so this figure give a more accurate comparison in terms of flight behaviour.

CAVOK

This is a piece of aviation weather jargon; it is actually derived from the abbreviation of "Ceiling And Visibility OK" and its definition is that there is no cloud below 5,000ft, visibility is at least 10km and there is no precipitation reaching the ground.

Windspeed, groundspeed and airspeed

Windspeed is simply the speed of the wind over the ground.

Groundspeed is the speed of the aircraft relative to the ground.

Airspeed is the speed of the airflow over the aerofoil.

A point worth noting is that, in flight, some pilots have trouble distinguishing between airspeed and groundspeed. Take a look at *Fig 6.4*.

A. The pilot is standing on top of a hill with an inflated canopy. The windspeed is 10mph, the groundspeed is 0mph and his airspeed is therefore 10mph.

B. Now he has taken off. The windspeed is still 10mph and his groundspeed is now 15mph. As he is flying into wind, the airspeed over the canopy must be 25mph. So far so good.

C. Now our pilot has encountered a 20mph windspeed; his airspeed is still 25mph. His groundspeed has now dropped to 5mph.

D. As he is a long way from the hill, he decides to turn round and come back. He does not alter his airspeed, which remains at 25 mph, and the windspeed is still 20mph. His flight path is now downwind and his groundspeed is now 45 mph. The sudden increase in speed over the ground can be disconcerting if the pilot is not prepared, particularly as he may now be heading straight towards the hill. Pilots have been known to slow down at this point by braking hard; the result is, of course, a stall, which can mean losing control and hitting the hill, with painful consequences. It is easy to avoid this mistake by knowing what to expect

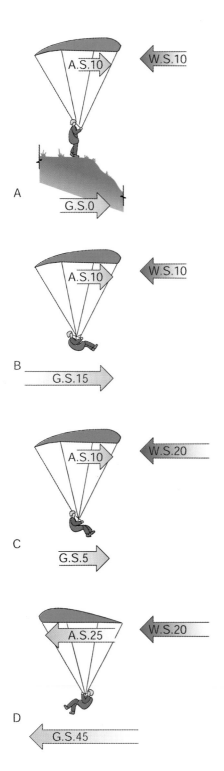

and by judging your airspeed not by the ground, but by the feel of the airflow in your face and the position of the controls.

In a school situation the instructor can mention these figures, but to really appreciate the acceleration in groundspeed you need to experience a downwind turn. Just for comparison, a 180degree turn on a typical paraglider takes around one second to complete, so your increase in groundspeed in the illustration above would be some 40mph in one second.... Unless you happen to be a racing driver, chances are this makes your car look a bit flat!

If the wind is not blowing directly onto the hill, the same thing occurs to a lesser degree as you soar along it. One "beat" will be slow relative to the ground as you pull into wind and the other very fast. Be careful to maintain airspeed on the fast leg! There are some other terms that are used in the sport and in this handbook - refer to the glossary at the end.

Fig 6.4: The interaction between windspeed, groundspeed and airspeed

The BHPA and the Pilot Rating System

The British Hang-Gliding and Paragliding association is the governing body of the sport in the UK. The Civil Aviation Authority, which controls all non-military flying in Britain, has allowed the BHPA to shoulder the responsibility of ensuring adequate training, pilot and instructor qualifications, aircraft airworthiness and accident investigation. In addition to this the BHPA liaises with other air-users' associations and with landowners, the government and the general public. It arranges insurance cover for members and publishes regular bulletins detailing safety notices and other information in the monthly magazine, Skywings. Together, these tasks represent a major undertaking, with a good deal of the work being done by unpaid voluntary officers.

We shall only retain our enviable freedom to fly if the BHPA and its members can act, and be seen to act, responsibly. Most nations where paragliding is established have a similar association. Membership is mandatory for anyone learning to paraglide at a registered school in the UK. There are three basic types of membership.

Full membership

This gives all benefits, including 3rd party and public liability insurance of 2 million pounds (at present). Membership incudes a subscription to the magazine Skywings, which is published monthly. Full members may also hold ratings, and have voting rights etc. This is renewable annually and can be "rolling" membership, paid for monthly or quarterly by direct debit. If more than one member of your family flies you can get family membership, which simply removes the duplication of copies of the magazine. There are concessions available for those in full time education.

Training membership

This offers the same insurance cover and benefits such as Skywings magazine, but does not allow for ratings to be held, or give any voting rights. This membership option is designed for those who are still trying the sport out and have not yet decided it is for them. It is valid for 3 months. This period is designed to allow sufficient time for a course to be completed. You cannot hold a rating with this type of membership, so when you have completed CP (Novice) level you will need to renew or upgrade to full member status.

Day membership

This is simply an 'insurance only' package for one day, and is designed to cover those who are having an air experience flight or "taster" day.

BHPA membership also confers a number of benefits that are less immediately obvious. The instructors who teach you have been through BHPA training courses and are examined for their licences. Officers and volunteers in the association investigate and report on any accidents or incidents to try and learn how best to keep the sport safe, and there is the inevitable administration work of dealing with insurers, producing exams and club bulletins, arranging competitions and events and dealing with government departments.

Outside the UK

You may be reading this book in a country other than the UK and using a somewhat different training regime. The exercises outlined here are designed primarily for the dynamic hill soaring conditions common in Britain. For mountainous terrain there is far less emphasis on techniques for dealing with strong winds and far more on thermalling technique and other factors. However, the outline of the system below is broadly relevant to most new pilots.

Training Overview

It is usual to begin the day early by ringing your school to check on weather conditions, and, in some cases, the meeting place. If you do not ring in, or if the school does not offer this facility, you run a far greater risk of a fruitless journey. Assuming that the weather is fine, the instructor will begin by answering any questions and giving a talk on the sport. He or she will check that everyone is in good health and fit to fly, and ask if anyone has had any previous experience in flying or parachuting that could be useful.

You will be encouraged to ask questions. It is not the sort of class where you can sit quietly at the back and nod even if you do not understand something - your safety can depend on your knowing what is going on so that you can decide what to do next.

You will be required to join the national association - this is mandatory in the UK and in several other countries. Membership confers third party insurance, which is necessary before you fly. Some schools will also provide you with a theory book or notes for you to use as a back up to your instructor's lessons.

This section is an explanation of the process of learning to fly a paraglider.

It is essentially an overview of the British Hang-Gliding and Paragliding Association's training programme, including a brief look at the alternative options adopted by other paragliding training systems.

A few words on starting paragliding

If you choose to enrol on a course, your instructor will very likely begin with an introductory chat about the sport and what you can expect. However, by that time you will probably have already paid for a course and it is a bit late to back out! The school has an interest in attracting you, and the instructors are all enthusiasts themselves, so all brochures and conversations tend to be on the optimistic side. (It never rains in brochures!)

The reality is that paragliding is a great sport, but the weather is fickle and you will almost certainly waste a lot of time and fuel trying to ensure you are at the right site on the right days. Each year many students are disappointed that they cannot complete their course during their holiday week, or on the days they have put aside. The weather risk is one you share with the school. Most schools will say somewhere in their literature that you are purchasing a course of instruction, not a specific weeks holiday.

If you are unlucky and it rains or blows all week, you can expect to be able to re-book for a later date, but you cannot expect a refund.

Paragliding is potentially dangerous. No matter how well you are trained and how good your gear is, you cannot entirely escape the risk of injury or even being killed.

Anyone can make a mistake, and the environment we fly in is not always completely predictable. However good your instructor may be, he cannot make you a more decisive person or help you (other than by advice) if you get into trouble.

Before you even pick up the 'phone to book your course you do need to understand and accept both these facts.

Paragliding can be successfully done by a wide range of people, and this is one of its greatest appeals.

Many "adventure" or "extreme" sports require a good deal of physical fitness or high levels of skill and technique to master. Some, like leading difficult rock climbs, or carve-gybing a windsurfer at high speed, are quite simply beyond the capabilities of many people.

By contrast, launching, flying and even thermalling a paraglider from a high mountain is really quite easy. Students taking the controls of a tandem wing can quite easily circle up to cloudbase on a good day, even if they have never been near a paraglider or flown anything prior to that flight. In this respect paragliding is quite often technically undemanding. (Many flights are not much more energetic than playing a piano).

The structured training programme possible in UK, starting with small flights on shallow slopes in good weather, and gradually increasing the height and demands on the pilot, is designed to get as many people through the course as safely as possible. However, it is possible to get a slightly unrealistic sense of security from this type of approach.

If you should make a mistake whilst flying and misjudge your landing pattern for example, you could find yourself trying to manoeuvre into a small or hazardous area. Hit some turbulent air, and the whole picture can change dramatically; the paraglider can collapse, drop dozens or even hundreds of feet, and be difficult or impossible to control within a very short time. These situations are not common, and can usually be minimised with good planning, and can generally be dealt with, but the experience can most definitely be an extreme one! If you keep flying long enough, it is inevitable that eventually you will experience an "event" of this type.

You may, like many of us who fly, consider the risks worthwhile, and be happy to take responsibility for your own safety. But just because paragliding is easy to do does not necessarily mean it is any more suitable for those who are less capable of dealing with the physical and mental demands it can make in certain situations.

With the extremely rare exception of an equipment malfunction, the primary causes of accidents and injuries in paragliding (and quite a few other activities) are pilot error, and almost all of them have their root in one of two situations.

1. Underconfidence

Especially being indecisive, or, at worst, "frozen" by fear.

2. Overconfidence

Thinking, "I will be OK flying this

Deathship Mk 3 prototype" or (more commonly!), "I am sure I can deal with these conditions, I am just as good as that pilot up there."

The ideal student pilot is confident, but just a little bit wary as well.

If you have any flying experience, this is very useful, and you should tell your instructor. Initially, even pilots with thousands of hours are just as hopeless at the alien skills of launching and ground handling, (kite flying is the closest related skill here). But, when you reach the approach planning stage, the pilots have an advantage.

Your brain is making decisions in three dimensions whilst flying, and although we are all used to judging speed and direction, most of us have little practice at judging altitude loss (or gliding). Pilots - especially Hang-glider or other slope soaring pilots - find this easier and may benefit from reduced training requirements.

The good news for non-pilots is you soon pick up the trick of judging approaches in just a few flights.

Before you venture onto the slopes, your instructor may well ask you about your medical fitness etc (see Chapter 3, Health and Safety). He or she may also tell you about special rules for the site; what paths to use, toilet facilities (if you are lucky) and advice, such as no smoking upwind of the gliders.

On arrival, your first lessons will be in assessing the site and the weather and an introduction to the equipment; these subjects are covered in subsequent chapters.

The BHPA Progressive training system

This is a brief introduction to the training system used at all approved schools in the UK. There will be some variation in style from school to school, of course, and in some countries the reverse launch that is used in windy conditions is not as critical. This syllabus refers to foot launching. There are some other disciplines to be mastered if you are launching from skis or being towed aloft.

The section below gives an overall view of the system and then a blow-by-blow explanation of each exercise.

The previous chapter mentioned how easy paragliding can be, and it is probably true that you could throw ten students off the top of a mountain and seven or eight of them would have mastered the basics pretty well by the time they landed an hour later. Unfortunately these odds are not quite good enough, and next of kin of the remaining 2 or 3 who do not make it might take rather a dim view of this arrangement.

It seems fairly obvious how to teach someone to fly a paraglider: simply start low down or with a tandem flight and work your way up steadily. That way you can catch any problems close to the ground and the instructor can assess each pupil's progress before going on the next task. That, in a nutshell, is how it is done.

Over many years, the BHPA has monitored training and the best practice has been gradually refined to concentrate on common problems, increase standards, and ensure vital elements are all included.

The most recent revision of the training

system is perhaps the most comprehensive of all, and specifies all the exercises that a student needs to complete, and the briefings required to ensure everyone coming though the system has had a comprehensive grounding in all the skills and knowledge they will need. This is laid out in a logical manner. You must have a lecture on the rules of the air before you fly with others, for example. In the BHPA model the pupils and instructors jointly "sign off" the exercises as they are completed.

It is always subject to revision, but the present (2003) system is reproduced below. The version shown is for Hill launched paragliding; there are other variants for Tow-launched training.

At this point you will be allocated a Student pilot training booklet. This is a vital log of all the training exercises, and you and your instructor(s) will work through each exercise and sign them off as you go.

The first page is a risk warning and a record of your BHPA membership type.

The risk warning is an important element. In the past, students have stated that they did not appreciate that there were risks involved in paragliding. This warning is included in order to ensure that no-one is misled into the mistaken belief that paragliding is totally safe.

The membership type is for administrative use so that your instructor can check at a glance if your membership is still current. The training pack is issued by the BHPA to those who have annual or training membership. It includes a copy of Training wings and literature on the association. Some schools add their own elements, such as details of holidays or feedback questionnaires on your course.

The notes are fairly self-explanatory. An instructor could, in some circumstances, be training as many as six pupils, and to some extent may rely on the students themselves agreeing that they are confident at a specific exercise. If you do not think you are ready to move on then do not sign the task, but discuss it with your instructor.

The instructor will give you an introduction to the equipment. (Photo: Northern Paragliding)

Surname:

Forename:

Student Training Record
Paragliding (Hill)

Student's personal details

Address:

Telephone:

Date of birth: Age: Weight:

Contact name:

Telephone:

British Hang Gliding
and Paragliding
Association

BHPA

READ THIS

Paragliding is a form of aviation, with all of the inherent and potential dangers that are involved in aviation. No form of aviation is without risk, and injuries and death can and do occur in paragliding, even to trained pilots using proper equipment. No claim is made or implied that all sources of potential danger to the pilot have or can be identified. No one should participate in paragliding who does not recognise and wish to personally assume the associated risks.

What is this Student Training Record?

This book details all the exercises which make up the training programme that you are following. Your Instructor and you must use it to record your progress both in the main section and in the log section at the back. You should also use it to ensure that you fully understand each new exercise before it is attempted.

Your Student Training Record will be retained by your school.

Student's BHPA membership record

Personal accident insurance taken out?:

Date Training Pack issued:

Membership type	Expiry date	Instructor's signature	Student's signature

Student Training Record ©BHPA 2002   Page 1

ELEMENTARY STAGE
Paragliding (Hill)

The exercises are arranged in sequential order (except the theory subjects in Phase 5, which may be tackled at any time). Ensure that each section is signed off before progressing to the next. The Instructor and student should read each objective carefully, and be certain that the exercise has been completed in full before signing that it has been achieved.

In certain circumstances environmental constraints may make it impossible to progressively increase height/turns exactly as indicated in the text. In such situations the Instructor may exercise reasonable judgement in accordance with the advice contained in the Instructor's Notes. These stress the need for height/turn increases to be progressive, and that extra consolidation flying is required if height/turn increases are to be larger than those indicated.

Phase 1: Ground training

Objective: The student should have a basic understanding of the sport and its risks, a basic understanding of the equipment and the site environment, and understand how to avoid/minimise injury as a result of a mishap. The student must also complete the mandatory administration steps.

1. **Introductory talk** - school and instructors - risk warning - student's health/medical conditions - clothing/footwear - the BHPA - the Pilot Rating Scheme.

2. **Site assessment briefing** - site and any site hazards - airflow and airflow hazards - weather assessment.

3. **Introduction to canopy and equipment** - parts and functions of canopy, harness, helmet - how an aerofoil creates lift - daily inspections explained, demonstrated, practised and understood.

4. **Avoiding/minimising injury** - safety techniques discussed, including parachute landing falls (PLFs), when and how to use them, demonstrated and practised to a good degree of competence.

The four ground training exercises above have been completed satisfactorily

Instructor's signature   Student's signature   Date

Phase 1: Ground Training

This covers the basic theory of launching and landing into wind, and how the airflow determines the flying environment, It is often covered on site. You then move on to looking at the equipment and being shown how to unpack and lay out the glider and harness. If the weather is suitable the instructor may well demonstrate a launch and a quick flight. This shows the class what to expect and also serves to allow a check of the conditions.

The next element in the ground training is pre flight checking the equipment. The checks swill be demonstrated and explained by the instructor before you have a chance to unpack more gliders and practice your own checks. Demonstration is an essential teaching technique, but there is substitute for doing it yourself when learning a new skill.

You should now have the site, weather and equipment all checked and ready to start flying. But before getting airborne the instructor is required to run through additional safety checks, most notably the parachute landing fall drill.

About Parachute Landing Falls (PLFs)

You cannot realistically learn a perfect PLF technique in a very short time, but the aim of this exercise to ensure that you have grasped the basics of dealing with a hard landing.

PLF's are, in fact, of no use in normal flying and you may well fly for many years without the need to employ this technique. So it is not realistic to spend a lot of time on it. However, if you do find yourself descending vertically or near vertically after a low level collapse for example, or under a reserve parachute,

then knowing about the correct position to adopt and rolling with the impact can help prevent a number of potential injuries.

This training also has a number of other purposes: if a potential student has a problem with quite gentle impacts or difficulty with co-ordination, then this exercise "flags up" such a problem to the instructor before he become airborne. If you cannot fall on the ground from a standing position without problems, then paragliding is not for you.

There is a mental preparation angle too. Paragliding can be very easy, and is of course great fun, but it is possible for students to forget that it carries very real risks. Starting a course by discussing the possibility of getting injured, and the steps to reduce this risk, is a reminder that proper training is a serious business, and that the instructor or school always has safety as the main priority.

Phase 2: Ground handling

Objective: Through ground-based activity the student should achieve a reasonable and consistent level of competence at preparing the equipment for flight; inflating the canopy; running with it whilst looking ahead; maintaining direction; flaring and collapsing the canopy.

5. **Briefing** - pre-flight checks - importance of taking off and landing into wind - airspeed control - flare/stall.

6. **Preparation** - putting on the helmet and harness - canopy layout - pre-flight checks.

7. **Inflation** - take-offs practised to stage of running with an inflated canopy (forward/reverse inflation method as appropriate to the conditions) - looking ahead - flare - collapsing the canopy - post-'flight' control and moving of the canopy.

8. **Directional control** - how the controls work for directional control - initiating turns - lookout and looking ahead.

The four exercises above have been completed satisfactorily

Instructor's signature   Student's signature   Date

Phase 2: Ground handling

Flying a paraglider is very easy, but getting airborne can be quite difficult! However, if you want to be a solo pilot, you have to learn ground handling and launch techniques before you can fly.

This phase covers the vital pre-flight checks, including the site, weather and equipment, and gives the opportunity to get to grips with the power of a paraglider and familiarise yourself with the controls before becoming airborne.

The instructor will usually help quite a bit at first, but the eventual aim is to get each pupil to be able to check, inflate and be ready to launch the paraglider himself. This section includes steering, flaring the wing to collapse it, gathering up the wing to carry it "posy" fashion and laying it out again ready for the next launch. This will include a lot of running down a gentle slope and walking back again. Do not be discouraged if this seems to be taking a long while to master: this is normal!

Phase 3: First hops

Objective: The student should combine the skills practised on the ground in Phase 2 to make straight ground-skimming flights (typically less than 5m/15ft ground clearance).

9. **Getting airborne**
   The student should reach a reasonable and consistent level of competence at taking-off, maintaining the correct in flight control position for good airspeed, the landing flare/landing, and post-landing control of the canopy.

Exercise 9 completed satisfactorily

Instructor's signature	Student's signature	Date

Phase 3: First hops

When your launch technique is good enough you may find that you are either "moon walking" (ie have only a part of your bodyweight on your feet) and can take huge strides with the wing supporting much of your weight through the harness, or possibly that you are leaving the ground completely and making small flights just a few feet above the ground.

The aim at this stage is to maintain a consistent airspeed and hold a course.

As your instructor sees you progressing he may move you to a steeper slope or perhaps help by adding a little extra airspeed with a well placed hand on the back! As the flights get longer, you will find it easier to judge your speed and direction and make course corrections and gentle landings.

These first three phases are a fair indicator of what can be achieved on your first day if the wind is OK and no-one has any serious problems.

Phase 4: Flight exercises

Objective: The student should be capable of acting as pilot-in-command at the Elementary level.

These exercises MUST be completed in the order listed.

10. **Eventualities briefing** - the need to prepare, before take-off, plans to deal with the unexpected.

11. **Commands and communications briefing** - this must include signal bats, radio, etc., as appropriate.

12. **Responsibilities briefing** - from this point the student becomes the 'pilot-in-command' and will be in a position to determine the course of the flight. The student must clearly understand their level of responsibility for the safe conduct of any flight and be confident of their ability to undertake this step.

The three briefings above have been completed and understood

Instructor's signature	Student's signature	Date

13. **Flights (i) - Maintaining course and airspeed**
    The student should reach a reasonable and consistent level of competence and confidence flying at a increased ground clearance (maximum 15m/50ft) and in making the directional control corrections required to maintain a straight course. At least 4 successful flights must be achieved. Direct communication from the Instructor must be available.

Dates and number of flights:

Flights attempted	/ /	/ /	/ /	/ /
Successful flights	/ /	/ /	/ /	/ /

Exercise 13 completed satisfactorily

Instructor's signature	Student's signature	Date

14. **Flights (ii) - Introducing turns**
    The student should reach a reasonable and consistent level of competence and confidence whilst flying with a greater ground clearance (maximum 30m/100ft), maintaining good airspeed control and making gentle turns. The student should be briefed on turns, the need to avoid low turns and the need for lookout. The turns should be of no more than 90° (i.e. less than 45° from directly into wind). Direct communication from the Instructor should be available. At least 4 successful flights must be made.

Dates and number of flights:

Flights attempted	/ /	/ /	/ /	/ /
Successful flights	/ /	/ /	/ /	/ /

Exercise 14 completed satisfactorily

Instructor's signature	Student's signature	Date

Continued

---

15. **Flights (iii) - Completing simple flight plans**
    The student should reach a reasonable and consistent level of competence and confidence when making flights with a further increased ground clearance. Flights should involve unassisted launches, turns of 90° or more with good lookout, good airspeed control and controlled landings within a defined area.

    The student should be briefed on turns and the need for lookout. At least 4 successful flights must be made. Any increases in altitude must be progressive.

Dates and number of flights:

Flights attempted	/ /	/ /	/ /
Successful flights	/ /	/ /	/ /

Exercise 15 completed satisfactorily

Instructor's signature	Student's signature	Date

Phase 4: Flight Exercises

This begins with the eventualities briefing. What if you start to drift to the left? What if you get lifted up 20m, etc? It is important to start considering the different options you have, as from this point on you will be the master of your own destiny, and though the instructor can advise you, he cannot directly affect your decisions by taking control, so you need to understand and accept this responsibility.

Some schools use radio communications, and some use visual signals, such as bats in the landing field. Whatever the system employed, you do need a check to ensure that they are working and that you understand the signals or commands.

The first flights should be quite low, although they can be quite long if the site is gently sloping. The first aim is just a continuation of the hops, to hold a course and speed. You must complete at least

Phase 5: Theory and examination

Objective: Through lectures, lessons, talks and personal study the student should achieve the required knowledge level in these subject areas.

	Instructor's signature	Date
16. Meteorology		
17. Principles of flight		
18. Rules of the air and air law		
19. Elementary stage examination completed and all incorrect answers de-briefed and discussed.		

Instructor's signature	Student's signature	Date

Phase 5: Theory & Examination

By now you will have been flying for two or three days, and unless you are very fit you will be getting a bit tired with all the walking back up the hill. Usually on day 2 or day 3 the instructor will call a break or two to discuss some of the theory of paragliding with you (and let you have a rest!). The subjects to cover include basic meteorology and airflow

Final assessment of Elementary Stage

20. I have checked that the training detailed above has been completed and confirm that, to the best of my knowledge, this student has the right attitude to flying and has reached the standard of airmanship required to continue training in this discipline.

Instructor's signature	Date

Final assessment (EP)

The final assessment is signed by a senior instructor to confirm that you are ready to start on the Club Pilot syllabus. In practice the progression can be fairly seamless; for example you may have already done some of the theory or have good enough reverse launches to have these CP tasks signed off before you complete the EP level.

four good flights like this.

The natural next step is to introduce gentle turns. To do this you will need a little more room, and you may be flying with up to 40m ground clearance. Again, at least four good flights with turns of up to 90 degrees is the standard.

over hills, the principles of flight and how your craft works, and the rules of the air (anti-collision rules) and the laws that govern our activity.

The remaining time on your Elementary course is taken up with polishing the basic skills i.e achieving more consistent self launches, planning and executing flights with good airspeed and smooth 90 degree+ turns, and setting up and completing controlled and reasonably accurate landings. You will need to take and pass the BHPA EP exam, which is a multiple choice paper covering all the areas mentioned. The Exam is only partially a test of you. It is also final check for the instructor: if half the class gets question 6 wrong something has obviously been missed and needs re-visiting.

The main reasons for having an EP then CP level are really to do with people moving schools, or doing half the course then having a break before continuing. It is just a convenient level to draw a line. It marks a national standard, and allows schools to market the course in two halves, as taking one week at a time off work, and paying in two parts, is more practical for many students. The EP is also a natural point to sort those who just want to try the sport out from those who are considering taking it up and perhaps buying equipment.

The school may have some CP gear, but it is quite common for students to buy their own at this stage and continue their training (perhaps at a reduced cost) on their own glider.

Achieving the elementary level usually takes about 4 to 5 flying days. This level means that the holder is ready to start on the Club Pilot course and soaring flight. It does not confer any kind of licence or insurance cover for flying without instructor supervision. EP level students are not registered as qualified pilots with the association.

This is an important point, as there have been cases of EP holders buying gear and flying without the supervison of an instructor, and this situation may well be viewed by the authorities (and life insurance companies) as negligent behaviour. In the worst case the air navigation order makes it an offence to operate any aircraft in a negligent manner. Negligent could quite easily be defined as "without a suitable licence".

CLUB PILOT (NOVICE) STAGE
Paragliding (Hill)

Before undertaking these exercises the student must have successfully completed the BHPA Elementary Stage Paragliding (Hill). Check flight/s may be required in circumstances where there has been a significant interruption in the training programme or a significant change of environment.

Whilst these exercises are laid out in a logical sequence, the Instructor may vary the order to suit site and weather opportunities. The Instructor and student should read each objective carefully, and be certain that the exercise has been completed in full before signing that it has been achieved.

In certain circumstances environmental constraints may make it impossible to progressively increase height/turns exactly as indicated in the text. In such situations the Instructor may exercise reasonable judgement in accordance with the advice contained in the Instructor's Notes. These stress the need for height/turn increases to be progressive, and that extra consolidation flying is required if height/turn increases are to be larger than those indicated.

Phase 6: Pre-soaring

Objective: The student should be ready to attempt soaring flight.

21. Theory
The student should have a refreshed and expanded understanding of site assessment (including hazards, turbulence and rotor), weather assessment (including wind strength measurement, wind gradients and venturi effect), flight planning (including the importance of building in options), Rules of the Air, ridge protocols, airflow around ridges, lift bands, soaring patterns, all turns away from the hill, the need to keep a good lookout.

Exercise 21 completed satisfactorily
Instructor's signature   Student's signature   Date

22. 180° turns
The student should reach a reasonable and consistent level of competence at flights involving unassisted launches and controlled turns of up to and beyond 180°. Instructor supervision to be advisory in nature (briefings and de-briefings).

Exercise 22 completed satisfactorily
Instructor's signature   Student's signature   Date

23. Planned approaches
The student should reach a reasonable and consistent level of competence at planning flights and landing approaches, by making a controlled landing within 10m/33ft of a designated target at least 4 times. Techniques should include the 'constant aspect approach' and 'S' turns. Instructor supervision to be advisory in nature (briefings and de-briefings).

Dates and number of flights:
Flights attempted / /   / /   / /   / /
Successful flights / /   / /   / /   / /

Exercise 23 completed satisfactorily
Instructor's signature   Student's signature   Date

Club Pilot (Novice) stage

It is not unusual for the Club Pilot level to be done at a different venue from the EP level or with another instructor, or with the same school but some weeks or months later. In such cases the instructor will need to refer back to the student's record book, and a refresher of some of the high flights and briefings may be needed to ensure that the student is ready to attempt the next stages. It is also quite likely that a new glider may be introduced at this stage, so a repeat of a couple of previous flight plans on the new equipment is a sensible precaution.

Accidents are very often the result of too many new things at once: new glider, new site and new task after a break of a few weeks is a classic recipe....

Phase 6: Pre-soaring.

The pre-soaring flights will involve 180degree turns, ie quartering the same area of ground in both directions and making planned approaches to a defined landing area. This skill is vital in using lift effectively and gaining height. Semi-soaring flights (ie following a soaring pattern but descending because there is not sufficient lift) are an excellent exercise for improving control, and once you are in a good lift band, the task of staying up will be comparatively easy.

You will be required to demonstrate a number of accurate landings. Accurate landings and approaches not only show that the pilot can land where he wants but are a very useful task in learning about the handling and turn radius of the glider. Once soaring you will extend the range of places you can fly to in order to land, so it makes sense to ensure this skill is of a reasonable standard before you start using lift to extend your flights.

This skill will be vital in setting up landings in a limited space on top of the hill later.

Phase 7: Soaring

Objective: The student should demonstrate a reasonable and consistent level of competence at ridge soaring and top landing.

24. Soaring flight
The student should reach a reasonable and consistent level of competence at utilising ridge lift to maintain or gain height. This will include flying beats in a controlled manner and with good lookout.

A minimum of 3 flights of approx. 10 minutes (or equivalent) must be completed, at least one of which must be completed either on a separate site or on a separate day.

Dates and number of flights:

Flights attempted	/ / ☐	/ / ☐	/ / ☐		
Successful flights	/ / ☐	/ / ☐	/ / ☐		

Exercise 24 completed satisfactorily

Instructor's signature	Student's signature	Date

---

25. Top landings
The student should reach a reasonable and consistent level of competence at top landings, demonstrating good airspeed control, good flight planning, accurate approaches, and good canopy control after touchdown.

A minimum of 4 top landings must be completed, at least one of which must be completed either on a separate site or on a separate day.

Dates and number of flights:

Flights attempted	/ / ☐	/ / ☐	/ / ☐	/ / ☐	
Successful flights	/ / ☐	/ / ☐	/ / ☐	/ / ☐	

Exercise 25 completed satisfactorily

Instructor's signature	Student's signature	Date

---

26. Flying with others
The student should reach a reasonable and consistent level of competence at flying with others, showing a good awareness of other craft and their characteristics.

This exercise must be strictly controlled with new elements and aircraft introduced gradually. The briefing must include checking the student's level of understanding of collision avoidance rules and wake vortices.

Exercise 26 completed satisfactorily

Instructor's signature	Student's signature	Date

Phase 7: Soaring (Dynamic lift)

Ridge soaring is not a new skill; it is simply a question of making controlled turns in the right place and taking advantage of the fact that the air is rising in this area faster than your canopy is sinking. The key skills, therefore, are an ability to read the site and anticipate the areas of useful lift, and having good enough control to make the most of it.

This is often made both easier and harder by the presence of other pilots: easier in that you can see where the lift extends to and is best, and harder in that you will need to have part of your brain working on keeping track of the other gliders' positions. If there are too many airborne for you to be able to process this information then it may not be suitable for your first soaring flight. Your flights must demonstrate that you are able to fly safely with other air users and know the rules of the air.

Your first flights will probably be with radio contact from your instructor. Hopefully he will be prompting you by saying things like "as you get towards that end of the ridge, check over your shoulder for traffic; if it is clear, turn when you feel the lift is strongest"

This kind of prompting ensures that you know what to do, but allows you the freedom to make your own decisions.

After a couple of successful beats, if you have joined the pattern and are managing well, your instructor will probably leave you get on with it for a while and make your own decisions.

Phase 7 requires you to make a minimum of 4 good soaring flights and these must be on more than one site or day. By this time you should be comfortable flying in dynamic ridge lift in good conditions.

As you are staying up, it seems rather pointless landing at the bottom and having to walk up, so if the site is suitable the next task is top landing.

Again, with gradually reducing input from your instructor, you need to make at least 4 good top landings. These must be well planned and executed, - being blown backwards, or inadvertently drifting sideways onto the top is not acceptable as a top landing!

Phase 8: Improving skills

27. Exploring the speed range
The student should be competent and confident at using the paraglider's normally used speed range. They should also understand the hazards associated with fast and slow flight, and be familiar with recognising the symptoms of a stall. The student should also have a basic understanding of the speed to fly concept. Approaching the stall and deliberate stalls must be avoided (other than during ground handling).

Exercise 25 completed satisfactorily

Instructor's signature	Student's signature	Date

28. Accelerator systems
The student should understand the uses and limitations of accelerator systems (and trim setting devices) and be proficient and confident at using an accelerator system. This exercise should include a warning about inappropriate use of accelerators to attempt to fly in strong conditions and a risk warning covering the effects of turbulence on accelerated wings.

Exercise 28 completed satisfactorily

Instructor's signature	Student's signature	Date

29. Forward launching
The student should reach a reasonable and consistent level of competence at forward launch techniques, with good control throughout.

Exercise 29 completed satisfactorily

Instructor's signature	Student's signature	Date

30. Reverse launching
The student should reach a reasonable and consistent level of competence at reverse launch techniques, with good control throughout.

Exercise 30 completed satisfactorily

Instructor's signature	Student's signature	Date

31. Weight shift and pitch-roll co-ordination in turns
The student should reach a reasonable and consistent level of competence at using weight shift and pitch-roll co-ordination in turns.

Exercise 31 completed satisfactorily

Instructor's signature	Student's signature	Date

32. Cross wind and slope landings
The student should reach a reasonable and consistent level of competence at cross wind and slope landings, should understand the problems and hazards associated with these manoeuvres, and know when and how they might be used.

Exercise 32 completed satisfactorily

Instructor's signature	Student's signature	Date

Phase 8: Improving skills

Soaring flight is a key goal for most new pilots; however, learning to soar is only one of the skills you will need to fly safely.

Phase 8 includes showing a familiarity with your glider's speed range, using the accelerator system and knowing its limitations and maximising your performance by making co-ordinated turns. This phase also includes a specific requirement to show competence, both forward and reverse launching (just in case you have managed to get this far without mastering one or other of these techniques). Also mentioned here are crosswind or side-slope landings. This is not a mandatory task, but is a very useful skill for many flying sites in the UK. 360° turns are not specifically mentioned in the task book, as they could be difficult to achieve at some sites and could cause long delays in completing the CP for some pilots. However, for schools with access to bigger hills or mountains, the 360° turn is a very useful skill to master and is commonly included.

Phase 9: Instability and emergencies

Objective: The student should understand techniques to recover controlled flight and be aware of techniques and procedures used during emergencies.

33. Theory

Emergencies: the student should understand water and tree landing procedures - PLFs - use of emergency parachute systems - uses and limitations of alternative control techniques such as weight shift and rear riser steering in the event of control line failure.

Instability: the student should understand recovery techniques for collapses, stalls, spins and spirals - paraglider certification - BHPA recommendations on pilot skill level requirements.

Exercise 33 completed satisfactorily

Instructor's signature	Student's signature	Date

34. Active flying

The student should demonstrate a good understanding of the concepts of active flying and coping with turbulence. Minor pitch oscillations should be induced and then stabilised. This exercise must be carried out at an appropriate altitude in smooth conditions and with effective communication.

Exercise 34 completed satisfactorily

Instructor's signature	Student's signature	Date

35. Rapid descent techniques

The student should reach a reasonable and consistent level of competence at using the 'big-ears' rapid descent technique and should understand its uses and limitations. This should include closing the tip cells on one side at a time, weight shift steering whilst in the big-ears mode, and safe exiting - no pumping! This exercise must be carried out at an appropriate altitude in smooth conditions and with effective communication.

Exercise 35 completed satisfactorily

Instructor's signature	Student's signature	Date

36. Dealing with an asymmetric tuck

The student should reach a reasonable and consistent level of competence at dealing with and recovering from an asymmetric tuck of more than 15% and less than 35%. This size of tuck is effectively one 'big-ears' and the exercise should be conducted on that basis. Initial training should be carried out on the ground first. This exercise must be carried out at an appropriate altitude in smooth conditions and with effective communication.

Exercise 36 completed satisfactorily

Instructor's signature	Student's signature	Date

Phase 9: Instability & Emergencies

Keep flying long enough and you will come across a situation that requires specific knowledge to deal with it. This section covers the commonest of these and your instructor will discuss all the calamities that may befall the unwary pilot and ask you to try out some of the techniques to cope with them.

Rear riser and weight shift steering mimics a situation where a brake line has broken or become tangled. Active flying is simply dealing with the air when it is not very smooth and so minimising the effects of turbulence.

Big ears is an invaluable technique in the dynamic conditions of the UK, as it is a relatively straightforward way of combating strong lift.

Dealing with small asymmetric tucks is equally vital and all these things will be discussed and practiced.

Perfect training conditions at Curium, S. Cyprus. (Photo: Northern Paragliding)

The more serious instability situations that can occur, such as spins and stalls, are not practiced at CP level for obvious safety reasons. In fact, if properly understood, these events should never occur at all. (Both situations are only possible in very severe turbulence or as a result of gross pilot input). This exercise is to impart the knowledge of how they can be avoided and to discuss what actions should be taken in each case.

The use of a reserve parachute should be properly understood so that, should the case ever arise where it was appropriate, the pilot would be prepared to use it knowledge yourself.

Exercise 40: A talk on human factors is of particular note. Human factors such as drugs, (including hangovers), tiredness and stress (including fear), have been implicated in several reportable incidents.

Much emphasis is placed on pre-flight checks and annual inspections of your gear. The test authorities and manufacturers spend a huge amount of time and effort improving the standard of equipment. But if the pilot decides to fly after a drink, or fly anyway when it looks a bit rough to impress his new girlfriend, it all goes out of the window!

Paragliding is very safe, but unfortunately the same cannot always be said of all paraglider pilots.

Phase 10: Theory and examination

Objective: Through lectures, lessons, talks and personal study the student should reach the Club Pilot (Novice) level of understanding in these subject areas.

	Instructor's signature	Date
37. Meteorology		
38. Principles of flight		
39. Rules of the air and air law		

40. **General airmanship knowledge** - the hazards of flying alone - human factors (drugs, tiredness, stress, lack of currency, etc.) - flying abroad - repairs and periodic inspections of canopy and equipment - the PRS - the need to join a recreational club - the coaching system - the limitations of the Club Pilot (Novice) rating and the routes to progress to "Pilot".

	Instructor's signature	Date

41. **Club Pilot (Novice) theory examination** completed and all incorrect answers de-briefed and discussed.

Instructor's signature	Student's signature	Date

Phase 10: Theory & Examination

This consists of the further theory and subsequent exam. Your instructor may give separate lectures to CP level, he may combine them with the EP level theory session, or he may provide material (such as this book) for you to improve your

---

Final assessment for Club Pilot (Novice)

42. **Declaration by Senior Instructor**

I have checked that the training detailed above has been completed and confirm that, to the best of my knowledge, this student:

■ has the right attitude to flying

■ has reached the standard of airmanship required to fly safely and competently as a Club Pilot (Novice) Paragliding (Hill)

Senior Instructor's signature	Date

Final Assessment (CP)

Just getting all the exercises signed off as complete and passing your exam is not the whole story. Your instructor must then sign you off as having the right attitude and standard of airmanship. What does this mean?

It means different things to different instructors no doubt, but a pretty good definition might be the answer "Yes" to the question, "Would I be happy knowing this pilot is out flying tomorrow on a new site?". If this is the case, then you will get the signature and will become qualified as a Club Pilot, ready to fly with just the informal advice or coaching of more experienced pilots. Many clubs have designated coaches who have been selected and had some training to offer support to new members.

Your record book is kept by the school. If you need it for any reason (such as going on a foreign trip with another school, or to transcribe information into your per-

sonal log book) they can usually supply a copy, but they are constrained to keep the original.

BHPA membership card.

Reverse side showing ratings held.

Different training systems

The method of training employed is determined to a great extent by the geography and weather of the region. The BHPA system has been refined in windy conditions where shallow slopes are common and walking back up is practical.

In many countries paragliding is a true mountain sport and the tuition is quite different.

In place of many short low-level flights, the initial training may be carried out on a flat or almost flat field. However, if there are no low hills, the next move is to fly from a large mountain.

In fact this is much easier in some respects, as there is plenty of time to think and space to get it slightly wrong and make a correction. Because the weather in mountainous regions is determined as much by the topography as the weather patterns, it is frequently possible to fly in zero wind, especially early and late in the day.

Whilst zero wind launches do require a committed run, the actual flights are very smooth and easy to control. Most instruction is by radio, and though the risk of the pupil finding himself in the

wrong place at the wrong altitude is significantly greater than on smaller hills, the advantage is that a pupil may make dozens of flight path corrections or turns on one flight and so progress very much more quickly.

Manoeuvres like the 360° turn are introduced almost immediately, as there is a lot of room and little wind drift. Students learning in an alpine environment typically progress in their canopy control skills very quickly.

Mountain flying does carry a significantly higher risk of accidents, primarily because of pupils having trouble judging their position when 1,000 metres above the landing field, and because the landing area is often quite restricted. In Ski resorts, the cables of the ski-lifts that make the sport possible, are themselves an additional hazard.

In Spring and summer the thermal activity and valley winds mean that flying for beginners is strictly a morning and evening activity. As the students progress the window of flyable weather becomes wider, but so do the challenges posed by turbulence and wind. A common problem is for pupils who have learnt in one environment switching to another. British pilots flying in the Alps for the first time find phenomena such as valley winds and lee-side thermals quite alien to their experience. Conversely, Alpine pilots may struggle to ground handle, reverse launch, and top land in strong dynamic conditions.

Tandem flights with an instructor are a much more common feature of mountain flying. However, in non-thermic conditions the flight generally ends up at the bottom of a mountain, requiring a long drive or cable car ride to get back up. As the instructor can only take one person at a time, the cost of training this way becomes prohibitively expensive.

The commercial pressure of earning money from taking members of the public for an experience flight, rather than flying students on courses, means that in popular resorts the tandem wings are often used full time for tourists!

Many countries with dry consistent climates and mountainous terrain do not have the soil and grass cover found in the UK and the resulting slopes are rocky and often covered in scrub. Whilst the local pilots may clear launch areas, flying and landing in such regions requires good planning (and good boots).

Other regions are covered in trees and flying tree-covered slopes has a significant effect on the airflow; again, conservative flight planning in such areas is vital.

Coastal soaring in sea breezes and landing on beaches is a worldwide phenomenon and many pilots with low airtime flying abroad would do well to explore the coastal sites available.

It is possible to learn many of the skills of paragliding without any hills. Tow launching is a popular option in some countries and regions where the right sites are not readily available. The BHPA have a slightly different syllabus and task book for tow launch training, including such vital areas as signalling, emergency release procedures, and flying a circuit over an airfield, which may be in use by other aircraft.

Tow launching requires a team to operate the winch or tow vehicle, lay out the lines and signal the launch. It is a great group or club activity but does mean you cannot suddenly decide to go and have a fly when you wish. In the busy skies of the UK a tow permit from the Civil Aviation Authority (CAA) is required before towing above 60m is allowed.

Towing does have the advantage of not requiring any walking up hills. Given a reasonable field you can often fly no matter what the wind direction.

The downside is that with a minimum sink rate of around 1.2m/sec your flight from a 300m tow will only last 4 minutes or so. You would need to be very lucky indeed to contact a good thermal in the first couple of minutes in order to get a longer flight. Flying from a mountain or a hill with ridge lift gives you far more airtime to play with.

The International Para-Pro System

Most paragliding countries with an association operate their own training systems, and instructors in each tend to be reasonably conversant with those of their near neighbours, making cross-over ratings fairly easy. The closest thing to an internationally recognised standard is the

FAI Para-Pro system.

The Para-Pro system recognises 5 stages and many associations affiliated to the FAI can "convert" your national rating to the appropriate Para-Pro level. This may make acceptance or conversion to a different standard simpler for those pilots who may wish to fly in a number of different countries.

The Levels are

Stage 1: Ground Skimming.

Stage 2: Altitude Gliding

Stage 3: Ridge Soaring

Stage 4: Thermal Soaring

Stage 5: Cross- Country

Comparsion of this system with the BHPA PRS would put a Student pilot at about half way between stage 1 and stage 2, and a Club pilot at just slightly short of Stage 3 (which requires 10 hours experience).

The BHPA Pilot and Advanced Pilot levels equate quite well with Stages 4 and 5.

The full text and detailed requirements for the International Para-Pro system can be found at http://www.fai.org/ hang_gliding/ documents/parapro.asp

An International Para-Pro licence card (IPPI card) is available, and even if your association is not using this system, it is usually possible to obtain one on the strength of your national rating. This is the case in the UK and in a number of other countries.

There is a small fee for issuing these cards.

Unassisted forward launch; one of the skills you will need to master.

Site Assesment

To assess when and where to fly safely you need to be able to understand the factors affecting a site. Foremost of these factors is being able to visualise how the air is behaving: where the good lift will be, where the wind will be stronger or lighter, what the likelihood of turbulence is. To understand its behaviour we need to know a little bit about the air.

Air is composed of molecules that are bouncing around all over the place, constantly colliding with each other and any nearby object. It has mass and weight, which is handy as it keeps the air stuck to the planet! We do not take much notice of the air in our daily lives unless the wind is very strong, but when flying, its behaviour is of crucial importance and great interest.

The air is gaseous, but it in many important ways its behaviour is similar to a liquid, so perhaps the easiest way to visualise its movement is by imagining it as water flowing over the landscape. Obviously there are some differences. For example, air can climb slopes more easily than water, but it gives you the general idea.

When you stand on a hilltop with the air moving along as wind, it is helpful to visualise the flow as broad river flowing towards and around the landscape. Ask yourself where you would see rough or white water. This is likely to be in and around woods and buildings, in the lee of hills, or wherever an obstacle interrupts the flow (see *Fig 8.1*). We have immediately established the major areas of turbulence. The reason why air (like water) has a turbulent flow is because it cannot make sharp changes of direction. Its mass and inertia keep it moving one way. This analogy also explains some other characteristics of airflow that are important to us. A small or conical hill cannot generate as much lift as a straight ridge, as the air will flow round rather than over it if it can just like a rock in a stream.

If you do have a long ridge but it has a gully or pass in it, (see *Fig 8.2*) the air will accelerate through the gap, and so this area should be treated with caution. One pilot flying along a line of hotels on top of a coastal ridge in Israel flew too close to such a gap and described the ex-

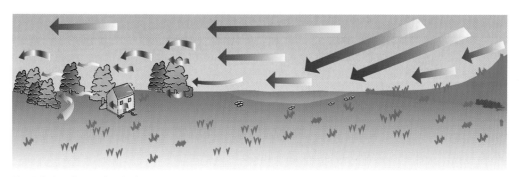

Fig 8.1: Mechanical turbulence

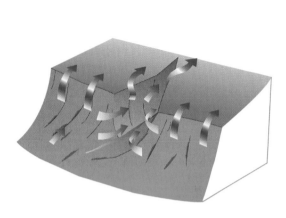

Fig 8.2: Airflow in a gully

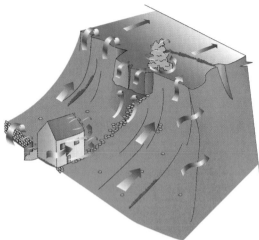

Fig 8.3: Airflow on a cliff and ridge end

perience as being "hoovered" backwards through the space. He ended up on the roof of a house (fortunately they are flat in that part of the world).

The same phenomenon is found at the end of a ridge (see *Fig 8.3*). The last few metres are often of no use, as the wind is escaping around the end of the ridge rather than being pushed over the top as lift.

In very mountainous areas, or those with narrow valleys, you may find that the airflow is affected more by the shape of the land than by the prevailing wind direction. Even in a light westerly breeze the wind in the bottom of a deep north-south valley is likely to be northerly or southerly. Even in quite small sites with a concave aspect like a bowl, the airflow is distorted by the terrain (*Fig 8.4*).

If the wind is forced to change direction suddenly by flowing over a cliff for ex-

Fig 8.4: Airflow in a bowl

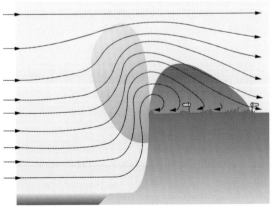

Fig 8.5: Airflow up a cliff showing lift band and dangerous areas affected by rotor.

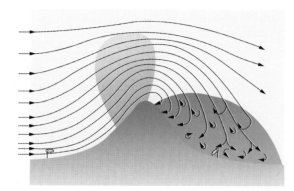

Fig 8.6: Airflow over a spine-backed ridge showing lift band and area affected by rotor.

ample the result of its inertia is for the airmass to "overshoot" in the same way as a waterfall in a fast flowing river, and to leave an area of relatively low pressure behind the obstacle. The air then curls back on itself to fill the space and the result is a rotating airflow or "rotor". *Figs 8.1, 8.3, 8.5 and 8.6* show such common areas of turbulence. The water analogy does become less applicable when dealing with vertical obstacles as, unlike water, air will flow up a cliff, for example, causing a rotor over the top edge. (*Fig 8.5*)

A "spine-back" ridge has an even greater effect on the airflow with a very large area of descending and potentially tum-

bling and chaotic air on the lee side. (*Fig 8.6*)

However, the advantages of the inertia of an airmass is significant to the soaring pilot. When wind comes into contact with a slope, it is forced upwards, and the flow has a vertical component we call lift. The steeper the angle the air climbs at, the better the lift. A 45° slope with a given wind speed will always create less lift than a 70° slope in the same wind speed as the vertical component is less (see *Fig 8.7*).

We also need to take into account the wind strength and direction. Is it too strong? Is there enough wind to soar? Is it blowing directly onto the hill? Very often the wind does not meet the hill at a right angle. If it is, say, 30° "off" the slope, less lift will be produced, as the air will climb the hill at a shallower angle. In this case a slope that looks like the steeper example in *Fig 8.7* will actually behave more like the shallower example in terms of the lift produced.

If the wind is "off" it also means that when you are soaring in the rising air in front of the slope, you will, on alternate beats, be flying on a downwind leg - this situation is addressed in the section on airspeed, groundspeed and windspeed. You

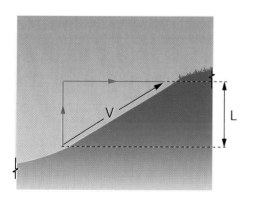

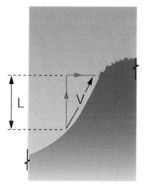

Fig 8.7: Steep and shallow slopes and the different amounts of lift (L) produced from the same wind speed (V).

must decide whether it is worth flying or moving to another hill, or not to fly at all. This kind of judgement can only be made with experience. If in doubt, do not fly.

As well as the shape and aspect (direction) of a site, a further variable is size. Bigger sites are better at producing lift as a larger body of air is being deflected upwards. This means that the "new" upward direction of the air mass is more established and the lift band will be higher and broader. The size criterion does not only apply to the actual ridge or hill itself; the upwind terrain also has a bearing on the effectiveness of the site at generating lift. A small ridge that is located downwind of gradually upward sloping ground will produce more lift than the same sized site with flat or undulating ground upwind of it.

Many apparently "perfect" ridges are in fact the sides of valleys, with another slope facing the opposite way just upwind. Such sites demand great caution, as many are dangerous to fly, or can only be used in very light winds, due to the downslope winds or rotors affecting the lift band of the potential site. If there is any doubt about such a site it is better to be left unflown until it has been checked out by highly experienced flyers. (In the UK most possible flying sites have already been investigated.)

A site will often have bowls or spurs that face in slightly differing directions; parts of the ridge may be higher than others and parts will be steeper; one section may have a nasty rotor behind the edge, and the shape of the lip may give a strong venturi effect at another point. If you have a basic understanding of airflow and lift production you should be able to predict where the site is safe to launch and land,

where the best lift will be in a given direction and if there are any areas that should be avoided or need extra height to cross.

While assessing the site there are other factors to consider. There may be hazards such as trees or power lines. The landing area should be large enough for your level of experience, and if you are planning to soar and top-land there must be a suitable area for this. The aspect of a site is very important, ie what is it facing? If the area immediately upwind is rough or down-sloping, or has high buildings, this will adversely affect the airflow. If it is has green fields the chances of thermals are less, and if it has a dry or rocky landscape the chances are much greater. Sites facing the sea often benefit from very smooth airflow and are often very suitable for early soaring flights.

Putting all this information together we can look at a site such as in *Fig 8.8*. With the wind coming from the north (a northerly) the ridge is pretty straightforward and looks easy to soar. Because it has a south-easterly face as well, it would be dangerous to drift too far back, so caution is required in stronger winds. The rocky gulley may be a good source of thermals, but it may also "trap" you in the venturi effect if the wind is strong. This is doubly dangerous, as the power lines are immediately behind this point.

If you fly beyond the gulley, the lift will weaken very quickly if there is any easterly component to the wind, as the wind flows around the face rather than along it. You may lose height and find it hard to get back, especially with the power lines between you and the landing area. Until you have a good deal of experience, the whole western end of the ridge beyond the trig point on top is best left alone.

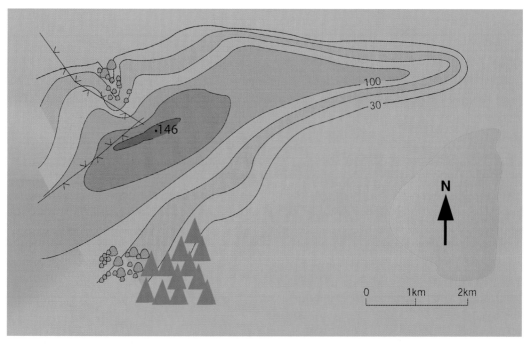

Fig 8.8: Topographic (map) view of a possible paragliding site.

In a south-easterly wind the ridge is longer and perhaps a little easier to use. The area of rocks that are sheltered from the wind by the trees and facing directly into the sun are a very strong trigger point for thermals to be formed. However, as the ridge gets shallower here, the ridge lift will be weak, and the best option may be to work up some height first, then go and loiter for a while in that area, before coming back to the main ridge if you do not find a good area of lift.

The lake is a good indictaor of the wind that is approaching the ridge, and ruffles or calm patches seen on the surface can help you "see" the approach of gusts or of thermals. Because the ridge is a spur, if you do gain say 500m of height above take-off in a thermal and follow it downwind, when you fly out into the flatlands behind it you will immediately

"gain" another 150m of altitude, making this an easy site to fly cross-country from. This can all be assessed simply from the map; when you can see the terrain and sky for yourself, there are many more clues you can glean as to how the lift will behave at a specific site.

A thorough site and weather assessment should give you enough information to decide if it is suitable for you to fly.

Wind gradient

Air is affected by friction as it moves over the landscape; all the grass and trees, bushes and buildings obstruct the flow, preventing the airmass from travelling the way it wants and slowing it down, so at ground level, where there is a lot of friction, the air is moving relatively

Fig 8.9: Wind gradient

slowly. A few metres above the surface, there is far less friction, though due to its inherent viscosity, the air will still be slowed to some extent by the slower-moving layer beneath. The higher you go, the less restricted and therefore the faster the wind will be.

The first 10 metres or so above ground level can exhibit an increase of 100% in the windspeed. At 200-300 metres or so above the terrain the relative drag decreases more slowly in most circumstances, and the effect becomes less apparent (though different meteorological conditions can have a marked effect on this pattern). See *Fig 8.9*.

Wind gradient is an effect of parasitic drag, and as the windspeed doubles, so the drag generated is squared. This means that in a light wind the gradient is barely noticeable, but as the wind gets stronger so the gradient becomes more marked. A wind of 5kph in the landing field may indicate a wind of 7kph at the launch site 200m higher. A wind of 20kph in the same spot is likely to mean 40kph or more at launch on the same site.

This gradient in wind speed is particularly noticeable on the hills we fly; the "normal" gradient of say 10kph in the landing field and 15-20kph at 100metres above it is exaggerated by a related phenomenon - the "venturi" zone (*Fig 8.10*).

Paraglider pilots choose to fly ridges that offer the best lift, that is to say hills which the wind is forced to flow over. And in addition to the wind gradient, the airflow is accelerated over the crest of the hill by being constricted between the ground and the weight and inertia of the horizontal wind above it. The effect is the same as airflow over a wing -the less space there is, the faster the flow must be. The result of this is that the wind speed at launch may be two to three times the wind strength in the landing field.

It is vital to appreciate this for two reasons in particular. Firstly, if you launch from below the top of a hill, you must assume that the wind will be much stronger than above you and that if you

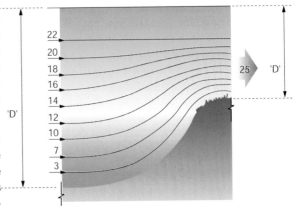

Fig 8.10. Wind gradient due to ground friction and venturi effect over the ridge crest.

ascend into this stronger zone you could have a problem. The second is to do with flight planning. You may suddenly find that you are approaching the bottom landing area more quickly than you anticipated, and with less headwind to reduce your groundspeed, your glide performance can improve dramatically. If you can anticipate this situation it is much easier to avoid an inadvertent stall caused by misjudging your speed, or an overshoot of your intended target.

Pilots who habitually fly dynamic soaring sites soon become used to the increase of wind strength with height, but can be caught out when flying big Alpine sites where the phenomenon of valley winds can make the wind strength in the landing area stronger than at take-off. This is also caused by the venturi effect, but in the case of a deep valley which is narrower at the bottom than the top the "squeezing" and subsequent acceleration of the airflow is most in evidence at the valley floor. This situation is covered in Chapter 33, Mountain Flying.

In addition to assessing the airflow patterns and dynamic lift characteristics of a site, there are some other factors that we also need to consider.

The surface of the slope can have significant effects on the way a site is flown. The first is physical: a rocky slope will be less forgiving of an inadvertent touchdown or a slope landing, and so will demand a wider margin between your feet (and wing-tips) than, say, a grass-covered slope. Trees also dictate a larger margin for error, for obvious reasons.

Flying sites are often the venues for transmission ariels and these may be supported with bracing wires. More than one pilot has caught a thermal and circled up the slope, to find their track is leading them straight at a mast. Such obstacles demand a wide margin, particularly as the cables are often almost invisible from certain angles.

In addition to the risks of actually touching your site, the physical properties of the surface can significantly affect the air. When snow covers the mountains and hills, the smooth surface and uniform temperature can offer some glassy smooth flying conditions.

However, a rocky slope facing south will soon start to heat up in direct sun, and powerful thermals will give good lift but turbulent air.

When flying over trees at a good height they are just like grass or bushes on a bigger scale and do little to change the airflow pattern, but if you get low, particularly on slopes with a "shoulder" or ledges, the trees can cause areas of sinking air or turbulence in their lee. It is very unwise to try and soar a ridge or work a thermal if that involves flying behind trees.

One very pleasant side effect of tree-covered sites is that, if they have been in sun for a few hours, and the wind drops in the evening, they may gradually release the warm air as the day cools, in a kind of huge, long-lived, slow motion thermal allowing an extended late evening flight, where you seem to be staying up as if by magic. Pilots therefore sometimes know this phenomenon as "magic lift".

A summary of site assessment is to check for: Shape, Size, Steepness, Surface, Aspect, Access, and Rules.

Weather Assesment

In addition to the properties of the site, we also need to know that the weather is suitable. The weather is a huge subject and there are some excellent books that are definitely worth reading if you wish to know more. To confine ourselves here to the fundamentals, we have three basic requirements.

Good visibility

It is self evident that it is dangerous to fly if there is low cloud or mist obscuring the hill. Even if you can see parts of the slope or the landing area, there is a very real danger of it thickening quickly, particularly if the temperature is falling, and

you can quickly become totally disorientated. If you are in cloud but well clear of the surface, you still run the risk of encountering another aircraft. In thermal generated cumulus clouds (especially near popular flying sites) there may be another glider taking the same gamble. Even far from flying sites you may encounter both civil and military traffic flying on instruments.

At dusk (or dawn if you are really keen!) the visibility may also be poor and make judging distances and altitude very difficult. Obstacles like power lines may be completely invisible. It is worth noting that if you are flying above a hill or moun-

tain it remains light much longer than in the valley or landing field. More than one pilot has been caught out setting up a landing in a dark field late in the evening.

For all these reasons it is illegal to fly in poor visibility, whether caused by cloud or darkness (see chapter 24, Airlaw).

Rain and snow

Flying in light rain or drizzle is miserable, but it is not dangerous for short periods as long as the visibility is OK. It is often easier and quicker to fly down than walk if the weather turns poor. If it means getting a nice dry canopy wet, remember it may be a long job to dry it out again. If there is heavy rain or snow, it becomes dangerous to fly. The water or snow is carried into the canopy with the airflow and cannot escape. It will build up in the trailing edge and eventually it will distort the canopy and disturb the flight characteristics. If sufficient weight builds up you could enter a stall from which you cannot recover. One pilot has already been killed in this way flying in snow. Heavy rain is often associated with squally or turbulent air, and this is another reason to avoid flying in very wet conditions.

Wind

We require a reasonably smooth breeze to fly. For training, it can be anywhere between zero and about 20kph (though not too gusty). For ridge soaring we need at least 10 to12 kph, but no more than about 25kph. We can check the wind strength and how smooth it is in several ways. The first and most important is by feel and experience. Standing on the edge of the hill for five minutes before

deciding whether or not to fly is never a wasted exercise. If you think it is near the top limit for you this is particularly true: you would not wish to launch only to find that you had taken off during a temporary lull. You can confirm your impressions with a wind speed indicator. These come in several forms and give you an accurate readout of the wind speed. They can only tell you what the wind is doing on the spot where you are holding them, so it is worth walking to the edge of the slope and angling them into the airflow to obtain the highest reading you can. This will be the most accurate. They can also assist in deciding just how gusty it is.

Gusts are the thing to watch out for: it is safer to fly in a steady wind of, say, 24kph (providing the site is suitable) than in one that is varying between 10kph and 20kph

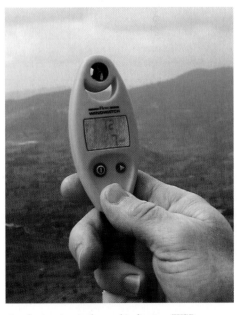

An electronic wind speed indicator (WSI)

There are also visual clues to the wind's behaviour. Among the most obvious are windsocks or streamers (every site should have one) and other pilots.

You will often be sharing the site with hang-glider pilots whose craft have a greater resistance to turbulence. If they are getting kicked about it is a good idea to wait a while. The best plan of action is always to ask those who have just flown (hang-gliders or paragliders): they are usually happy to give you their impressions. Model aircraft and birds can also be useful indicators.

Clouds offer perhaps the best way to assess the wind from the ground. Look first at how quickly they are travelling; if there seems to be just a light breeze on the surface, but the clouds are hurtling by only a few hundred metres above your head, some further investigation is required before you consider flying. The other way in which clouds can help you assess conditions is that each cloud type is an indicator of the air's behaviour. Thermals - rising columns of warm air that create lift and associated turbulence - are frequently marked by cumulus (cotton wool) clouds, formed when the moisture in the air condenses when it cools. Lenticular clouds are indicators of atmospheric waves set up by the flow of the air over the hill or mountain ranges. Such waves are a source of both lift and, at their fringes, turbulent air. Perhaps the most noticeable of all clouds are cumulonimbus (cu-nim for short) which are associated with heavy rain and storms and in which the turbulence has been known to tear the wings off sailplanes. Thermals and wave lift are discussed in chapter 26, Cross Country.

The greatest single cause of accidents is flying in poor or unsuitable weather conditions (especially strong winds). If in doubt, always ask for advice. Remember, the mountains will still be there tomorrow.

An approaching cold front.

The Parachute Landing Fall (PLF)

A paraglider is unlike any other aircraft in that it offers no protection at all to the pilot in the event of a hard landing or a crash. If you do approach the ground too fast or in the wrong direction, it is certain that you are going to be the thing that hits hardest.

There are a couple of things that we can do to protect ourselves: the first is always to wear sensible clothing, boots and a helmet, and to have a foam pad of some type installed in the harness.

The second is to become proficient at the parachute landing fall. The PLF, as it is usually known, was developed in the UK by the military when the number of injuries sustained by paratroops on landing was becoming a cause for serious concern. There is no doubt that the technique has subsequently saved many potential injuries in the parachuting world. Whilst the horizontal component of a paragliders landing approach makes it less applicable in most cases, there are a number of situations in which it works equally well for us (a low level collapse, being "dumped" by turbulence or deploying a reserve

for example); and for this reason it is a mandatory part of the BHPA's training programme.

The PLF works by reducing the shock to any one part of the body by ensuring that the shock is absorbed over a large area. A PLF cannot be learnt from a book, but the basic position and the roll are illustrated here.

A good technique and airbag combined can do a lot to minimise injury.
(Photo: f8 photography)

The important points to remember are:

● **Tuck in your elbows and chin.**

● **Bend your knees and keep them together.**

● **Bend slightly at the waist.**

● **Twist away from the direction of travel (45° or so is best).**

● **Try to go "floppy" (blowing out your air and "deflating" may help).**

● **PRACTICE - It's no good if you can't remember what to do when the ground is coming up too fast.**

Common faults when practicing PLFs include:

● **Not bending at the waist enough (the feet do not end up going the right way if you do this).**

● **Not turning as you flop: the sides of your knees, not the front of them, should touch the ground.**

● **Being too stiff; try to "crumble" into the ground, not fall over like a felled tree. The calves should touch first.**

● **Legs coming apart as you roll- don't let them -gripping something like a glove between the knees may help you practice.**

In conclusion, the PLF is rarely used in a real situation, but when it has been, it has certainly prevented injury. It should be practiced regularly. If you cannot remember anything else, always twist away from the ground, so you do not hit head-on, and bend -the foetal position will do the job. Shouting something just before contact (you can choose your own word!) is helpful as it empties the lungs and helps you "deflate", but do remember to keep your tongue in and your mouth shut as you impact.

Pre-Flight Checks

Like any aircraft, a paraglider must be pre-flighted before launch. The reason is very simple: the air itself is not inherently dangerous, but it is an environment that is very unforgiving of mistakes.

The consequences of (say) failing to do up a buckle are liable to be a lot more serious than falling off a windsurfer.

Pre-flight checks fall into three categories:

Canopy inspection.

To be carried out at least once a year or after any damage. This should be an exhaustive check of all the fabric for tears and excessive wear, all the lines of stitching, and all the lines, including attachment points. It is normal to measure a selection of lines to ensure they conform to the original specification. Ideally, the fabric should be tested for its air impermeability (porosity) and a line broken to check the reduction in breaking strain. If the canopy is faded, it may be suffering from ultra-violet degradation, particularly in hot climates.

The annual check should be carried out by a professional dealer or manufacturer. The German DHV airworthiness certification and most glider manufacturers specify that an annual check by a professionally authorised person is a requirement of the certification and the warranty.

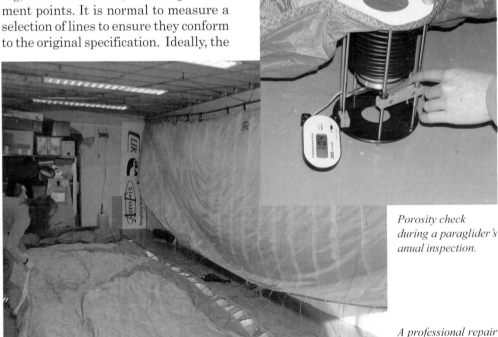

Porosity check during a paraglider's anual inspection.

A professional repair facility carrying out glider inspections.

Daily inspection (DI)

These are visual checks that are to be carried out each day before flight.

Helmet ~ Correct size, on and done up?

Harness ~ Check stitching. Check for wear, especially where any metal touches webbing. Ensure buckles are functioning correctly - it is possible to misthread some types. Quick-lock buckles can be unreliable in sandy or snowy conditions. Ensure that any protective padding is correctly installed. Check that the reserve parachute locking pins are securely in place.

Maillons/karabiners ~ All should be fully done up (large and small). Note that all maillon gates should be exposed. If they are "turned over" and hidden inside webbing loops they can be unscrewed by the motion of the risers.

Risers ~ Check stitching, especially where it is "bar-tacked", as this is very prone to abrasion.

Control lines ~ Are they secured correctly to the handles? Do the last two metres show signs of wear? Make sure they are free running and not wrapped around the risers.

Lines ~ Check for damage and tangles.

Canopy ~ Check the fabric for signs of wear and tear. Any rips or punctures? Check stitching, especially around the highly stressed leading edge. Make sure there are no obvious internal ruptures and that there are no objects in the envelope (stones, sandwiches etc).

Instruments ~ Is your battery life OK? Are all attachments secure? Have you zeroed altimeter and set stopwatch?

Checking the glider (above) and the risers (below) during the Daily Inspection.

Pre-launch inspection

To be completed before committing your-self to each flight:

1. Wind and weather

- Is the strength and direction still OK?
- How is the sky looking?
- Is visibility good?
- What is on the horizon? (Upwind weather)
- How are other pilots doing?

2. Kit

- Harness: On correctly? Leg and chest strap(s) done up? Both carabiners locked?
- Reserve pins securely seated.
- Is my helmet correctly fitted and done up?

Pre-launch checks (here being assisted by an instructor).

- All canopy cells fully open?
- Lines all clear? No tangles, no line-overs?
- No riser twists, Check which way you will rotate for reverse launches.
- Controls lines. No twists or tangles. Are the lines free running?
- Instuments/ Radios On?

3. Airspace.

Is the space you are about to launch into clear of all other aircraft and hazards? Check in front, above and behind.

4. Pilot.

- Are you feeling OK? Confident and focused?
- Have you got an outline flight plan?
- Have you remembered your PFUP? (Pre-flight urination procedure)

Many pilots use mnemonics to help them recall all the main points of their pre-launch check. Common ones include : **W**ill **G**eordie **H**ave **H**is **C**at **A**board

Wind & weather
Glider
Helmet
Harness
Controls
All clear

Another is : **S.H.O.W.B.I.Z.**

Straps and buckles(4, including helmet)
Helmet
Observation
Wind
Brakes
I'm OK
Z There is no "Z"

Or feel free to make up your own!

The Forward or Alpine Launch

Introduction

This method is used if there is a light (less than 10kph) wind, or no wind at all. As the name suggests, it is commonly used in alpine countries where the majority of launches are on slopes with little wind. It can be used in stronger winds if an anchor-man is used to help hold the pilot while the canopy rotates up.

Preparation

Do your pre-flight checks. In zero wind, or on flat ground, you may be helpful for a fellow pilot to hold up the centre of the leading edge. Make sure you have enough room to have a good run and to check the canopy before you are committed. If launching from an area with rocks or vegetation that could snag a line, you can vary the technique by placing all the lines on top of the canopy and standing with your heels touching the trailing edge. Take care not to stand on the lines.

The launch procedure

1. Lay out the canopy flat on its back (top surface) with the trailing edge into wind.

2. Stand with your back to the canopy, facing into wind.

3. Hold the control handles as you would in flight and allow all the risers to drape over your forearms. (You usually need to identify and pick up the

front A risers in your hand at this point.).

4. Step forward until the "A" lines are fully stretched and evenly tensioned; check the air to make sure that it is clear. Note : several glider models with "split" A risers may launch more easily in light winds if you ignore the outer A's and hold only the inner front risers.

5. If there is any breeze you may be able to pull the risers a little to create a "wall" and ensure the cells are inflating evenly.

6. Run strongly and smoothly forward - keep your head down and lean forwards. At the point of maximum rearward pressure you may need to check your forward motion to allow the wing to "catch up" and fly above your head; however as the pressure reduces you will need to continue your forward run, releasing the front risers when the canopy is almost overhead (you can feel the rearwards pressure reducing). You may very well need to add some brake at this point to stabilise the canopy in the correct position above your head.

Leaning forwards helps your hands follow the natural arc of the front risers - do not pull them down or push them forward. The power should come from your run, not your arms.

7. Turn your head to one side then the other to check the canopy - cells open? Lines clear? Try not to break stride or slow down as you do this: the more pressure and speed you maintain the better. If a cell or two are collapsed on one side, give a firm pump with the control on that side to reinflate them, do not launch with collapsed cells.

8. If you have time, you can double check that the controls are running freely. Apply pressure to the controls smoothly and evenly as you clear the edge of the hill.

In stronger winds some pilots still prefer to use this launch method, where there is very restricted space, for example. In this situation an experienced helper is useful to prevent the pilot being pulled backwards during inflation.

Alpine, or forward launch, using an anchor-man.
(Photo: Northern Paragliding)

The Reverse Launch

Introduction

The reverse launch is generally used when there is a breeze that can support the inflated canopy without the pilot needing to continuously move forward. This is usually the case when attempting to ridge soar on hills rather than mountains. There are a few more elements than with a forward launch, and therefore more to go wrong, but with some breeze there is also more time to play with, and you can inspect the inflated canopy at leisure before deciding whether to fly. It is far easier to inflate and pull the canopy up without being pulled over by the wind when you are facing it, so this type of launch allows you to manage alone in a wind that would require help if you were forward launching.

However, if you have any doubt about your ability to control the canopy in a good breeze it may be appropriate to ask an experienced pilot to act as your anchor man and hold you while you inflate your paraglider. Though if the wind is simply too strong for you to managed an unassisted launch then it is likely to be too strong to fly safely.

Preparation

Do your pre-flight checks. Make sure there is plenty of slack in the lines as you prepare and put on the harness - it could be em-

The reverse launch pull-up. (Photo: Sup'Air)

barrassing and painful for the canopy to start inflating and for you to be dragged along with only one leg in the harness!

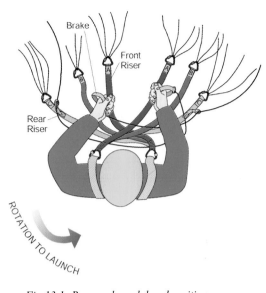

Fig 13.1: Reverse launch hand position.

1. Lay the canopy out flat on its back in a gentle arc with the trailing edge into wind.

2. Stand with your back to the wind, facing the canopy. To do this you will have to lift one complete set of risers over your head. You should now have the risers crossed in front of you. See *Fig 13.1*- look carefully at which way they are crossed. When you come to turn back again (the rotation) you will need to "follow" the lower set of risers around. If you decide at the start of your flying career which way you will turn, and do it the same way every time, you are less likely to get it wrong.

3. Grasp at least a metre of control line in each hand (do not cross your arms, just take the line that is controlling the same side as your hand). There should still be no tension on the rest of the lines at this point.

4. Without letting go of the control lines, hold the corresponding front riser in each hand as well.

5. By pulling on the front risers, inflate the cells to form a "wall"; if it is uneven or tries to lift too soon, you can alter its shape, or lower it, by pulling on the trailing edge with the control lines. If you need to lower the wall quickly, walk towards it at the same time. Ideally, the centre of the wall should be higher than the tips. A low wall of 2-3ft high is adequate in most conditions. If the cells are squashed on one side it means the wind is coming from that direction and you need to move yourself and the wall round a few degrees until it is inflated evenly.

6. Once the wall is prepared you can set up the launch. There are a few variations on the exact method and each has some strengths. However, the commonest is the "continuous control method" or "crossed brakes" technique outlined below.

7. Now you need to collect the brakes - there shouldn't be too much tension on lines while you do this; step forward if you need to. Look down at the crossed riser sets. Visualise how you want your controls to be when the glider has come up and you have turned. You will need to reach under the crossed set of risers and take the control handle from the lower set. This is the "shortest route" and

seems quite natural as your hand is just following the riser.

8. The other arm follows the "longest route" and reaches over the top of everything then around the back of the riser set to take the other control handle. Do not be tempted to put your hand between the risers or you will get tangled as you rotate. This control handle can now be brought back over to a more comfortable position with your arms uncrossed. You will see that the control line you have just collected is now wrapped around the riser set and looks a mess, do not worry, this is normal and it will unwind as you rotate later.

9. You can now take the front A riser on each side. There is no need to cross your arms - simply grasp the riser on the right side with your right hand and vice-versa. Each hand is now controlling one front riser and the brake for the opposite side.

10. Complete your pre-launch checks by seeing if your airspace is all clear. If all is well you can fully inflate the wing by pulling on the front risers.

11. As the wing reaches the flying position you may need to add a dab of brake

You can then either turn and launch immediately, or remain facing the canopy while you feel the wind, or wait for an opportune moment to turn and launch.

15. Turn to face into wind. Take care not to reduce the pressure on the canopy - it

to stabilise it in the correct position. You now have time to check that the canopy is fully inflated and has no tangles. When happy, you can then simply pivot on one foot and rotate under the wing to face forward for your launch.

12. If the wing begins to "fall" one way you can correct this very simply by stepping sideways towards the centre of the canopy and simultaneously applying brake with the hand on the **same** side (this will of course apply brake to the "high " side of the wing). i.e, if the wing is slipping right, you step right and brake with your right arm. This seems a little strange for the first few attempts, but quickly becomes a normal reaction.

13. If the pull-up has been too weak, the canopy will simply fall backwards and you can re-start. If it is coming up too fast, you can apply brake as it climbs. A big advantage of this technique is that you can apply brake and steer at any point during the launch, as you always have the controls in your hands..

14. When the canopy is stable above you, check for full inflation, clear lines, etc.

is common to collapse it at this stage by stepping back under the wing as you turn. An effective technique is to reach out behind you with one leg as you rotate so keeping your movement constantly into wind, and the canopy evenly loaded. Before you turn, check the risers again: you need to follow the lower (obscured) one around. Apply pressure smoothly and evenly to the controls as you clear the edge of the hill.

NOTE -If you find that you have turned

the wrong way, the risers will now have a 360° twist in them. If you are on the ground, you can simply go around the other way. If you have been lifted off, as can happen on slopes, do not worry. Simply continue to use the controls to fly the canopy away from the hill until you are well clear. If you then let go of everything, the risers will naturally untwist themselves. Once sorted out, reach casually

"...and fly off as if that's what you meant to do all the time..."

for the controls and fly off as if that was what you meant to do all the time.

Other reverse launch variations

The cosss-brake launch outlined above became widely popular in the early 90's when canopies became fast enough to require continuous brake throughout the launch procedure. Prior to that, pilots would often pull up the risers with the controls from the same riser in their hands.

That system has a big disadvantage, in that you must drop at least one control handle at some point, or pass it from one hand to another whilst you rotate.

It was not uncommon for pilots to find themselves airborne without one (or both) control handles in their hands, or if they dropped one under some pressure the handle could fly up and hitch itself around the control line.

However, this technique is very good for extended ground-handling, as there is no line wrapped around the risers (which can cause damage and excess wear) and the natural tendency of the risers to untwist is reduced. For this reason, using the "uncrossed" technique, in which the right hand controls the right tip while the wing is facing you (exactly like kite flying), is very good for extended ground

Reverse launch variation. (Photo: Sup'Air)

handling practice and for walking an inflated glider back up a slope, for example.

Certain older pilots are reluctant to change from this original technique, as it very familiar to them.

Inflating the canopy with one hand con-

One handed variation.

trolling a front riser while the other hand controls the brake on the same side is a very useful technique in strong winds.

In this variation, the pilot stands slightly to one side of the canopy as it is pulled up and the canopy generates much less pressure as it flies up the side of the "window", so it is easier to control without you getting dragged. Once in the stable position, the controls do have to be located after the rotation as above.

This technique is very good for strong conditions, or pilots without great physical strength or body weight, and is rightly popular with tandem pilots who are handling a larger wing for the same reasons.

Essentially, all ground control is concerned with modifiying the speed of the wing and its direction. It is possible to do this with almost any combination of brakes and risers, you can hold both brakes in one hand and both front risers; in another - though this technique

Both front risers in one hand and both brakes in the other hand variation.

offers very little lateral control and needs fast footwork to stay under the centre of the wing at all times.

You can simply hold both rear risers and steer with those, but because you cannot speed the wing up in this situation, but is easy to stall and drop it, this technique is well suited to use on a steeper slope where the wing is always trying to fly (useful when walking up a steeper slope, for example)

There is no "right" way to control a paraglider on the ground and it is very useful and informative to try out a few of these variations when you have an opportunity .

Launch Problems & Ground Handling

Some common launch problems and how to deal with them:

Problem!
The canopy will not climb overhead.

- Too much wind? If the problem is that you are being pulled backwards as the wing comes up during an alpine launch, try switching to a reverse launch.

- Not enough wind? If you are having to walk backwards when reverse launching, try an alpine launch.

- Have you remembered to drop/ fully extend the control lines before reverse launching?

- Not physically strong enough to pull the wing up? Try the "One side" technique mentioned in Chap 13.

- Some outside factor, such as sand or snow or other debris in your wing,

- Is your paraglider wet?

- Are you running on completely flat ground, uphill or in turbulent air? It may help to begin closer to the edge if this is safe.

- How old is your wing? A sign of increased porosity is increased difficulty in launching. If your canopy often seems to "hang-back", it is well worth having it professionally checked, particularly if it getting old or the colour is fading.

Problem!
Canopy tucks (collapses forwards).

- Is there enough wind? Try an alpine launch or run faster.

- You may need to be adding brake if the canopy is overflying you. Try the continuous control method.

- Are you pulling on the front risers too hard or for too long? Or are you shortening them by pulling them down? (This is quite a common problem and can be hard for an instructor, to spot unless he is holding the risers with you). Are you "punching" and pushing them in front of your body? Guide the risers up with open hands.

● Are you stepping back towards the canopy when rotating, thereby reducing pressure? (This is probably the favourite method of cocking up a reverse launch!). Before you rotate, consciously reach back with your foot towards the edge of the slope/ into wind, before putting it down and pivoting on it.

● If the canopy is climbing too fast for you, try pulling it up holding the A and B risers together in your hands. Stepping towards it as it comes up also helps to de-power it to some extent, but this must be done as it is part way up, **not** as it reaches the zenith position or it will collapse.

Problem!
Canopy slews to one side.

● Turbulence in launch area?

● Canopy not laid out neatly?

● Canopy not laid out into wind, or not running into wind?

● Uncommited launch - insufficient pressure.

● Are you standing on the centre line of the canopy compared to the wind.?

Problem!
Canopy collapses in the centre (claps hands).

● Poorly laid out? Try laying it in a tighter arc.

● Uneven ground? Try using a helper to hold up the centre of the leading edge.

● If you have split A risers, launch with just the middle A's.

● This can happen on snow or other slippery surfaces, where the tips of the inflated wing start to slide away from you the moment you relax pressure on the controls. You can dump a few handfuls of snow on the trailing edge to pin it down until you are ready.

Ground handling

Many pilots find that the hardest part of paragliding is controlling the machine while still on the ground. The reason for this is that when flying, your weight will automatically swing below the canopy, and, except in turbulent conditions, there will always be a load on the lines. On the ground however, the canopy can slide over to one side of you or the other; it can drop behind or in front of you and the load can vary from moment to moment. The more you can minimise these variations, the better the canopy will behave.

To keep the paraglider above your head

in the proper position you will often need to use the controls and sometimes the risers as well. A lot of problems can be eliminated by good preparation, making sure the canopy is into wind, knowing which way you will need to turn during a reverse launch, etc. Treat the canopy as hostile! If you give it the opportunity, it will try and drag you through the nearest cow pat or fence! You must stay in charge and not allow yourself to be pulled around. If this proves to be impossible, collapse it immediately and start again. If this is not possible to control effectively, it may simply be too windy for you to fly.

Remember that until the wing is flying correctly above your head the controls will serve only to pull it down further, not as effective steering devices. If it is well off to one side you will need to walk back under the centre as you brake, or use the brake and front riser from the high side to pull it back up to the correct position. The other way you can help yourself is by keeping the load constant. This often means that you must correct and check your canopy while running or walking (often backwards) to maintain pressure through the lines. Take care not

to walk backwards over the edge of the hill by mistake!

Many people actually find it easier not to look at the canopy once they have rotated and are facing forward ready for launch. Try to develop control just by feeling what your wing is doing above you.

Inevitably sometimes you will lose the battle and the canopy will end up in a heap on one side or on top of you, and you will have to lay it out again. In a breeze you may find that a little careful manipulation of the brakes and risers can do this without the need to go and move the canopy by hand. An example of this is when the canopy has dived over and is "nose down" with the leading edge and the cell entries pointing into the ground. It is often possible to lean back a little on the risers to give a pivot point, and with a long pull on one brake handle, make the canopy fly back over into the correct starting position.

Ground handling skills are very useful and are something that many pilots, eager to fly, often spend too little time perfecting.

Ground handling practice. (Photo: www.sunsoar-paragliding.com)

First Flights

By about the second or third day of training you will have completed several low level flights or "hops". You should have mastered use of the controls, and hopefully your instructor will have sorted out any bad habits (looking at the canopy as you fly along is a favourite one). It is likely that you have been responding to commands from an instructor or to "bat" signals from him as he stands in the landing area. Now you are ready for your first high flights.

Flight planning

The higher you get, the larger the radius of the circle within which your possible landing sites will lie. Unless you are very lucky this means that you are now able to reach stone walls, barbed wire fences or the field with the bull in it. You can no longer wait for the ground to simply come up and meet you - this is where you really start to pilot the aircraft and make decisions for yourself. Your instructor may

well be on the radio, but he will only be a back-up and he certainly won't be able to do anything if you do the wrong thing. The secret of being a good pilot is to think ahead.

A pilot has been heard to say, "Well, I can console myself with the thought that the best pilot in the world could not have avoided crashing." This was in a deep valley with trees, a river, a railway line and no obvious landing area. The answer, of course, is that the best pilot in the world would not have put himself in that situation.

In range of some unsuitable landing areas! (Photo: APCO Aviation Ltd)

Preparing for the first high flight.

The first point, then, about flight planning is that it includes planning not to fly. The next point is that you should think about any hazards and how you can avoid them before you take off (see Chapter 8, Site assessment). This reduces your mental workload when airborne.

A third and slightly contradictory element of flying un-powered aircraft, is that you must be prepared to revise your flight plan as you go along. If you decide to fly over that wall, and you start to sink low as you approach it, do not blindly follow your plan (or even your instructor's).

Decide on an alternative and do it. It is far easier if you think of these alternative flight plans, along with your intended plan, before you launch. The worst thing you can do is still be trying to make up your mind when you get there. Pilots

have been seen to approach a huge field with one obstacle such as a tree in it. They veer left as they come in, then right, then left again and end up narrowly missing it simply through indecisiveness.

"...a huge field with one tree in it..."

Bill Lehan

The first high flights.

Usually done with radio contact from an instructor, the aim is to achieve a good clean launch, fly at a suitable airspeed, and be able to initiate a number of turns in order to follow a basic flight plan and arrive in the right position for a straight-forward landing approach and a reasonably accurate and well controlled landing.

The flights may be made from a smaller slope with some lift, or may be from a higher hill or mountain. The bigger the "jump" in altitude the more preparatory hops are required first.

The progressive nature of flying training means that the first few flights may be lower and contain as few as two turns, and later flights may require many turns to arrive in the right place at the right height. Simply being in the air, and making the control inputs to follow your flight plans teaches you to anticipate your wing's responses and gets you used to the sensation of gliding flight. Because the paraglider is trimmed to fly straight and at a suitable speed if left alone, it is often a good policy to do less rather than more on the early flights. You may have slightly elevated adrenaline levels in your bloodstream on early high flights, but try and remember that effective piloting is more about technique and progressive input than about strength!

As the "I am really flying" sensation hits you and the ear to ear grins start appearing, it is worth remembering that actually flying in smooth air is very easy; it is launch and flight planning elements that need the most work, so your instructor may be keen for you to complete several lower flights, whilst pupils are often keen to go higher and have longer flights as soon as possible.

First high mountain flights. (Photo: f8 Photography)

"...*your instructor may well be on the radio*..."

As you become more confident, new elements like larger turns are introduced, and planning your approaches becomes more critical. Your instructor may well give you rather less input as you start making decisions for yourself, and new exercises such as slope landings and weight shift steering may be added to your flight plans. Some of the useful exercises are included below and many form a part of your training syllabus.

Setting up a short field landing. (Photo: f8 Photography)

Exercises

People take part in paragliding courses for different reasons. It's certainly a more memorable way of spending the day than staying at home to wash the car. However, if you are interested in becoming a pilot, the best way to progress is to learn as much as you can from each flight. It is easy to waste a lot of time (and money) by undertaking training flights with no eventual aim. There are several exercises you can set yourself, or your instructor can set for you, to make the most of each day.

Ground handling.

If the weather is poor - mist on the hill, for example, or strong winds at launch - you can still learn a good deal by practicing your ground handling and emergency collapses. PLF's can be done without even getting your paraglider out.

Launch practice.

Almost everyone finds flying easier than launching. You can practice this on a small slope and fit in as many launches in an hour as you would get in a day on a large hill.

Short field landings.

This is an excellent one to practice - imagine an obstacle such as a fence across your usual landing area. Try to plan your flight to land short of it. When you have done it with an imaginary fence a few times, a small field with a real fence is far less of a problem.

Spot landings.

As above, but try to hit a specific target - you learn a lot about yourself as well as about the capabilities of your wing. Don't forget, it is an exercise - it's not much

Using an accelerator.

use claiming from your hospital bed that you were the closest.

Soaring beats.

This is perhaps the most valuable of all the exercises. In order to prepare yourself for soaring flight, try to fly parallel to the ridge, execute an efficient 180° turn and fly back over the same ground in the opposite direction. If you can do this in light winds near the hill, or in stronger winds further out beyond the lift band, you will find that doing it when there is lift is far easier.

Some of these exercises are listed in the Pilots training record (Phase 8 improving skills) and your instructor will help you work your way through each one.

Exploring the speed range.

Try to make changes to your airspeed as you fly. Stalls are dangerous, so discuss this with your instructor before you try it.

Accelerator systems.

This is also an exercise in the training

syllabus, but too many students try it once or twice in order to get signed off and then never use their accelerator system again until they find they are pinned by strong winds. By using it from time to time in smooth air you become much more familiar with locating and activating the foot stirrup and with the effect it has on your speed and stability.

Weightshift and pitch roll co-ordination in turns.

Even on quite early flights the roll (turn)

response of the wing can be improved by weight shifting; ie leaning your body weight into the turn. This is normally done by moving the C of G to one side with a simple leaning motion, or (for maximum effect) by lifting one buttock from the seat and leaning the outside leg over the inner one, to load the inner wing. Because the wing is being banked and loaded due to weightshift, less brake input is needed to complete the turn, and as braking is inefficient (as it works by adding drag to one wing) the turn effi-

Weightshift steering. Note how the wing is deformed. (Photo: UK Airsports)

ciency is improved.

Pitch- rolling means allowing the glider to speed up slightly, which in turn will improve the roll response of the canopy; then initiating the turn, which can be a little tighter than normal if done with some airspeed in hand; then slowing down again as the wings level on the new course. This process converts some of your speed back into height and so re-gains some of the altitude lost in the origi-nal speeding up and turn.

Done properly, a well co-ordinated turn can be noticeably more efficient than just pulling on one brake line as a way of changing direction or reversing course, and is therefore particularly useful when you are trying to remain in (or get back into) a defined patch of lifting air with minimum height loss.

Cross wind and side slope landings.

You may need to land on a slope one day, and it is often a useful technique when you do not want to end up with a very long walk. This involves landing cross-wind - which is likely to mean faster - so start on a gentle incline and work your way up. There is usually one beat that is more upwind and therefore means a lower ground speed than the other way. Always choose the upwind beat for slide landings.

Do not try to land on a slope of more than about 45° or in a strong wind. You could partly collapse or stall the canopy, then find yourself airborne again.

360 Degree turns.

If you have plenty of altitude and space, 360° turns are a very useful tool, both for re-positioning yourself, prior to start-ing a landing approach for example, and for using lift. Efficient and co-ordinated

360 turns are vital for using thermal lift. The term 360 degree turn is used, as that is how many degrees you turn through, but it is rather misleading as it implies that you are flying in a circle. While this may be true in still air; because you need to fly downwind during a 360, you will drift with the wind, and so your actual ground track looks more like a fishhook! If there is a breeze you will need to en-sure you are well away from the hillside before trying this manoeuvre. As always, check with your instructor before trying this task.

Instability exercises.

Generally these are part of the later sylla-bus, and are tackled when you are soar-ing. However, in some training systems (from high mountains etc), they are added at an early stage in the training.

Asymmetric tuck practice is an important safety skill, but must be carried out un-der direct radio supervision of an instruc-tor. This is usually covered in the later stages of training. If you fly long enough, you will experience an unexpected tuck, and if you are properly trained and react quickly and appropriately, most tucks can be dealt with easily and with little disrup-tion to your flight plan. Dealing with more major collapses is covered in the instabil-ity section.

Rear riser steering.

This is also an exercise in the BHPA PRS. The purpose is to simulate a control line tangle or break. You can achieve limited steering by pulling slightly on a rear riser and combined with weight shift steering you can steer your paraglider quite effectively.

DO NOT PULL DOWN STRONGLY OR ON BOTH REAR RISERS AT ONCE - YOU CAN ENTER A DEEP STALL.

See Chapter 28, Instability and Recovery.

Note that you cannot control pitch or speed very well, or recover from a tuck without your controls, and therefore it is not advised to attempt this exercise in rough conditions.

Photo: Neil Cruickshank

Active flying.

Active flying is a term used to mean making small control inputs in order to "smooth out" the bumps in the air. The canopy only flies at its best when it is directly above you, so by braking to slow it down if it pitches forwards, or by adding speed if it drops back, you can minimise the effects of rough air. The small adjustments are similar to the subtle inputs made on a car steering wheel when driving down a straight road. A small input at the right time may avoid the need for a big one later. Active flying is something that becomes automatic with practice and is directly linked to the time spent airborne.

Rapid descent techniques.

Big ears, Spiral Dives and B line stalls should all be carried out under the supervision of an instructor. Big ears in particular is a useful skill that is part of the BHPA Pilot Rating System, but it does have some associated hazards. See chapter 28 for more information on these manoeuvres.

Landing

Preparation

First you must decide where to land. The earlier you think about this, the more options will be open to you. The landing field should, preferably, be a flat area with no obstacles, clear of any turbulent air-flow from upwind obstacles such as woods or buildings or other hills. The bigger the landing field, the better. Other factors to consider are animals or people in the area and how easy it will be to get out of (is there a gate?) Are there any power or telephone lines to avoid?

Approach

Having followed your flight plan, you need to decide what kind of approach to make. There are several options.

All landing approaches are basically a question of arriving near your chosen spot with excess height and burning it off in a controlled manner to leave you in the right position for an into wind glide to touchdown. *Fig 16.1* illustrates how you can judge whether you will clear an obstacle or not when on final glide.

If high or if there is little wind you can opt for the classic aircraft approach. This usually starts upwind of your intended area and consists of a circuit, with downwind leg off to one side of your touch down point, a cross-wind base leg and a final approach into wind. This option is designed to allow an aircraft to join a pattern at an airfield with other craft launching, and with a high base leg it can take advantage of changes in your approach speed or descent rate to give an accurate touch down. This is well suited to aircraft with power or aerodynamic controls such as airbrakes that can be used to degrade the glide angle on approach. The system can work well for paragliders, particularly for outlandings from cross-country flights, or flights from big mountains in little wind.

If there is much wind (or you do not know how strong it is), the lack of penetration into wind can make loitering downwind of the landing spot impractical.

Starting from high downwind and using linked S turns or beats to lose height is very effective, and is the system used by most new pilots from a training hill

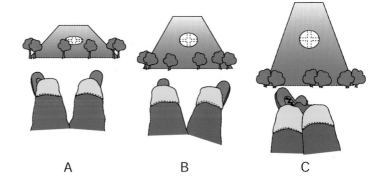

Fig 16.1: Relative motion; Flight A-B-C will clear the wires and land on the target. Flight C-B-A will land short.

A   B   C

Making a landing approach to avoid hazards.

where landing areas are typically huge. However, it is difficult to be accurate with this system, and the descent through different areas of lift and sink can cause pilots to easily undershoot or overshoot.

The constant aspect approach, is a modified version of the aircraft approach, starting slightly upwind and approaching in a curve It is very effective in allowing flexibility to accurately adjust your altitude if wind and lift conditions are variable.

The constant aspect approach (*Fig 16.2*) relies on conscious noting of the signs that most experience pilots use automatically

to judge their glide path and approach to a bottom landing field. Previously you will have used S turns to approach landing fields that your instructor had kindly placed pretty much where your glider wanted to land anyway.

Once you start playing with lifting air, or bigger flying sites where a short landing is required, you must refine your

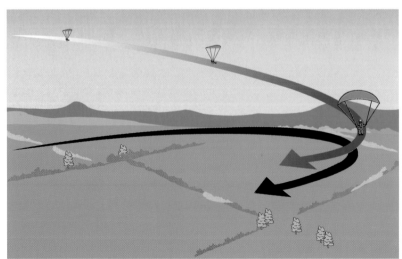

Fig 16.2: The constant aspect approach

technique.

When you look down and sideways at your intended field or landing spot you should be able to judge the glide you need to reach it. Of course you should be too high to fly straight in at this point (or you will need a closer field!) You must then fly past or parallel to the field you have chosen, checking constantly that the glide looks OK.

When it seems right, you simply start your long curving approach to maintain the correct glide angle. If you are climbing above your intending glide-path, widen the turn; if you are sinking, tighten up to get back on track. The idea is to end up some 20-30m above your target and slightly downwind, so that the final approach is straight glide into wind.

If you are high and well clear of a hillside then the approach can be usefully started at about 100m whilst flying downwind, but it can be "joined" at any point on the curve.

If you are in mountains or have flown away from the hill and are unsure of the state of the valley wind or your drift as you approach, you can do a whole circuit, beginning slightly upwind of the target and flying down in a lazy constant aspect circle like a spiral staircase - just the opposite, in fact, to circling upwards in a huge 2m/sec thermal.

It is important with any landing approach to keep checking the sky around you; do not get target fixated!!

This broad curving approach has a big advantage over S turns as it gives you almost infinite flexibility - get a bit high on an S turn approach and you are forced to do a whole new beat, perhaps involving a slight downwind leg close to the

ground.

Pilots with sufficient experience may approach from vertically above the landing area by circling or spiralling down, or in some cases by using a rapid descent technique like big-ears to regulate their sink rate or glide. However, these are not recommended techniques (except in very specific circumstances such as powerful lift conditions).

Not a particularly recommended approach! (Photo: Red Bull)

Whatever your approach, you should be turning into wind at a minimum of five metres from the ground, for a final glide directly into wind. Let the controls up if you have not done so already, so that you are flying at around 1/4 brake position or, in no wind, at maximum trim speed. Just before the touchdown you need to flare by braking strongly and smoothly. The exact amount of brake is determined by the wind. If there is no wind, a full flare is required. If there is a breeze you will need less. Every flight is different and you will have to practice to discover exactly when, and how hard, you need to flare.

One cause of problems with landings is that pilots seem to be accelerating towards the ground on approach (due in

*Flaring at touchdown,
Epidavros, Greece.*

part to the effect of wind gradient and in part to their reaction to the optical illusion created as the ground fills more and more of their field of vision). Some pilots' very natural reaction to this is to brake more and more as they near the ground and in an often sub-conscious attempt to keep their groundspeed low. The result, unfortunately, is that they can inadvertently stall too early and are "dumped" as the canopy stops supporting them.

A different problem is that some pilots lift up their legs as they come in. Your legs are your landing gear and much better equipped to withstand shocks than your backside. You need to make a conscious effort to sit up in the harness and actually reach down for the ground with one foot.

If one foot touches first it is easy to run off any excess speed. If both touch together it gives a very neat landing if you have no forward speed. But, if you are still moving forward, the next move is to fall over.

Touch-down

Once on the ground it is easy to relax, but the flight (and the danger of something going wrong) is not over until the canopy is safely wrapped up. If there is little breeze, the act of "flaring" the canopy to land will induce a stall as your feet touch down and the paraglider will start to collapse. To ensure that it does not drape over you, it is wise to continue to move forwards and hold the flared position with the controls. This makes the canopy fall behind you and, by keeping the lines stretched, helps to prevent tangles occurring. It's only necessary to flare sufficiently to touch down gently and so, in a breeze, you may only need to brake gently. In this case the canopy may remain inflated above you. There are several options open to you at this point. With some practice you can turn to the reverse launch position, and given an appropriate slope you can use the inflated wing to help pull you back up the hill.

You can continue to walk or run with it still inflated (provided you move more or less into wind). This can be useful if you have touched down in a muddy or rough area or if you need to clear the area for others coming in to land. If you wish to collapse the canopy, the best method is to turn and adopt the reverse launch position and then flare with the brakes or rear risers whilst moving towards the canopy.

If the wind is strong, a very good way of collapsing the canopy is to pull down sharply on the rear risers as you step towards it. This method offers the most effective means of "killing" most canopies.

The act of flaring a canopy has two effects. The first is to generate massive drag and slow or stop the forward motion through the air as the wing stalls. The second is to add lift as the angle of attack is increased. The most effective flares utilise both properties by approaching with some spare airspeed and then strongly but progressively "rounding out" by applying brake, finishing with a hard stab of the brakes to stall the wing as you contact the ground. It is common to see pupils (spurred on by their instructors command to "flare") simply whack the brakes down from their shoulders to their knees in one motion and shock stall the canopy. A slightly more subtle approach as outlined above is actually more effective, as it takes advantage

of the lift as well as the drag available.

Experienced pilots landing in very calm conditions, or those flying tandem, will often initiate a slight dive to speed up as they approach the ground, and by converting this energy to lift will actually be climbing when they flare for a touchdown. This "swing through" technique is very effective when done correctly. But do not be tempted to try it in wind or you may find yourself stalled 3 metres off the ground!

If you should lose your footing or find you have fallen and the canopy is trying to drag you, try to turn so that you are facing the glider, and releasing one control completely, pull the other control hand over hand. This is messy and may make your wing spin once or twice, but it is the best way to kill the wing's power completely if you are being dragged.

More details of landing in strong winds and subsequent canopy control are outlined in Chapter 21, Soaring Flight.

After Your Elementary Course

Once you have completed your initial course you have slightly different options open to you. You may decide that the sport is not really for you, but you'll take your certificate home, and hang it on the wall. For many people this is the best and most sensible decision.

You may continue as before, working your way up to the next level as a club pilot, using the school's equipment. This will give you the opportunity to decide for certain that you have found your vocation, whereupon you can consider buying your own equipment.

You can do this with your original school, which does have some advantages of continuity, or you can change schools, possibly to one that has a range of larger sites, or possibly one that teaches abroad. This option is discussed in more detail below.

Another variation is to buy a canopy of your own. If you are to continue learning on your own canopy, you may be able to do so at a reduced cost. (If you buy from the school who will be teaching you then a combined kit/ tuition deal may often save you a proportion of the tuition fees.

Whether you are using the school's, or your own equipment, you will now need to join the national association as a full member. You should also think about making contact with your local club, as, once qualified, it will be the club members you will be meeting out on the slopes. Most clubs run a variety of social events and have meetings each month or so, in addition to meeting when out flying. They may also publish a guide to your local sites, showing their status and suitability, nearest phones, who to ask for permission and any hazards or rules, etc.

Training in the Alps. (Photo: Sup'Air)

Training abroad.

You can learn with a foreign school, and many offer excellent tuition. However, do be aware that unless you are fluent in the local language, or the tuition is conducted in your language, the subtleties of some technical discussions may escape you. It will also add a further dimension to passing the exams!

Most importantly, however, you must be fully confident you can understand any radio commands clearly (even when you and the instructor may be under stress!)

Returning to your own country, you may find that some aspects of air law or site protocols are different, and that your qualification may not be quite the same as the local one, requiring a few more tasks to be completed and new exams sat.

Typically, learning in a mountainous environment produces pilots with far better Alpine launch and flight planning skills, but much poorer reverse launching and dynamic soaring and top-landing skills than those training on lower and breezier hills.

If you learn abroad on a holiday, do be aware that the fees you pay may be for a course, and if you cannot complete it due to weather etc, and cannot return, you may have to pay again to complete somewhere else. Always get a signed log sheet or record of your flights, so that you can show your local club or instructor what you have done.

Another way is to learn abroad but with a school from your own area. In the UK the Foot and Mouth Crisis in 2001 prompted a relaxation of the BHPA's training abroad regulations, and some schools teach all courses in various locations with good sites and better weather than the UK.

This seems like a very good idea, provided the school concerned has applied for the correct permission from the BHPA or their own country's governing bodies, and has established good relations with the flyers and schools (if any) in the host country.

In this way you can benefit from the training system you are used to, and also the better weather and holiday atmosphere of a foreign trip.

Caution: Some school trips have proved

Pilots-eye-view of soaring in South Cyprus.
(Photo: Pete Gallagher)

less than suitable because of problems with challenging sites or poor research by the providers. The BHPA ask for the following criteria to be met:

● A history of successful trips to the area.

● Liaison/permission from the local school/club/ site owners.

● Suitable sites.

● Proper preparation for incidents. Knowledge of local emergency services, local guide or person who is fluent in the local language.

Your best bet if considering this option is to check with the BHPA or previous students that the school is conforming to these criteria.

If you are a British reader, the ratio of good days for teaching in the UK is around 20-25%. In several countries with more reliable climates it is three times as high, and you get a sun tan! Wherever you go, it is unrealistic to expect to get perfectly flyable weather every day. (Despite what the brochure might say!)

Whichever route you take you can expect to need around 6- 9 days to complete a course from Elementary to CP level.

By the end of the course you can expect to :

● Be able to assess weather conditions and sites.

● Conduct good pre-flight checks.

● Be safe and reasonably competent at forward and reverse launching.

● Be able to soar in dynamic lift and top land where appropriate.

● Plan an approach and land reason-

Soaring the Grand Dune de Pyla near Bordeaux in France. (Photo: John Brettoner)

ably accurately.

- Deal with minor incidents like tucks.

- Understand and be able to use your accelerator system.

- Be able to combat strengthening lift and get down when you need to.

- Land and control your canopy in a variety of conditions.

- Understand your limitations and that of your equipment.

- Have a knowledge of the actions to take in various emergency situations.

- Know how to fly safely with others.

Or to put it another way, you should be capable of flying safely without an instructor. Parapro stage 3 is similar in scope, but requires more high flights and does not specify top-landings as a requirement.

First soaring flights in the smooth sea breezes on the S. Cyprus coast. (Photo: Mike Stiff)

Once you have reached this stage you are an independent pilot. But you are of course not an experienced one! Exercise caution, especially when assessing conditions, ask advice. It is much easier and safer if you have joined a club and go flying with more experienced pilots. Many clubs operate a voluntary coaching scheme for the newly-fledged pilots and these are well worth taking advantage of.

After spending lots of money and holiday time training, new pilots often then have a break for several weeks or months (over winter for example) before they fly again. They are rusty and the spring conditions are often powerful, so great care is needed after a break.

The best advice is to try and amass a few hours fairly soon after qualifying, or if you have had a long spell off, go back to school for a day or two.

Buying a Paraglider

The pace of paraglider development is very rapid and therefore it is impractical to refer to specific models in this section. However, there are a few questions that you should ask both yourself and the seller to make sure that you purchase the correct product.

How much can you afford?

When budgeting to buy a canopy remember that you must allow for a harness, a helmet and probably some extra training too. It will not be long before you will need a reserve and possibly a variometer. However, the newer the wing the longer it will last you, and as changing is an expensive business it is a false economy to buy a worn out or basic wing.

How much do you weigh (fully clothed)?

It is very important that you get the right size. Pilot weight and wing-loading is a vital factor in determining stability; too large and it will be slow and may behave badly in turbulence; too small and it will have poor sink rate performance making soaring difficult. Most manufacturers give an optimum weight range of around 20kg for each size. It is important that your all-up weight (that is, you with all the gear, including the wing) falls within this range. If you are in the middle of the range, that is clearly ideal, but all good paragliders will fly and behave well, even if you are at the top or the bottom of the range. Some pilots who are keen on racing or who habitually fly in windy conditions, will choose to be close to the top; others who float around on smooth coastal sites in sea breezes may prefer to be towards the light end.

As a rough guide, a basic set of gear will add 15kg to your body weight, or 20kg if you have a reserve or a bulky harness and winter clothing. If you have a large glider, a high spec harness with back protection, a reserve, instruments, boots

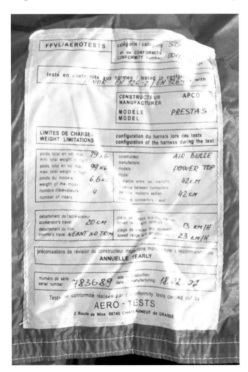

An Afnor certification label

A DHV certification label

and a flying suit you could be looking at as much as 25kg on top of your body weight.

What airworthiness classification does it have?

If you are a first-time buyer only consider a canopy with the appropriate classification. All suitable canopies will hold one or more of the following ratings: DHV 1 or 1/2, AFNOR Standard, or CEN A or B. However some unsuitable canopies may also have Standard rating, and a high proportion of DHV1/2 's (especially those certified after 2000) may also be unsuitable. More information on these classifications is given below.

Buying a Used Glider

There are a huge range of models available, ranging from very basic designs which have dreadful performance by current standards, to some excellent models that have only recently been superceded. Avoid wings more than about five years old as their useful life will be fairly limited.

Prices of some older or unpopular models can be very low, but this may be a false economy, as the resale value in a year or two is likely to be next to nothing, and in the meantime airtime may be more difficult to achieve. It is vital with a used machine that you get a recent service report. Internal damage, porous material or shrunken lines are often impossible for a visual check to detect.

Buying from a dealer is likely to cost a little more than privately, but you do have some comeback if there is a problem. Most dealers can offer you a choice; a

No matter how good a deal it seems at the time, buying a glider the wrong size is never a good investment! (Photo: Julian French)

private buyer is going to try and sell you the wing he has..

Buying a New Glider

All the same advice holds good, and with new you will have no trouble choosing a wing that is not only the right size and certification level for you but even get one in your favourite colour.

You will get a warranty of some kind, these range from an informal 12-month warranty on faulty workmanship or materials, up to a proper transferable guarantee of the specific properties of the fabric or lines for anything up to 3 years. Some manufactures offer so-called "lifetime warranties" However in reality it is hard to pin the makers down to exactly what that means!

There are a number of purpose-built canopies designed for the new pilot.

They are ideal for the first time buyer and many recreational pilots. This sector of the market is very price conscious, with gliders costing less in 2003 than they did in 1998!

They are usually good value for money. The only problem with this group is that the certification classes are so wide that it is hard to make meaningful comparisons.

About airworthiness certification

It is arguable that a canopy should either pass or fail a universal test. However, this would give the customer no information about the wing's behaviour or who it is suitable for. In the real world some pilots with experience are happy to fly wings that other pilots may not be, and of course the relationship between performance and security is always a compromise. At present, we have the rather muddled situation of two different systems, both of which are continually evolving, and manufacturers who are producing better and safer wings each year, making comparisons by test results very tricky. The encouraging element of all this is that the testing is getting better and more rigorous and the two systems are (hopefully) close to amalgamation (see *Fig 18.1*)

This is a far cry from only ten years ago, when the same glider could score 12 x A's at ACPUL (the forerunner of the AFNOR system) but be graded at 2/3 by the DHV.

The tests are far from perfect; they only report a glider's behaviour at a certain maximum and minimum payload on a certain day. In 2001 a tandem wing fully certified at DHV 1 and tandem level was found to spontaneously enter a deep stall when flown at a certain weight and with the ears in. This was only discovered after an accident and subsequent exhaustive "searching" for this problem. Be aware that the tests are an indicator of the canopy's likely behaviour, not a guarantee.

Many pilots and instructors rely quite heavily on the certification to show that a wing is "safe". In fact statistics show that whilst the grade of the wing is significant, it is far less critical than the conditions you fly in, in determining your chances of an accident or injury.

Making sense of it all!

Some manufacturers market DHV 1 models that are a bit basic for more ambitious flyers, whilst several wings with the DHV 1/2 placard are actually very high performance machines. This is not a problem in itself as they have proved their safety in unstable situations. But the faster and more energy efficient models do tend to get into trouble a bit faster, if they are "spat out" of a thermal, for example, as the very speed that makes them desirable means that they dive more readily and are therefore more prone to tucking. Whilst it is by no means a rule, if a manufacturer has more than one DHV 1/2 model it is usual that the "higher" end model is aimed at a second time user.

If the model is both certified at 1/2 and "Standard" this is a hint that it may be more suitable for a first time buyer than if it has the 1/2 rating alone. (Some 1/2 models have the performance certification.) The New CEN certification system is due to come on line by 2004, but it has been "imminent" for at least three years, so don't hold your breath!

Read the recommendations of the manufacturer, but always get advice from your instructor on the pros and cons of each machine before deciding.

Canopies designed for the more experi-

AFNOR/CEN 2003	Description	DHV	Description	Proposed CEN	Draft Description
Standard	For inexperienced pilots and pilots seeking relaxed flying Very stable, rapid recovery with no pilot input, easy predictable handling	1	Paragliders with simple and very forgiving characteristics	A	Paragliders with very good passive safety.
		1/2	Paragliders with good natured flying characteristics. (Recommended minimum: BHPA Club Pilot rating)	B	Paragliders with good passive safety.
Performance	For the very experienced pilot who flies frequently, flies 'actively' and is familiar with normal recovery techniques. Generally stable with straightforward recovery though this may require pilot input, predictable handling. (Recommended minimum: BHPA Pilot rating)	2	Paragliders with demanding characteristics and potentially dynamic reactions to turbulence and pilot errors. For regularly flying pilots. (Recommended minimum: BHPA Pilot rating)	C	Paragliders with reasonable passive safety.
Competition	For the very experienced advanced pilot who flies almost every day. This pilot will need very highly developed skills at avoiding and recovering from all departures from normal flight. Possibly only minimal stability, recovery may require skilled accurate piloting and may need time. Possibly demanding handling. (Recommended minimum: BHPA Advanced Pilot rating)	2/3	Paragliders with very demanding characteristics with potentially violent reactions to turbulence and pilot errors. For experienced and regularly flying pilots. (Recommended minimum: BHPA Advanced Pilot rating)	D	Paragliders with minimal passive safety.
		3	Paragliders with very demanding characteristics with potentially very violent reactions to turbulence and pilot errors. Little scope for pilot errors. For expert pilots.	Fail	FAIL.

Fig 18.1: How the two existing airworthiness systems compare and how they will be integrated into the new CEN system due out soon.

enced pilot fall into two broad categories. The high-end 1/2 types are designed for recreational flyers who have reasonable skills and a year or more of experience, some suitable canopies for this group may feature "performance" or DHV 2 certification. They are not suitable for first time buyers.

Top performers

The state-of-the-art canopies as used by competition and experienced cross-country pilots, these wings represent the cutting edge of paragliding technology and deliver excellent performance, particularly in glide and speed range. They are not suitable for first time buyers with even the more docile models needing some expertise to fly well if the air should be turbulent. A few may require a great deal of skill to fly safely. Usually DHV 2 or "performance" rated, though some may feature DHV 2/3.

If you do have plenty of experience and are seriously competitive, then of course you have got to have one!

Anything with DHV 3 or "competition" written on it is strictly for highly skilled or professional pilots who are very comfortable in unstable situations outside the normal flight envelope.

General Pointers

If you can afford to buy new, that is usually the best policy. Although the improvement curve is flattening out a great deal compared to few years ago, the newest canopies are noticeably better than even two or three-year old ones. Not only do you get more flying because of this, but it may well cost you less in the long run as older canopies depreciate very fast. The exceptions are if you can find someone who has quickly got bored, or moved up and has a "nearly new" machine, or an ex demonstrator, etc. When buying new, always buy from an approved dealer; your instructor may well be the best choice (providing he is offering a good range of products - some schools are tied to one manufacturer and may sell that model even if it is not necessarily the right one for you).

It is often possible to get reduced cost training to soaring standard if you purchase a canopy from the school and fly on your own machine. Buy the right size; you will regret it if you do not. This is especially important advice to remember if buying second hand.

Get a harness you know you are comfortable with: a few older harnesses do not accept the soft foam back protector pads which are now almost universal. Your dealer should advise you.

Never buy used without first seeing the canopy flown and secondly flying it yourself. Always get a second opinion if it is a private sale. If the dealer or seller is not a competent pilot then his advice is not going to be worth much. Do not buy a canopy that has been repaired or modified unless you are 100 per cent satisfied about its history (i.e. who did the repair and whether the manufacturer approves of any modification). NEVER buy a canopy without certification.

Airworthiness Testing

As the previous section makes clear, the certification level of a canopy is a vital indicator of its suitability. Very few canopies are still available new that have not been submitted for an airworthiness test. Those that have not are generally confined to competition prototypes and development gliders. Some countries (usually outside Europe) have small builders who make a few of their own designs or "clones" of other models for sale to their local pilots.

All reputable manufacturers display a classification by an independent body on their products and advertisements. The major European systems are the DHV Guteseigel (German) and the AFNOR system which is (apart from in Germany) fairly universally accepted. The SHV (Swiss) certification is part of the AFNOR system and the tests are identical. Hopefully, all major manufacturers will soon conform to the proposed Pan-

European CEN classification system.

One of the most common questions asked by students and first time buyers is, "What does the test actually do and what do the classes mean?" There are a number of routines through which the test canopy is put and its reactions noted by the pilots and by a panel of judges from a high definition video recording.

The ANFOR certification is designed to be as objective as possible; the glider passes each test or it does not. The results are recorded in the user's manual and on a sticker fixed to the glider so that

A glider being put through its paces. (Photo: Swing Gliders)

the pilot is able to be fully aware of the results. The first test is a load test. The wing is steadily loaded to eight times the maximum recommended weight (8g). This is done by pulling it behind a truck. The canopy is also shock loaded with a slack line and a 6g weak link in the system. The truck accelerates away and the canopy is snatched with an instant 6g load. It must pass these tests with no failure. In the second part of the test the glider is put through a range of manoeuvres by a test pilot.

The tests are constantly being evaluated and new exercises are added or existing ones are altered as necessary. See Chapter 38, How a Paraglider is Designed, Built and Tested.

Airworthiness classifications

If you wish to check out the test pilot report on any canopy they can be found on the DHV website at www.dhv.de.

When referring to these tests do remember that they are designed to give a benchmark indication of the relative behaviour of different models. Passing a test at level 1 for example, where a wing recovers from a 60% asymmetric tuck in less than 4 seconds and with a turn of less than 90 degrees, does NOT mean the wing is necessarily going to recover in the same way in turbulent air. The canopies are tested in ideal conditions (still air) by highly skilled test pilots.

Make sure you are the right weight for your wing.

IF YOU FLY OVER OR UNDERWEIGHT THEN STABILITY IN SOME SITUATIONS CAN BE SEVERELY COMPROMISED.

If this is all a bit much to take in, as is probably the case if you are looking for your first paraglider, here is a shortened guide:

- If you are a new pilot or are not particularly interested in competitions, buy a wing with DHV 1 or Standard (STD) certification. Some DHV 1\2 wings that were certified before about August 2000 may be suitable but some are definitely not... take advice.

- If you have a few hours under your belt, are an ambitious XC pilot and you have had some training in dealing with tucks etc. then the wings that have Performance rating (PERF) or DHV 1/ 2 or possibly 2 may be suitable for you.

- If you are an experienced pilot and have good SIV experience and are interested in top-level competition, then the Perf or DHV 2 (or possibly 2/3)level wings are likely to give you the edge you need, albeit at a price in reduced security and massive depreciation.

- "Comp" and DHV 3 wings are now rare and it is unlikely that manufacturers will now bring many more models of this type to the market. They are not recommended.

- **Best of all, get advice.**

Additional Equipment

Harnesses

The right choice of harness can make a huge difference to your flying. A good harness needs to be comfortable to fly in, but must also be easy to get in and out of, provide adequate storage for your glider bag and other items, offer the facility to allow back protection to be fitted, and have a suitable arrangement for mounting a reserve parachute system.

Finally, the harness is also part of the foot-operated speed systems that almost all paragliders are fitted with.

Comfort in flight means that you have no pressure points and that the fit is close enough so that you do not slide around on the seat. Make sure that you can sit back easily on the seat when launching without undue problems, or needing to wriggle about too much as you launch. Even more importantly, you must be able

to rotate easily into the upright position as you approach to land. If you are too supine, this can be a struggle, which can have serious consequences.

The harness must be a good fit; most are available in 3 or 4 sizes; too small and it will not be comfortable for long. On the other hand, if it is too large, you will tend to "slide about" when the harness tilts. The seat plate, or articulated support flap, should extend to a point around 10-15cm short of the backs of your knees - much shorter than this and the pressure point caused by the edge of the plate will be noticeable on a long flight - much longer and you may find it hard to rotate upright or to run effectively whilst wearing it.

All modern harnesses are adjustable –

Cam-lock adjuster

make sure that you are sitting well back on the seat plate, that the straps do not slip off your shoulders, and that you are not too upright or too supine.

The attachments for the risers should be at least 6mm stainless steel maillion rapide quick links. Some climbing karabiners are also suitable, but perhaps the best option are karabiners made especially for the job. These can be of the screw gate (manual locking) or twist-lock (automatic self-locking) types. These are available from all good dealers. They are usually made of aluminium and have stainless steel pins in the mechanism. This is worth noting as prolonged contact with salt water or a salty atmosphere may result in corrosion where the materials are in contact. If flying on a coastal site regularly, or if they are immersed in sea-water, a thorough rinse with fresh water is strongly advised.

Virtually all harnesses offer the option to adjust the straps and so alter your

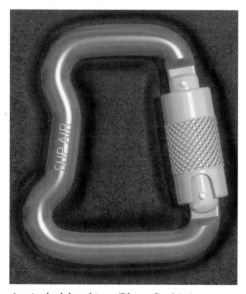

A twist-lock karabiner (Photo: Sup'Air)

angle of recline, and possibly the tilt of the seat. The waist strap is also adjustable, allowing a range of different sized pilots and offering the option to fly "cross-braced" by tightening the waist strap in flight to help reduce the impact of turbulent air. Some harnesses feature a small strap or handle to allow easy adjustment of the waist strap in flight.

The certification class of your paraglider will specify the distance apart of the karabiners when tested. All harnesses will adjust to conform to the tested distance and in many cases it is not very critical. However, it is worth noting that a very much larger distance can adversely affect the recovery behaviour in the event of a large collapse. A shorter distance can adversely affect the spin characteristics.

A critical feature is the ability to mount a reserve system neatly into the harness. Check that the reserve handle is going to be visible and easily reached when fitted. A good reserve container should be closed with one or more curved pins; systems relying on Velcro alone are no good.

Many models have clear "windows" so that you can check the pins without disturbing the container. Reserves may be mounted on the side, under the seat, over the small of your back, ventrally (on your stomach) or between your shoulder blades. There is no "right" position, and all these options have some advantages and some drawbacks. The important point is that the handle is easily accessible at all times and that the reserve is easy to deploy but not likely to be activated by mistake.

Fig 19.1 tabulates the possible options and their relative advantages and disadvantages.

Harnesses generally feature three buck-

Position:	Top (Shoulder-blades)	Side	Front (Ventral)	Underseat	Rear
Advantages:	Reserve out of way. Good storage space. R or L hand deploy.	Easily visible handle position.	Easiest handle to find. Most storage.	Good handle position. Lots of Storage.	Right or left hand deploy. Reserve out of way.
Disadvantages:	Handle may become detached making deployment impossible.	May effect symmetry & balance. One hand deploy.	Cumbersome & awkward to do up. One hand deploy.	More liable to damage & damp.	Less visible handle. Less storage.

Fig 19.1: Relative advantages & disadvantages of reserve parachute positions.

les to secure them onto the pilot. There are two basic varieties of buckles the simple "interlock" type and spring loaded "quick-lock" buckles. Interlock (or pass-through) buckles are a slight nuisance to connect, especially if you have gloves on or cold hands; however, there is no known case of them failing once connected. In an emergency situation such as water landing, the time taken to disengage them may be a problem. For this reason they are not recommended for use where there is a significant risk of a water landing.

Quick-lock or automatic buckles are much more convenient; however, as they are more complex, they can malfunction

–usually because of sand or snow in the mechanism. It is important that you check that these buckles are fully engaged before flight by testing them with a good tug.

If you habitually fly in sandy or snowy areas it may be worth considering using interlock buckles (pass-through). Note quick-locks must be of the "two opposed buttons to release" type. A few early harnesses used a single "press to release" button, like a seatbelt, but these are considered unsuitable as the risk of an unplanned release and falling from a harness is too great.

The two pictures both show harnesses

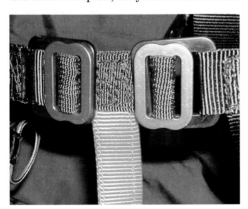

Harness interlock buckle.

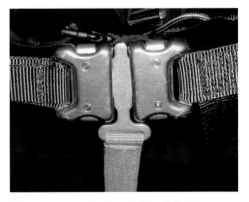

Harness automatic (or quick-lock) buckle.

with an "anti–forget" system. This essentially means that the waist strap cannot be fastened without a strap between the legs also being engaged. This is to prevent the situation of a pilot finding himself starting to slide out of the harness if he launches after forgetting to do up his leg straps. … it has happened more than once!

Another important consideration is back protection. A number of harnesses on the market feature some kind of passive protection system that is designed to minimise spinal injury in an emergency situation. These are essentially bags of air that are kept inflated either by being full of foam padding (the airfoam or Bump'Air), or by being inflated though a valved entry and pressurised by your airspeed (the Cygnus airbag).

The disadvantage to all these protective devices is added bulk and in some cases weight. However, as many paragliding injuries are either minor or involve the spine, they are a major step in making the sport safer. The foam types are rather bulky, but are very effective (except for sharp "point" impacts). They basically hold the shape of the air-bag so that a sudden stop causes the air to escape through the seams and fabric in a controlled way, increasing the stopping distance and so minimising the deceleration force. The "Cygnus" types are even more effective and are less bulky to transport as they function in the same way, but without any foam. The disadvantage is that they take a few seconds of steady airspeed to inflate, so are of little use in a zero-wind- launch-closely-followed-by-crash scenario. These systems are improving however, with stiffeners added to hold the air-void open before launch. (Ground impacts, by definition, always happen at launch or landing!)

Polystyrene of other "solid" materials are also very good at deforming under shock load, and at least one protector is made of this substance. However, unlike air, it is not re-useable, and it only needs to be sat down on once or dropped by an airline baggage handler to lose much of its effectiveness..

An unwelcome side effect to good protec-

Airfoam protector. (Pic: Sup'Air)

Cygnus airbag protection system.

tion in harnesses is that some pilots behave as if the airfoam padding is an alternative to landing on their feet. It is not.

The DHV testing to determine the effectiveness of these devices tests for a reduction in deceleration from a situation equivalent to falling 1.85m (6ft) squarely onto the padding. The resulting G force transmitted should be sufficiently low to prevent permanent spinal damage. Note that a sideways or angled impact is not tested for, and these devices will offer far less protection in that (much more likely) situation. Some of the more well-appointed harnesses include lateral impact protection as well, but it is by necessity much thinner and less absorbent. Its principal function is to minimise the likelihood of the pilot sliding off the main protector in an angled impact.

By contrast, falling from 1.85m onto your feet and bending your knees (or better still, performing a Parachute landing fall) is many times more effective in preventing injury. The message is pretty clear: rotate into an upright position in your harness whenever you are close to the ground and go for a feet-down landing every time...

A few years ago there was a vogue for rigid protectors made of fibreglass, Kevlar and similar materials. Research has shown that in some circumstances these can actually increase the risk of certain injuries, and if found in older harnesses these protectors should be removed.

Harnesses are available in many shapes and sizes, and there are specialist models for those seeking ultra-low weight or volume, harnesses for tandem use or those that allow the competitive pilot to adopt a fully reclined position to mini-

mise drag. These are not ideal for the first time buyer.

The Vamp'Air harness by Sup'Air featuring enclosed legs for greater aerodynamic effect! (Photo: Sup'Air)

Helmets

It is impossible to entirely rule out the chance of an accident, and/or hard landing where the pilot falls over or is dragged. For this reason a suitable helmet is a mandatory piece of equipment. There is a CEN standard for airsports helmets to which any paragliding helmet should conform. (Recognised by the CE966 mark on the shell) .

Full-face helmet with the CEN markings.

Helmets can be either of the open face variety, which are cooler, lighter and usually cheaper, or the full-face type. These offer greater protection and warmth to the lower face, and can be a good place to mount a microphone.

Whichever type you choose, it is important that it fits correctly, allows good all round visibility, is in good condition and of course is CE966 certified. Visors or peaks can restrict vision and are not usually a good idea; if glare is a problem good sunglasses are a better bet. Heads come in a variety of shapes, and some helmets can be "rolled" either forward or backward right off the heads of some people, even with the chin strap fastened. It is worth spending a minute ensuring that this is not the case with yours, as a helmet is clearly useless if it is not on properly.

Helmets designed for other sports such as motorcycling are as good or better in terms of ultimate protection, but are almost always unsuitable, due to restricted upward vision and hearing problems. Those designed for cycling or climbing may not offer adequate protection.

The materials used for flying helmets are generally polycarbonate or carbon fibre (kevlar). Both of these are very intolerant of knocks and care must be taken not to drop them onto a hard surface or much of the protection may be lost. Also take care not to crush the helmet by stacking heavy items on your packed bag or allowing your helmet to go in the hold of an aircaft packed in your glider bag. Never buy a used helmet for this reason.

Primarily because of UV degradation, helmets also have a limited life (around 5 years or so if used regularly) so they need to be replaced periodically. Some stickers or solvents can also damage the integrity of the shell. Never paint or add stickers to your helmet without being certain that the glue or paint type is compatible with the helmet materials.

Reserve parachutes.

It may seem strange to carry a reserve system when we are already flying under what is effectively a parachute. However, because our wings require constant air-pressure to remain inflated, excessive control movements or turbulence can collapse them. In these cases, recovery is often quite straightforward. However, there remains a possibility of "wrapping-up" the canopy to the point where it is impossible, or may take too long, to recover. We are not alone in the sky, and there is always the possibility of a mid-air collision, either with another canopy or (perish the thought) with something a lot heavier and faster.

Reserves are rarely used, but they are a second chance: if you fly in a variety of conditions or with groups of other pilots, you may one day need it. They are mandatory equipment for cross-country or alpine flying. A paragliding reserve is usually a small (24-40 sq metre) round parachute.

A quick glance at the marketplace reveals that some reserves of quite different sizes are sold for the same weight pilot. How can this be? Size (whilst very important) is only one of the criteria in how well a reserve decelerates you. There are a number of other design factors that can affect the coefficient of drag of a reserve system.

Flying diameter, for example, is usually

A pulled-down-apex reserve parachute.

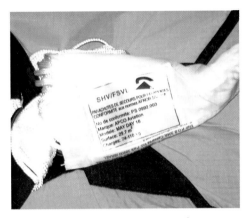

Certification label on a reserve parachute.

a much better measurement; to visualise this consider a plate which may have a smaller surface area than a bowl yet have a greater flying diameter (or "projected" area). In fact, some shapes have higher drag coefficients and better sink rates than others, even with the same diameter. Some designs use "drive" to generate lift, and there are variations such as adding a central cap over the vent, or depressing a circular area rather than a single point at the apex.

Another factor is fabric. Some reserve designers use more porous fabric for stability and other reasons, so the reserve needs to be correspondingly larger than one using zero-porosity fabric in order to have the same sink rate.

The criteria used by the DHV and AFNOR testing bodies demanded a certain sink rate at a certain payload (6.8m/sec @ 106Kg for DHV and 5.5m/sec @ 85Kg for AFNOR .)

Amazingly, they do not currently specify a maximum load for the reserves. This is left to the individual designer or manufacturer to determine, and some calculations are more optimistic than others.

The CEN system is virtually in place at the time of writing, so newer systems with this certification should offer any user a maximum sink rate of 5.5m/sec in still air, provided there is no interference from the paraglider itself.

What do these figure actually mean? A 5.5m/sec rate equates to the impact experienced when stepping from a height of 1.5m and 6.8m/sec when stepping from around 2m.

The BHPA recommend the 5.5m/sec figure as likely to minimise injury, and a rate of a 7.5m/ sec as a maximum acceptable figure. Of the 20 or so emergency reserve deployments recorded by the BHPA in the last few years, using a reserve that is correctly packed, and where the pilot is within the manufacturer's payload limitations, all have been successful and resulted in no injuries. (Hanggliding is a different story, unfortunately.)

Reserves are mounted in or on the harness, with the deployment handle within easy reach. All should have an airworthiness test (ACPUL/SHV or DHV label) and come with instructions for use and repacking.

A reserve should be mounted so that when it is opened the pilot is suspended by both shoulder straps.

Reserves must be aired, inspected and repacked at least every year, or more often if they have been exposed to damp or compression. Many pilots attend re-pack sessions run by their local club with a BHPA licensed re-packer each spring, or you can send your reserve to a licensed packer who will check and pack your kit for you.

Parachutes are available in a large number of sizes and formats; these can broadly be divided into five variants.

● Hemispherical or tri-conical reserves

These work well and were very popular until around ten years ago. They require a relatively large fabric area and are correspondingly more stable in their descent, and somewhat slow in their deployment (opening) time. Perhaps the main reason they have fallen out of favour, however, is that they are quite bulky and heavy to carry around. These types are now rarely seen in the UK.

● Rocket or ballistically deployed reserves

These are not a different canopy type but a different method of deployment. The rocket, once activated, can blast right through any paraglider fabric or, for that matter, several layers of hang-glider or microlight sailcloth, and will stretch the lines of the reserve and speed up the deployment time significantly. If you are wrapped up in fabric, or need a very fast deployment (say near the ground) and, this could be very useful. There are a number of disadvantages to this kind of system, however, in that the weight, and especially the cost, is greater and the rocket is a lethal weapon (actually some are modified military mortars) and could kill someone in a mid-air collision situation or even if fired accidentally (ground handling in gusty winds, for example). Another problem is that commercial aircraft prohibit carrying devices of this type, so you cannot take it on holiday with you. Finally, they require expert maintenance to ensure that they perform perfectly when you need them. Apart from certain specialist requirements like testing prototype wings for example, it is difficult to see the attraction of such a system. Other options have been to have a deployment system propelled by compressed air or a spring; however, none of these options has (to date) made much impact on the market.

● Reserves with drive

Some designs have slots in the envelope that give the reserve forward motion or "drive", and these have two purposes. The first is to aid stability by controlled bleeding of excess pressure and therefore reduce excess oscillation. The second is to allow the pilot to "steer" by converting the forward momentum into a turn, using brake handles or weight-shift through two or more risers. In order for the drive to work, however, the parachute must be allowed to fly correctly, which is a very difficult situation to achieve when a main canopy is flapping around behind it. Some reserves may be relatively unaffected by this (although you obviously cannot steer them without either dumping completely or at least wrapping up your main wing).

Some reserves with drive are true wings

and actually fly just like the paraglider, and a likely result of deploying them is that the reserve will stall or fly away from the main (downplaning), which can cause a very dangerous situation – perhaps worse than that which caused the deployment.

A pilot who threw a "square" reserve was very lucky to survive a 2,000ft descent of stalls and swooping dives as the main and reserve fought it out, taking turns to stall each other.

You cannot steer a reserve whilst still attached to even a partially inflated paraglider – despite the misleading wording of some advertisements that may seem to imply otherwise.

● Pulled down apex reserves

These are systems in which a central line holds down the Apex in a shape rather like an inverted saucer. This gives a relatively large flying diameter for relatively little fabric and therefore a good low sinkrate combined with a small light package. Another advantage is that these types operate at high pressure and therefore inflate very quickly – a great bonus as many deployments occur at a surprisingly low altitude (the most common situation is a mid-air collision while ridge soaring).

The pulled apex design does tend to oscillate more than a tri-conical or hemispherical type. Also, in the early days of paragliding the reserves went through a phase of being built very small indeed with correspondingly high sink rates. This was, to a great extent, due to the very optimistic 6.8m per second allowed by the German DHV test – at that time the only recognised standard. Experience has shown that this is a rate that will

give the pilot a pretty fair chance of injury, and as a result the newer AFNOR/ and now CEN test demands a sink rate of no more than 5.5m/sec

● LARA, CONAR, and other variations.

In order to decelerate the pilot a reserve needs to generate a significant amount of drag, or lift. Lift is created when the reserve can fly forwards through the air like a paraglider, and this is the type that is used by sport parachutists. However, a true flying reserve is problematical for use with a paraglider as the main wing can stall it, causing it to malfunction. This leaves drag, which is generated in proportion to sheer size, but can be enhanced by altering the shape, such as pulling the apex, as discussed above.

There are additional design techniques too, that may improve slightly on the classic pulled apex design. One is the apex being depressed in a ring rather than at a single point; this is the basis of the LARA design. This is not as different aerodynamically as it may appear, as, due to the central hole in the apex of the reserve, the inner edge is effectively a ring already. However, it does allow an even flatter profile and a corresponding increase in the flying diameter.

An apex hole of some type is necessary to prevent oscillation, but inevitably reduces the drag efficiency of the reserve; the Conar and similar designs seek to minimise this problem. This can be done with a "cap" immediately above the apex hole which acts to deflect and slow down the escape of the air. Using mesh or making the central part of the reserve with more porous materials has a similar effect.

At the time of writing, the UK is one of the very few countries that still does not insist on an independent test for reserves. To a great extent this is due to the fact that market forces dictate that Certified reserves are almost universally used anyway, However, there are other systems for sale and it is advised in the strongest possible terms that you ONLY purchase a reserve with a CEN AFNOR or possibly DHV certification.

The factors that determine reserve performance are quite complex. One leading manufacturer discovered their larger model had a worse sink rate than their small one with the same payload! It is therefore not really possible to determine from the adverts or calculations which is best for you. Fortunately, just about every deployment of a correctly sized reserve (i.e within the manufacturer's recommended range) and properly packed reserve has resulted in a successful save; so it is fair to assume that the manufacturers of these systems have got it about right, (or that paraglider pilots are very tough or have been very lucky so far).

Instruments

It is perfectly possible to fly a paraglider well with no more equipment than your harness, helmet and senses. However, to use the available lift to its maximum potential, to thermal efficiently and to navigate cross-country you require some senses nature has not provided. The higher you are above the ground, the less reliable your senses become as the visual clues become less useful.

Variometer

A vario measures how fast you are rising or falling and displays this information as a sound, on a meter, or both. Most work by detecting changes in air-pressure. A human can detect acceleration, such as flying into a thermal and shooting upwards, but smooth constant gains (or losses) of altitude are undetectable. Your senses can actually work to fool you. Lift of 500ft per minute may suddenly decrease to only 200ft per minute. To the pilot this feels exactly the same as sinking at 300ft per minute and, without a vario, he may make a bad decision and leave the lift. A vario is therefore essential to know what is really happening.

Altimeter

An altimeter tells you how high you are above a specific pre-set point (see Chapter 24, Air Law). You may think it is obvious how high you are, but until you

Vario in flight.

work out beforehand that you can reach point B if you are at 3000ft or better, at point A.

In practice, most variometers and altimeters are integrated units in one case. Most of these will give you very accurate information and allow you to switch between altimeter settings. For example, you can check your height above takeoff and at the touch of a button check your altitude relative to airspace (see details of altimeter settings chapter 24, Air Law) Many units will also remember details of your peak altitudes and other information from your last few flights. Some more sophisticated units function as a barograph, that is, record a complete trace of your flight that can be downloaded into a computer or printer, and which can form the basis of an official record claim.

All of these functions have a use but only you can decide what is necessary for you.

have had a good deal of practice most people are amazingly bad at judging altitude, especially from great heights. Why do you need to know your altitude? There are three main reasons:

● Personal interest – "I made my best height of four grand today!" etc.

● To help you navigate your position relative to controlled airspace – are you under the Airway or in it?

● It complements the vario when thermalling. If you are flying in broken lift; that is up, then down, then up again, it is soon impossible to know if you are gradually losing height or gradually gaining. An altimeter gives you this information at a glance. It could occasionally be of use in some competition tasks where you can

Compass

Useful for navigating – it is easy to get lost or disorientated after a cross-country flight involving several hundred circles over unfamiliar territory. Again, good navigation is required for avoiding airspace etc. It is a useful tool if you get caught in a cloud, and invaluable simply as an aid if you get caught in the mountains on foot.

Barograph

A barograph is essentially an instrument that records a flight. This information is displayed as a trace that can be read to ascertain your duration of flight and also your altitude at any point during the flight. Modern barographs are electronic and display this information as a print out, or by downloading onto a computer screen. Barograph evidence is a requirement for a flight to be recognised as an official record.

Map

Mandatory for cross-country flights. Rather than carry an air chart, a practical plan is to mark all the relevant parts onto an ordinary route-planner map. Good for finding your way back to the car too!

GPS (Global Positioning Systems)

Originally developed by the US military, the GPS system currently comprises a constellation of satellites whose relative orbits ensure that several are always above the horizon. The GPS units are small handsets that can plot a position from these satellites and give a very accurate fix as to your position anywhere on the earth's surface. If enough satellites are above the horizon they can even give you a reasonably accurate altitude. A further facility is that you can program "waypoints". These are positions that you can use as turn points or targets and the GPS can then advise you of the heading to take to navigate accurately to these points. These are very useful indeed for aircraft flying on instruments or for maritime traffic, for which accurate positioning is essential.

The falling price of these units has meant that some pilots, especially those undertaking long-distance flights over unfamiliar or featureless terrain, have found them irresistible as a safety and navigational aid. The fact that they can tell you exactly where you are, and therefore how far you have left to go, what your ground speed is, what heading to take to reach your goal, and even whether you've already broken that record before you've even landed are powerful incentives to own one!

Many competitions now accept GPS data a proof of the completion of a task. Only some models have the facility to record tamper-proof data, so if you wish to compete it is important to you ensure you buy the correct one.

GPS data can be overlaid onto mapping information held in a handheld PC to give real-time positioning on an airchart, for example. More sophisticated GPS's have this facility built in.

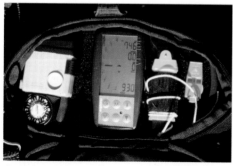

An instrument console such as this Cockpit by Sup'Air are convenient ways of grouping instruments together.

GPS

One problem with GPS is that they are very battery hungry, so you may need to have a map as backup against battery failure mid-flight.

Radios

It is only legal to transmit from the air on specific airband frequencies in the UK, and you may only use the specified channels if both you and the equipment are licensed. Details of Airband radios are discussed in chapter 24 "airlaw".

There are two other types of radio that deserve a mention. The first are 2-metre VHF radios. They have a good range and are a fraction of the price of airband equipment. They are very common among paraglider pilots, and certain frequencies have been unofficially adopted by groups of pilots. In France and some other countries, the weather information

from automated stations at major launch sites is transmitted regularly on a 2m frequency which is very useful in choosing a site.

In the UK (at present) it is not legal to transmit on the 2m frequencies without a radio amateur's licence and not legal at all to transmit from the air. The *De facto* situation is that for safety and convenience many pilots choose to use this system anyway, and make every effort to stick to the "clear" frequencies which are not allocated, and stay well clear of the frequencies used by the emergency services.

A recent innovation has been the introduction of Ultra high frequency (UHF) radios on the general market. Whilst these have a slightly shorter range than a 2m radio, they offer superbly clear reception, and best of all they are both legal and very cheap. (A pair cost less than £100 including chargers)

UHF (left) and 2m (right) radios.

Packing & Care of Your Glider

How you repack your canopy depends on what sort of terrain and wind conditions you are in and whether you have anyone to help you. You will need to decide which method is most appropriate to your situation. If there is any wind, your first move should be to orientate your canopy so that one tip is pointing into wind. This makes it less likely to blow around while you fold it. Next, make sure that the canopy is laid out flat on its back with no lines underneath it. Place all the lines on top of it (under-surface). The harness is best left attached in most circumstances, and can either be passed over the wing so that it is next to the leading edge, or placed close to the trailing edge.

Fold the canopy as neatly as possible. If you are alone, or if the terrain is rough and you do not wish to drag the fabric over the ground, this is best achieved by folding the tips into the middle, then each end into the middle again, and so on. If you have help, you can either fold the canopy from each tip, one panel at a time, or concertina fashion, one panel at a time, starting at the centre and pulling each panel in as you fold. When the canopy is arranged as a double pile of folded panels, press out the air trapped inside. This must be done working from the sealed trailing edge towards the leading edge where the air can escape easily through the cell entries. Fold one side onto the other and press out any remaining air in the same way.

The long "tube" of fabric can be folded concertina fashion to form a square pile of S folds. This should give you a fairly tidy package to which the harness is still attached, but not wrapped up in the fabric. Try to avoid carrying it around like this, as the bundle will inevitably split apart. This is best secured with a strap, or can be slipped into a stuff sac if you have one. The secure bundle can now be

Photos: Paul Currer

placed into your rucksac with the harness. Many modern harnesses take up a lot of room, so the best way to manage this may be to place the canopy in the seat and secure the waist strap around it.

If you are expecting to use the canopy shortly but do not want to leave it lying in the sun, a "clinch bag" or "quick pak" is a useful bit of kit. Simply lay the disc of material and drop your bundled canopy on top, then carefully pull the drawcord tight as you stuff any loose bits inside. This is no substitute for a proper canopy bag for carrying your kit any distance, but is excellent for keeping it dry and protected from UV between flights.

Care of the canopy

The fabric used for paragliders is prone to damage by repeated exposure to ultraviolet light, so do not leave it lying out in the sun for long periods. This is particularly important where the suns rays are

very intense, for example at high altitude or at low latitudes. The fabric and lines are of synthetic fibres and are easily damaged by heat. Take care not to smoke near them and never attempt to dry a canopy by applying direct heat. It is advisable to avoid getting the canopy wet, but inevitably it sometimes happens. If so, dry it out fairly soon afterwards, as it is possible to get mould or mildew on fabric that has ben left damp for long periods, and this can leave unsightly marks. Paragliders dry in a matter of minutes in a breeze, as long as the water is not trapped in the cells.

Never store the canopy near chemicals or fuel as this could affect the material. If you are flying in a hot climate, take care to pack your canopy into its bag and protect it from great heat. Canopies with Dyneema lines risk them shrinking if the temperature exceeds 100° C – this has happened where an unpacked canopy has been left inside a car. Never use chemicals to try and clean the fabric or the lines: some cleaners that will remove oil will also attack the fabric.

A damaged wing; torn at the line connection point.

Blown internal cells after a severe nose-down landing.

Sometimes, of course, paragliders do get damaged. If the damage is to the lines or a riser, or the webbing or metal of the harness, do not fly it until it has been professionally checked and repaired. If the damage is a small tear in the fabric of the harness, it is unlikely to be critical, but it should be attended to as soon as possible. If the tear is to the canopy fabric, then minor tears, that is to say those less than 10 cm long that are not on a seam or line attachment point, can be repaired using self-adhesive rip-stop tape. This is available in a variety of colours from camping shops and sailing equipment shops. If applying this kind of tape, there are a number of pointers to get the best results:

1. The canopy must be completely dry and clean.

2. The tape should give a generous overlap around the damage.

3. The edges of the tear should be carefully aligned in their original position, otherwise there will be creases and additional strain on the area.

4. Always round off the corners of patches.

5. A patch should always be applied to both sides of the fabric.

6. The internal and external patches should be of different sizes to prevent stress lines.

7. Do not forget to make a special point of checking the repaired area as part of your pre-flight checks.

Lines also need maintenance – tests would indicate that they get weaker with use and over time. At least one manufacturer recommends that you change the main load bearing lines (lower A and B) every 100 hours. As the canopy is ground handled the lines do tend to get wet and dirty. This can have the effect of shrinking the outer sheathing of the line and shortening it. As the A and B lines take much more of a load than the other lines, they may be stretched back again each time you fly. As a result canopies with old and dirty lines may fly at a slightly higher angle of attack, as the rearmost lines shrink the most. Stalls and spins become easier to induce and the top speed decreases. A moderate pull of 10 – 15 kg on a line may reveal that they can be re-stretched by anything up to 2 or 3 cm to achieve their proper length. If the lines appear excessively dirty, stretchy, or at all worn – replace them.) Line measurement and load capacity is hard to check without proper equipment, and this is another reason for ensuring your wing receives its annual check.

NEVER ATTEMPT TO REPAIR A LINE BY KNOTTING IT.

IF YOU ARE IN ANY DOUBT, SEEK PROFFESIONAL ADVICE.

Major damage should be referred to your dealer. All good dealers should be able to supply lines and other basic components. Apart from physical damage, canopies can be rendered unsafe through material degradation. The major cause of this, already mentioned in the section on fabric, is ultraviolet light. UV, a constituent of sunlight, gradually weakens the fibres of the cloth, and prolonged exposure will make it increasingly porous and more prone to tearing. This problem is associated with a severe fading of the colours, so, if your canopy appears very faded, ask a professional to check it for you. The tenacity and air-permeability of the fabric at critical points like the leading edge top surface is an integral part of a professional annual service.

Soaring Flight

Soaring can be defined as flight where altitude is maintained or gained purely from natural lift, i.e. without any outside input such as an engine or tow line.

As we already know, a paraglider is just that – a glider. It must be gliding down

through the air constantly to fly. So how can we soar? The answer is to find some air that is going up faster than we are going down.

Let us assume that your canopy sinks at about 300 feet a minute.(1.3m/sec) If

*Soaring flight at the
Dune de Pyla, France.
(Photo: John Brettoner)*

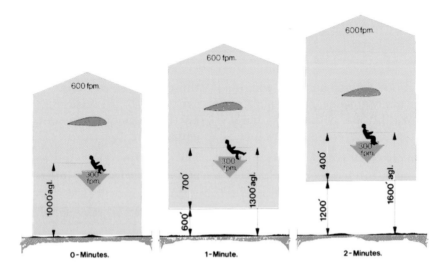

Fig 21.1 Flying down through a block of rising air, ie a thermal. The glider with a sink rate of 300fpm is flying through a block of air that is rising at 600fpm. The net result after two minutes is a 600 ft height gain.

we fly in air rising at 600 feet a minute, (2.6m/sec) after one minute we will have gained 300 feet (80m) of altitude. (See *Fig 21.1*).

Rising air is known as "lift", and there are several sources that a paraglider can use. The most common is ridge lift. This is produced when the wind is forced up over a ridge or cliff and forms a band of rising air we can fly in. (*Fig 21.2*)

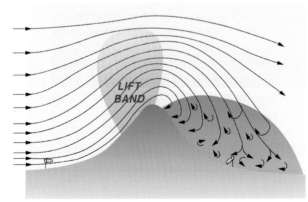

Fig 21.2. Section through ridge showing lift band and dangerous region of turbulence in the lee of the hill..

From what we know of site assessment and air behaviour we can visualise the "pressure wave" of air forming the lift band in front of the ridge. All we have to do is fly around in this area and we can stay up as long as we wish. This sounds very easy and often it is. However, it can require considerable concentration and effort to visualise and utilise this invisible force effectively. The best advice is to watch and learn from those who are already proficient. Birds of prey or gulls generally seem to have the right idea.

When soaring a ridge always make your turns facing into wind – see *Fig 21.3*. Try to follow a smooth extended figure-eight pattern, remember your site assessment and look for steeper sections of slope or those most into wind for the best lift.

Some useful hints:

● Always try to turn in a lifting patch.

● Watch out for gullies or the very end of a ridge where there may be no lift and you can be "hoovered" backwards.

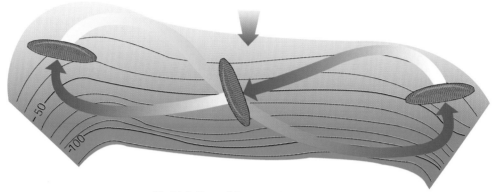

Fig 21.3. Typical figure-eight soaring pattern.

- The higher you get the further out the lift will extend. See *Fig 21.2*.

Other sources of rising air

These include thermals, wave and convergence, which are described in other sections of this book. A primary difference between ridge lift and other sources is that whilst it is easy to visualise and explore the position and strength of a static wave of ridge lift, the other sources are moving, and usually have no visual clues as to their dimensions. It must all be done by feel, making use of these types of lift more challenging than ridge lift alone.

Because humans have never evolved the senses to fly (or the sense not to) we can only judge our vertical motion by visual means, and if you are not close to the ground or a ridge this is very difficult.

A variometer gives you the missing information on your vertical movement, so flying thermals or other "random" lift sources means you need a vario to help define the limits and strength of the lift and fly effectively. The base criteria remain the same: to soar you must manage to locate and remain within airmasses that are ascending more quickly than your wing is descending. In the case of thermals, which drift with the wind, this often means circling continuously to stay within the confines of the lift.

Birds have successfully used this technique for millions of years.

In practice, the sources of lift are often mixed or less easy to define. A ridge may have weak dynamic lift, but be a source of thermals you can use. A sunny valley may have a lifting area well away from the slope that remains reliable for several hours, and so on.

Top landing

So, you are soaring. The view is wonderful and after a few minutes you can relax and concentrate on exploring the lift and perfecting your control. You are now

Always keep a good eye on other pilots. (Photo: Patrick Holmes, UK Airsports)

ready to land back on the top (just think, no more long slog up that hill). First, look in the area that you intend to land in. Is it suitable? Are there any potential hazards? Has anyone parked a hang glider there while you have been flying? (Most clubs have defined areas for landing that are kept clear if possible). If it is not a recognised landing area, could it suffer from turbulence and rotors? If in doubt, don't try it – land at the bottom. Ask other pilots and read your site guide to make sure it is advisable before attempting it.

If everything is OK, you need to plan your approach. Look at *Fig 21.4*; this is perhaps a little exaggerated in terms of good and bad choices, but gives you a good idea of the decision-making process involved. You have three choices: track in from the left (C) or the right (A) or approach directly downwind (B). All three approaches end up, of course, with a turn into wind. For your first top landings, a downwind approach (B) is not usually recommended; this is particularly true when it involves overflying a hazardous area such as the spine back shown in the diagram. So, left or right? If the wind is at 90° to the hill and the ridge is straight, the approach will be similar from either direction. Look at the area again; if you overshoot will it take you into the launch area or off the end of the hill? Choose the direction that gives the greatest margin for error – there are often unexpected patches of lift or sink above the top of a hill. Often the wind is not quite straight onto the face. This makes the choice easier – track to the end of the downwind leg and start your approach from there. In this example track (A) is the best choice.

1 Decide in good time that you are planning to top land (a good pilot always reads ahead). Do you have enough height? Do not assume that you will be lifted up as you approach the ridge - a painful collision may result if you do. Plan your turn carefully for the approach leg.

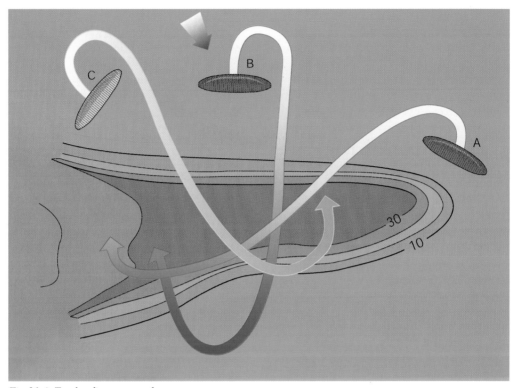

Fig 21.4. Top landing approaches.

2 Commence your turn as you would if you were intending to carry on soaring, then continue the turn until your track will crab you across the hill top Be careful not to turn too much with insufficient height, or you may not have room to turn back into wind.

3 Continue to crab until you are over your planned landing area, then turn into wind.

4 As you turn into wind and continue to sink, ease your brakes up, then ease them down if you need to lose any excess speed. Do not forget that you will be landing in a reasonably strong breeze – something you may not have experienced previously - so feel your way with the controls. Do not flare

hard unless it is obviously necessary. If, on your final approach, you find yourself too high, then a few gentle "s" turns will help you lose height. If in any doubt, overshoot and try again. With practice you will learn to judge more accurately and be able to spot land in a pre-determined area

Touchdown and canopy control

Once your feet have touched the ground you have a choice to make. You may be able to "walk" the inflated canopy to a suitable area to pack it or to launch again, or you can choose to collapse it where you have landed – if there is only a light breeze you can collapse it as normal – see chapter 16, Landing. If, however, there is a reasonable breeze, your first action should be to release one control completely and turn to face the canopy. In this position you have far more control (as per a reverse launch) and you can see where the canopy will end up.

To collapse it, pull down hard on both rear risers. This will effectively stall the canopy and it will collapse. If the canopy is a simple two-riser system, pull down hard on both controls and run towards it. In severe circumstances (you have fallen over), to prevent the canopy from dragging you, pull hard (hand over hand if necessary) on one control. This will cause the canopy to rotate and dive nose first into the ground. Once it is dropping nose first, do not pull any more as it may go right round and fly back up again. It is very important, if you are doing these manoeuvres, that you should run towards the canopy to reduce the pressure.

If the canopy dives into the ground with a good load through the lines to you, it may hit very hard and this could damage the internal cell walls. The more wind there is, the more important it is that you run towards the canopy while collapsing it.

Occasionally you may find that the wind is strong enough to re-inflate the canopy whenever you stop running towards it. In this case, the only safe position is behind (downwind) of it. If you should find yourself landing moving backwards or in a gusty wind, sprint round to the back of the canopy as soon as it is down. Being dragged by a paraglider is an unnerving and potentially dangerous experience. If you should fall over and find yourself being dragged, try to roll onto your stomach so that you can see where you are going and again, collapse the canopy by pulling one control hand over hand (until you get the fabric if necessary).

Soaring in the Lake District. (Photo: Patrick Holmes, UK Airsports)

Accelerator Systems

Often referred to as "speed systems" these are simply a way of changing the angle of attack of the wing in flight.

Some high performance gliders and tandem wings feature "trimmers"; these are small cam-lock adjusters on the rear riser which can be applied and locked in place to alter the length of the rear riser, and set the trim-speed of the wing.

This is very useful on fast wings, as it allows the angle of attack to be set to the optimum for conditions, and tilting the whole wing is far more efficient at maximising lift than adding lots of drag with the brakes alone. On a tandem wing this system is used because the brake pressures are greater.

Because of the harnesses arrangement tandems cannot use a foot operated speed system. Virtually all other canopies use a foot –operated stirrup to activate a speed system which lowers the angle of attack of the whole wing. (*Fig 22.1*)

When the foot stirrup is pressed the front riser is shortened. This would collapse the canopy's leading edge if done alone, but to prevent the airfoil "breaking", the B riser is also pulled down a proportional amount to maintain the even loading of the lines and keep the wing solid. In 4 riser systems (as shown) the C riser may also be shortened very slightly. This basic pattern is how all speed systems work, but there are variations on the theme: some may allow the rear riser to be extended as the A's & B's are shortened, for example.

A lower angle of attack means that induced drag is reduced, and the wing can travel faster and on a steeper glide path. The lower the angle of the canopy, the less resistance it has to diving further if

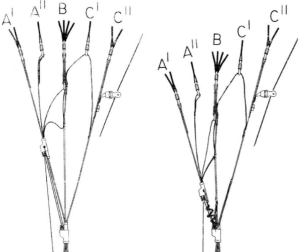

Normal position   **Activated position**

Fig 22.1: The stirrup is connected to your front risers by cords that run through pulleys mounted on your harness. The cord usually passes through another pair of pulleys on the front riser that gives a 2 to1 or 3 to 1 reduction advantage to make its activation progressive and to reduce the load, ensuring it is easy to operate.

it encounters a lull or any turbulence, and if it gets too low the airfoil can deform and have little resistance to collapse. For this reason, it is wise to use the speed system sparingly in rough air, and to maintain a little pressure on the brakes, so that you can slow and counter any sudden tendency to dive forward.

To actually use your speed system you need to locate the stirrup with your feet. Some systems are quite hard to find, as they are snug against the bottom of the the seat in normal flight. If you lengthen the lines the system cannot be fully extended, reducing your top speed (and the stirrup will get in the way of your legs as you launch).

The best solution is to use a stirrup extension. This can be a simple loop of cord in a plastic pipe or a stiff wire extension that is easy to locate without using your hands. A small patch of velcro is a handy

Photo: www.sunsoar-paragliding.com

way to keep the stirrup itself against the harness when not in use.

Speed system cords should be adjusted so that the system is not activated at all when the risers are tensioned. If they are too short, the wing will be hard to launch and prone to tucking. Pilots with long legs sometimes worry that they can "over-accelerate". However, this is not the case, as all the speed systems are limited by the distance between the pulleys.

Some pilots prefer to remove their harnesses when packing up. In this case the speed system must also be disengaged. The cords are often secured at the riser end, by either a small maillon, or by a pair of brummel hooks. These interlocking devices are easy and effective, but you must be very careful that lines cannot get trapped in the slots. (A number have been fitted that have a 1mm slot that has proved wide enough to make this a problem).

Any system with snap hooks or any spring-loaded gate must be discarded as the hooks can trap a line during ground handling.

Speed bar with a cranked ladder extension for easy 'footing'.

Accelerator systems are there to give a bit of additional speed if you should need it; they are not provided so that you can fly in winds that are too strong to cope with otherwise.

Apart from competition use, your speed system (like big ears) should be thought of as a safety device that you keep in reserve for dealing with situations where you have misjudged the conditions.

Photo: Swing gliders

Site Discipline & Rules of the Air

Paragliders are subject to the same rules as any other aircraft *(see chapter 24, Air Law)*. But, in addition to these, there are some other disciplines that must be observed for us to fly safely without causing problems for others.

Sites

In the UK at least, all land is owned by somebody, and before you fly from it you should find out whose it is and seek permission. Obviously, you must use common sense. If you are flying down from a remote mountain in the Andes it is unlikely anyone is going to worry. However, people flying in areas where grouse shooting takes place or where there are sheep during lambing time have already lost sites. There is certainly nowhere in England or Wales that should be flown without permission. It is vital for the future of the sport that pilots follow sensible guidelines when out flying. These include:

- Keeping away from stock.
- Not taking dogs onto hills where there may be sheep.
- Not climbing over fences, walls or hedges.
- No lighting fires.
- Closing gates.
- Checking there is no shooting or lambing taking place. (February to May).
- Parking sensibly.

- Leaving no litter.
- Flying with third party insurance, (see below), and paying for any damage.

These rules, of course, are designed to help others. We also need to help ourselves directly by observing a sensible attitude on the site. For example:

- Do not leave equipment in the landing area.
- Make sure everyone knows the site rules.
- Offer to help to act as anchorman for other pilots.
- Do not launch if the sky is crowded.
- Always do a pre-flight check.
- Only fly if you are in good health.

There are also some mandatory safety rules (failure to comply could invalidate your insurance, for example). These include:

- Wearing a suitable helmet.
- Having the relevant qualification for the flying you are undertaking.
- Being adequately covered by third party insurance (BHPA membership currently gives £2,000,000 cover).
- You may not fly when under the influence of drugs or alcohol.
- Do not fly in a modified paraglider or harness unless the manufacturer agrees to the changes.

Do not launch if you consider the air to be too busy for you. (Photo: www.sunsoar-paragliding.com)

Anti-collision rules.

For your own safety and that of others it is vital that you are aware of these rules. There is a certain amount of general air-law required to be a pilot, but the fact is that the people we are most likely to collide with are each other.

1 When approaching another aircraft head-on, break right. If this is impractical or unsafe because you are too near the ridge, allow the other pilot only to brake – if you should go left while he goes right you are likely to collide.

2 When approaching another aircraft on a converging course, the one on the right has the right of way (on your right – in the right).

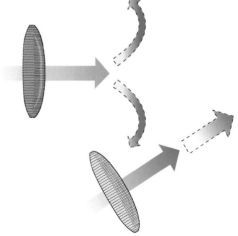

3 Give way to pilots below you (they have less room to manoeuvre and may not be able to see you).

4 When overtaking while ridge soaring always pass between the other pilot and the hill. They are most likely to turn out from the hill so this reduces the risk of collision. It also prevents you from "cutting them off" from their landing area.

5 When in thermals, always circle in the same direction as pilots who have joined the thermal before you. This means that your closing speed will be small and visual contact can be maintained.

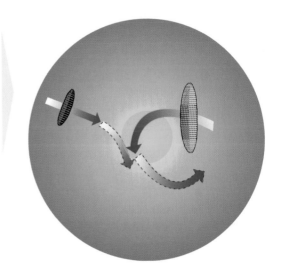

6 Notwithstanding the above, it is the duty of every pilot to take any and every action necessary to avoid a collision. In other words, even if it is your right of way you are expected to take action if the alternative is a collision. **This is the overriding rule!**

Site Discipline & Rules of the Air

 Look <u>BEFORE</u> you manoeuvre! This is not written down anywhere as the law –but it is probably the most useful and important discipline of the lot. Manoeuvring includes doing almost anything, from letting go of a control to scratch your nose, to taking off or commencing a turn.

Although it is critical that everyone knows and follows these anti-collision rules, the fact is that most pilots rarely put them into practice. The reason is that they only become important in situations where there is an imminent risk of collision and the sensible pilot never allows this situation to develop.

When you are flying it is useful to imagine that you are in the centre of a sphere or bubble which is your personal space, as long as you keep your bubble away from everyone else's the anti collision rules never need to be activated.

The size of your own "sheilded" area varies depending on your own experience, who you are flying with, how smooth the conditions are and other factors. If you do not think that your have enough space to fly without compromising your space, then the wisest move is to stay on the ground.

Note – Because of the low relative speeds and the fact that the pilot is exposed (not in a cockpit), it is often practical simply to shout at the other pilot if you are not sure that he has seen you.

One final point – some paraglider pilots seem to think that because their canopies are slow moving, faster aircraft such as hang gliders, sailplanes and so on should give way to them. While there is some truth in the suggestion that those craft have a greater speed to call upon, it is an EQUAL responsibility to avoid each other.

FreeX gliders

Air Law

Paragliding is a sport; it is often advertised alongside alternatives like climbing or mountain biking, and most flying is done with a few kilometres of recognised flying sites. Perhaps because of this there is occasionally a misconception that paragliding is not really "aviation" in the same way as flying a light aircraft, for example, and is therefore somehow less subject to air law. This is not the case, and all aircraft, including gliders of all types, are expected to know and conform to any relevant airspace regulations and restrictions.

At school, or when flying on recognised club sites that we know have no airspace restrictions, it is sufficient to know the visual meteorological conditions (VMC) required and the anti-collision rules, to be able to fly safely with others. When thermalling, and flying cross-country away from a known site, the situation alters. We are sharing the air with a wide variety of other users and having laws and regulations helps to keep both us and them safe.

Firstly we need to build up a mental picture of the way airspace is arranged.

The information given below is relevant to the UK only, though a very similar arrangement is common in many countries. If you need further information on another region, you are best advised to contact that country's association for advice.

The air in the UK is divided into two broad chunks – that above 24,500ft and that below. The top chunk is known as the upper flight information region (UFIR). This is not particularly relevant to us as no one has yet managed to fly anything like that high in the UK. In any event, you would be busy trying to cope with lack of oxygen and cold on a paraglider at this altitude.

The lower chunk is sub-divided into the London and Scottish FIRs. Within these flight information regions there are seven categories of airspace, designated types A to G, each with separate requirements for their use.

Airspace Categories

As far as paraglider pilots are concerned these seven categories can be contracted to just three, as types A,B,C,&D can all be considered the same. All of these require air traffic clearance to enter and are therefore prohibited to us.

The remaining types are E, which is very rare, and F & G; these categories do have slightly different rules for the craft entering them.

Note that the requirements are different for altitudes above and below 3000ft AMSL.

In order to conform to the airspace regulations that apply, a paraglider pilot requires the skills to be able to navigate sufficiently accurately to know his or her own position and altitude, and to have knowledge of what restricted or prohibited airspace is in the vicinity, and be able to avoid it. This generally means carrying a suitable map and instruments.

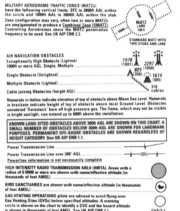

Fig 24.1 (above): 1:250000 airchart extract. (Reproduced with the permission of Civil Aviation Authority, Ordnance Survey)

Fig 24.2 (left): Key to symbols for a 1:250000 airchart. (Reproduced with the permission of Civil Aviation Authority)

A guide to the different categories

Categories A,B,C and D are prohibited.

Category E :These areas are accessible to us in full Visual Meteorological Conditions (VMC) : 5km visibility, (increasing to 8km above 10,000ft) 1,500 metres horizontally clear of cloud and 1,000ft vertically). Yes, metres and feet are mixed!.

Category F (advisory routes) and category G (the open FIR); these both have the same VMC criteria as E when above 3,000ft AMSL.

Below 3,000ft AMSL the rules are relaxed for aircraft moving at less than 140knots. VMC becomes: Clear of cloud and in sight of the ground with visibility of 1,500m. In other words, you may circle to Cloudbase if you are within this category, but may not enter the cloud.

However, uncontrolled airspace is exactly that: uncontrolled, and civilian and military aircraft are free to make use of it just as we are. There is also the possibility that temporary category A airspace may be may be notified at short notice. This is a royal flight path (previously known as "purple" airspace) and any penetration is not permitted. There are some paragliding sites in the UK located near to royal residences which are periodically affected in this way.

Airways

These are the roads of the air. They are (usually) ten nautical miles wide and have a lower and upper level. These levels vary and for each one you need to consult an air chart. The levels are printed along each one like road numbers and may say (for example) FL75. This means that the base of this particular airway is at a Flight Level of 7,500ft. The airways are designated on the chart by a single heavy broken blue line which marks the centre of the airway. A glider (that includes paragliders) is permitted to cross only a very few airways, though this is prohibited for the vast majority. Even if you are permitted to cross one (you local club will advise you of the situation locally) - your position is rather like a hedgehog crossing the road.

Therefore, the rules are self-evident – keep a good lookout, cross quickly and in a straight line at 90°. For obvious reasons you must be flying in full visual meteorological conditions; that is 8km visibility, clear of cloud by 1500 metres horizontally and 1000ft vertically.

Control Traffic Area (CTA)

Control areas are found above aerodromes. They are the roundabouts of the sky where the airways meet. Very often, the airways descend in steps to the control area.

Some of the control areas are known as control zones. As a general rule, a "zone" is airspace that extends from the ground upwards. An "area" is one that is from one given altitude to another. As always there are exceptions to this – Danger areas, for example, (over military ranges, etc) start at ground level.

Penetration is prohibited to paragliders (except where prior permission has been obtained) or when the area is stated as being inactive at specific times.

Terminal Manoeuvring Areas (TMA's)

These are a sort of aerial motorway junction found over major airports. They are generally category A airspace, which means that all flying is done under instrument flight rules. Within them, air traffic is controlled by the airport control tower. While it is possible to have radio contact if you have the right equipment and a suitable licence to use it, it is clearly impractical for a paraglider to manoeuvre to order, so of course they are prohibited to us.

Air Traffic Zones (ATZ's)

These comprise the restricted airspace belonging to smaller aerodromes. They start at ground level and go up to 2,000ft, within a radius of two nautical miles of the aerodrome. If the longest runway is longer than 1,850metres, the boundary is considered too close to the runway (less than one and a half nautical miles) and so the ATZ is increased to a radius of 2.5 nautical miles. There are a variety of grades of ATZ, ranging from prohibited through those requiring prior or radio permission to penetrate. Your club can advise you of the situation locally.

Military Aerodrome Traffic Zones (MATZ's)

As the name makes clear, these comprise the controlled airspace surrounding military air bases. They are made up of two parts – the inner Air Traffic Zone (ATZ), which is prohibited to us, and an outer "shell" that you are permitted to penetrate. That is the law: however, it would be extremely unwise to spend any length of time in an area where pilots who have a tremendous workload and are probably under training are very likely to be encountered. A MATZ typically has a radius of five nautical miles from the centre of the longest runway and extends to 3,000ft above ground level. In addition, there is usually a stub (see *Fig 24.3*) five nautical miles long and four wide, extending from 1,000ft up to 3,000ft above ground level.

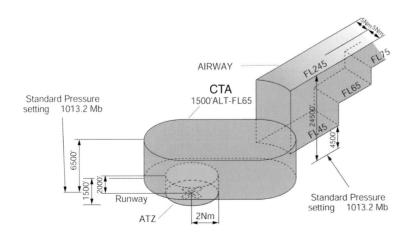

Fig 24.3: Aerodrome showing the air traffic zone, and an airway "stepping down" to meet it. The illustration shows only one airway stopping at the boundary. In fact, there may be more than one and they may well continue above, through and beyond the controlled area. Both airways and CTA's are visible on fig 24.1.

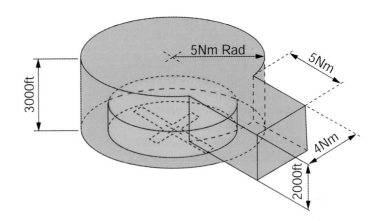

Fig 24.3: The dimensions of a typical military aerodrome traffic zone. (The ATZ is shown in orange). Note the "stub" is in line with the longest runway. More than one MATZ is visible on the aircraft extract shown above.

Areas of Intense Aerial Activity (AIAA)

This is a catch-all for any other area where there is a high risk of encountering other aircraft, such as an area used for aerobatics. Whilst not specifically prohibited to us, the same provisos apply as for a MATZ.

Danger Areas, Prohibited Areas and Restricted Areas

Dotted all over your air chart you will also find areas of prohibited or restricted airspace. These reflect ground-based activities such as sensitive military bases or ranges, nuclear power stations, etc.

Danger areas are often military ranges or similar hazard. They can be active permanently or only at certain times. If you have certain prior knowledge that they are inactive, they can be crossed (this may mean being in radio contact with ATC to request permission. Otherwise, they are prohibited. Each danger area has a code, for example, D503/12. This means

this is danger area number 503 (in fact number 03 above 50^0 latitude) and extends to an altitude of 12,000ft.

Examples of Danger areas are shown on the aircraft extract *Fig 24.1.*

High intensity radio transmission area

Airspace of defined dimensions within which there is radio energy of an intensity that may cause interference or even damage to radio and navigation equipment. Certain areas emit signals (microwaves, radar, etc) that can be harmful to pilots.

Bird sanctuaries

Usually these are breeding colonies of rare birds. Unfortunately some, such as gannets, like to nest in areas of good ridge lift! Some are out of bounds in the breeding season and a few are prohibited at all times.

Sharing uncontrolled airspace

The major risk of collision in uncontrolled airspace is with other gliders (whether rigid, hang or para) as we all fly the same terrain and in the same way. *The anti-collision rules are reproduced in chapter 23.* The second group of air users that concerns us comprises military aircraft with crews under training. Their operations are often carried out at low level, high speed and with their pilots doing their best to remain hidden by the terrain. They are concentrated in the more remote and hilly parts of the UK – exactly those areas most used by paragliders. Fortunately, the Royal Air Force usually operates on weekdays, except for major exercises, which are usually well publicised through a NOTAM (notice to airmen). As a sport, paragliding is predominantly a weekend activity. However, there is still a very real possibility of conflict. A number of steps have been taken to minimise the risk of collision.

Many of our major sites are marked on the air charts. *(such a site is marked with a hang-glider symbol on the chart extract shown above)* and some have a voluntarily agreed "avoidance" zone (again, your club will advise you). It is obvious that this is no protection if you are flying a minor site or have left the ridge on a cross-country flight. If this is likely to be the case, you should use the Civil Advance Notification Procedure (CNAP) by dialling 0800 515544. You will be asked where you will be planning to fly, the grid reference of the site, the nearest town, the time and area of intended activity and the scale of that activity. Given five hours notice, the information should appear on all pilots' notice boards.

Even if you cannot give that much notice it is still worth ringing. Note that the resultant CNAP *(like an avoidance zone)* tells pilots of your presence so that they can be careful to keep a look out for you. It does not deny them the right to fly there.

For details of royal flights, air displays or other short-term airspace restrictions, phone 0500 354802.

ALFENS (military automated low flying enquiry and notification service) is basically a computerised method of distributing CNAP information and could be of benefit, as it should speed up the time taken to relay information received on 0800 515544.

General flying rules

1 A glider should not be operated in a negligent or careless manner so as to endanger life or property, nor be flown in such proximity to other aircraft as to create a danger of collision, nor in formation without the prior agreement of the pilots.

2 No person may be carried except in that part of the aircraft designed for the purpose, or be drunk in the aircraft.

3 Nothing shall be dropped from the aircraft other than a person by parachute in an emergency, articles for life-saving, or ballast in the form of fine dry sand or water. (Or tow ropes at an airfield.)

4 A pilot, on meeting hazardous conditions in flight, shall, as soon as possible, report to the appropriate Air Traffic Control, information helpful to the

safety of other aircraft

5 Gliders shall not fly over built-up areas below either such height as will allow it to land clear, or 1,500ft above the highest fixed object within 600m of the aircraft, whichever is the higher. In any case, an aircraft may not be flown nearer than 500ft (150m) to any person, vehicle, vessel or structure except when taking off, landing or hill soaring.

6 An aircraft may not fly over or within 1km of an outdoor gathering of more than 1,000 people or below such height as will enable it to land clear. i.e. No dropping in on football matches!.

There are a couple of other rules designed for powered aircraft and not directly relevant to paragliders. However, because they may help us to understand the likely actions of other air users, they are worth knowing. The most useful of these are:

● When following a prominent ground feature (a motorway, railway or river for example) the aircraft shall keep the feature to its left.

● When not ridge soaring, and when following the same course, an aircraft shall overtake on the right.

Altimeters

Knowing about the airspace is totally useless if you do not know where you are. Firstly you must know your height, and for this you require an altimeter. This can be set to various references (see *Fig 24.4*).

1 QNH. This means that zero on the altimeter is equal to sea level.

2 QFE. This means zeroed to specific altitude, for example the takeoff point or the anticipated landing field.

3 Pressure altitude. This means set to a standard pressure setting (1,013.2mb). All the airspace above 3,000ft is based on this setting, so this will tell you where you are relative, say, to an airway. As the pressure

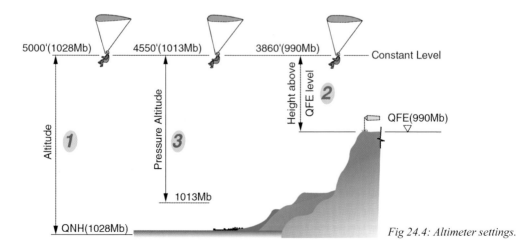

Fig 24.4: Altimeter settings.

changes this means that airspace effectively moves up and down, so using air pressure as a datum prevents different aircraft having different readings when they are, in fact, at the same height.

Air charts

Air charts are the maps that contain all the information outlined above. While it is invaluable to become familiar with them, actually using them to navigate is extremely difficult. The practical solution is to copy the airspace relevant to your planned flight onto an ordinary Ordnance Survey map, or similar, to refer to in flight.

UK aircharts come in two flavours.

The 1: 500,000 (half million) show every type of airspace and cover a large area. However, they are very difficult to read accurately in the air, and much of the high level stuff is not relevant to us anyway.

The 1: 250,000 (quarter million) show all airspace up to 5,000AMSL. They are obviously a better scale for local navigation, except that on that long epic you may find yourself flying into the unknown as you reach the edge of the map.

(Example shown in *Fig 24.1*)

Aircharts are updated regularly and it is each pilot's responsibility to ensure his information is up to date: see the reference section for further information.

Radios

It is illegal to transmit from the air with other than an airband radio. To use the vast majority of airband frequencies requires a radio telephony licence. This is necessary if you wish to talk to ATC controller to get permission to enter his ATZ for example. There are, however, a few frequencies that are available to us without this requirement: the main frequency used is 118.675Mhz and this is allocated hang-gliding and paragliding.

You do not need to pass an exam to obtain a licence to use these gliding frequencies, but you must maintain radio discipline and not use them to "chat". The frequencies currently available in the UK are:

129.900

129.950

130.100

130.125

130.400

Note that these may be used by other aircraft types, especially gliders, balloons and parachutists.

The emergency distress channel 121.500 is constantly monitored.

For the purposes of clarity there is an ICAO phonetic alphabet that is used to ensure accurate transmission and reception, particularly when reception is poor or vital information such as call signs etc being sent this is given in **table 24.1**.

There are other types of radios available and details are given in chapter 19, Additional Equipment.

A	Alpha	J	Juliet	S	Sierra	.	Decimal
B	Bravo	K	Kilo	T	Tango	5	Fife
C	Charlie	L	Lima	U	Uniform	9	Niner
D	Delta	M	Mike	V	Victor	0	Zero
E	Echo	N	November	W	Whiskey		
F	Foxtrot	O	Oscar	X	X-Ray	No	Negative
G	Golf	P	Papa	Y	Yankee	Yes	Affirmative
H	Hotel	Q	Quebec	Z	Zulu	Will Comply	Willco
I	India	R	Romeo			Wait	Stand by

Table 24.1: The ICAO phonetic alphabet.

When setting off on an XC flight, it is important to be aware of other aircraft as well as any airspace restrictions. (Photo: Patrick Holmes, UK Airsports)

Meteorology

The weather is a colossal subject. In this section the intention is to consider the basic weather patterns that affect us, and look at the local "micrometeorology" systems that a paraglider pilot is likely to encounter or that are of particular interest to us.

Forecasts

Weather forecasts are available from a variety of sources. The most obvious is television. The UK BBC forecasts are excellent for establishing a visual picture of what is happening and, if you are familiar with the synoptic (pressure) charts (see *Fig 25.1*), you can glean a good deal of information that the presenter does not have time to spell out. Satellite photos are useful for assessing cloud cover. The downfall of these forecasts from our point of view is that they are very general and give no indication of the change of wind speed with height, and they rarely mention convection, though code phases such as "sunshine and showers" can give a clue.

Radio forecasts fall into three main categories. General "it will be a nice day in the south" are of little use to us. Specific forecasts, particularly the shipping ones, are good for approaching weather and

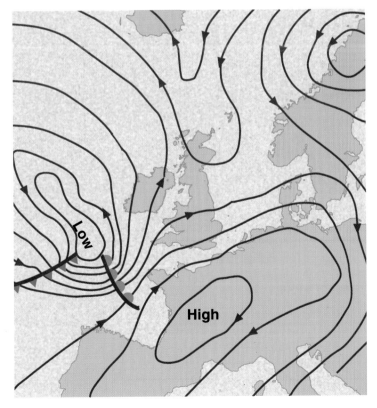

Fig 25.1: Synoptic chart

surface winds., especially for coastal flying. You will need to know where the coastal stations and sea areas like "Dogger" or "Fastnet" actually are.

Volmet is a constant transmission of actual weather data of interest to air-users and is possible to receive if you have an airband radio.

However, it has a number of disadvantages. It tells you what is happening right now at the airport mentioned, rather than forecasting what is going to happen, and you may have to wait some time to hear the weather for your specific region. In many parts of the UK it is difficult or impossible to receive. Frequencies for the Volmet service are :

North 126.600 Mhz

South 128.600

Scottish 125.725

National 135.375

Internet Forecasts

There are a huge number of weather information providers on the net. A list is given in the useful addresses section. But a good place to start is.

www.bbc.co.uk/weather

or

www.met-office.gov.uk

Telephone forecasts

Again, there are the general type which are often available for a small region. This does not make them more useful as local conditions, such as a hill or coastal fog, etc, may be mentioned. There is also a

service in the UK known as Airmet.

Airmet offers two services. One gives the weather for the following 24 hours, and one for the following 12 (i.e. that day). These are excellent as they give the most valuable information from our point of view – wind speeds at different heights. They also warn of turbulence, freezing levels and cloud types and coverage. The latter is expressed in octares (eighths). Airmet can also be subscribed to as a written forecast if you have a fax machine. A gliding supplement is available which gives information about wave or thermal activity, cloud types etc.

UK Airmet telephone number (9 regions) (2003)

These forecasts are updated each day at 0600hrs, 1200hrs and 1800hrs.

Tel: 09003 444 900

The airmet service are also introducing a "mountain weather" guide which should be useful.

The numbers are: 09068 500 ***

Where *** depends on the region:

Scotland East 442

Scotland West 441

Snowdonia 449

Lake District 484

Using the forecasts

As a general rule, pilots look out of the window first then watch the TV. If the forecast is good – "a bright sunny day with light westerly winds" – then they set out. If it is poor – "gales and sleet" – they obviously do not bother. If the forecast implies that it may be OK, then a call to Airmet may be advisable. If you are planning a cross-country flight it is worthwhile obtaining the gliding supplement. This is also the usual procedure for competition organisers, etc, who may even call their local airports to request the "actuals" (actual current weather), though this is not a general service to sport fliers.

The latest developments in forecasting involve hang gliding and paragliding clubs actually building their own weather stations, which they site in a suitable spot and which use a portable phone or are wired to a nearby line. Current technology allows the forecast data to be converted into a simulated voice that can be rung to give us our own "actual" data. (The publishers of this book have provided the necessary facilities for such a service in the Yorkshire Dales and on the East coast.) In France weather data from popular take-off points is transmitted regularly on 2m radio frequencies. A few sites, usually at skiing venues, now feature webcams so that you can log on and actually see who is flying and how they are doing! The ultimate forecast (or torture if you are stuck in the office).

Fax Forecasts

If you have a group 3 fax machine, it is also possible to obtain an Airmet fax forecast, including synoptic charts and spot winds at altitude in the UK. With a suitable dish antenna and a personal computer, you can even grab data and weather information direct from satellites. However, the scale of the images means that it is not really very useful for forecasting for a small region.

Text Forecasts

You can get a 6 hour local weather forecast texted direct to your mobile phone if you message your postcode to the met office. Call 0845 3000500 for details of this service.

Cloud types

Clouds are categorised according to their altitude and shape. There are three main categories:

Cirrus

These are the highest clouds, at 16,000ft (5,000m) or more, and they are composed of ice crystals.

Stratus

These are featureless layers of cloud.

Cumulus

Heaped piles of cloud caused by convection.

The latter two categories can be sub-divided again by height. The prefix "Alto" is added to identify clouds above 6,500ft (2,000m) and the prefix "Cirro" to identify those at cirrus levels. The term Nimbus (or Nimbo as a prefix) indicates rain bearing clouds.

As a general rule, the high level clouds do not affect us directly, though they do of course affect the amount of sunlight reaching the surface and are a valuable indicator of what the weather is likely to do in the next few hours.

The cloud types that directly concern us are, firstly, low stratus clouds. Are they going to cover the hills or cause visibility problems when airborne? A specific type of low stratus is orographic cloud.

This is a blanket of cloud that clings to the surface, usually on the windward face of a hill. It is worth pointing out that these clouds can form quite quickly, and if you are already airborne, and notice wisps forming over the surface of the hill, you should land immediately.

Orographic cloud. (Photo: f8 photography)

Cumulus cloud. (Photo: f8 photography)

The second type of cloud we are concerned with is cumulus cloud. Cumulus clouds are formed by the condensation of water vapour in rising air (convection) and therefore indicate areas of lift. Where there is lift there is also turbulence, so

Radiant fog over the Yorkshire Dales (Photo: RAD Aviation)

they also signal caution for the inexperienced pilot.

Cumulus clouds vary from the tiny "balls of cotton wool" that have little or no effect on us, through weak, medium and strong thermal clouds right up to the dark-bottomed cumulo-nimbus clouds which mark violent updraughts and severe turbulence. *Cumulus clouds are mentioned again under "thermals" and in chapter 26, Cross-Country Flight.*

Another cloud type that directly concerns us is a type of alto-cumulus known as a lenticular. Lenticular clouds are easily identified as they are smooth and lens-shaped and they do not move across the sky with the wind. They are usually arranged in "stacks" or as a series of "Bars" at 90° to the wind direction. These clouds mark the presence of atmospheric wave, which is an important source of lift and turbulence. Wave is discussed in detail later in this chapter.

Depressions, fronts and high-pressure systems.

The dynamics of weather systems make up an interesting but complex subject that is well explained in several books. Very briefly, the sun heats the earth more at the equator (where its radiation passes through the atmosphere at almost 90° to the earth's surface) and a much lower angle at the poles. This sets up a circulation as the heated air rises, moves horizontally, cools and then sinks and flows into regions of lower pressure again.

Large continental land masses and large areas of ocean also generate large and predictable airmasses. In some parts of the world this gives rise to regular and settled weather patterns.

In those areas sandwiched between "competing" polar and equatorial systems, or between oceanic and continental regions, the weather is changeable and much more difficult to predict. The UK (as we are only too aware) falls into both these categories. We can, however, read the weather as it approaches if we have some understanding of the main features.

Depressions and fronts

Depressions or 'Cyclonic' regions are areas of relatively low atmospheric pressure. Air can rise easily in these regions and, as a result, depressions are frequently associated with cloud and rain. Depressions often form where air masses

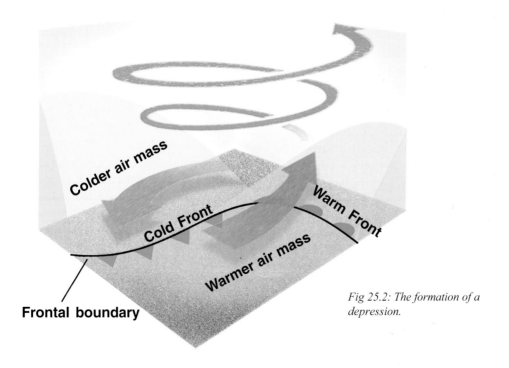

Colder air mass

Cold Front

Warm Front

Warmer air mass

Frontal boundary

Fig 25.2: The formation of a depression.

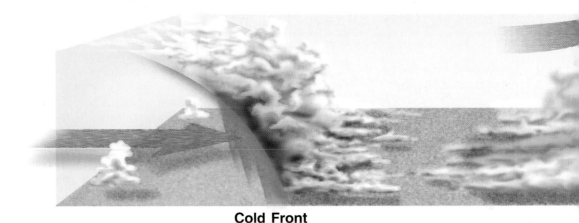

Cold Front

Fig 25.3: Cross-section through typical warm and cold fronts.

of different temperatures meet. The division between these air masses is known as a front. Because of the different characteristics of the air masses on each side, these fronts may develop "waves" along their length. The actual process is triggered by the Jetstream and is beyond the scope of this book. A wave on a front is the first sign of a depression being created *(Fig 25.2)*. As the depression develops and the airmasses rotate, the pressure drops and the winds increase The air masses are now arranged in sectors and are divided by a warm front followed by a cold front. As the depression gradually fills and weakens, the cold front overtakes the warm front and the result is an occluded front.

An occlusion can be active, with the warm and cold fronts passing 'back to back', or it can be quite weak especially as the depression is in its later stages and can be marked by no more than a band of high cloud.

To clarify the different characteristics, *Fig 25.3* shows a cross section through a simple example of a cold and a warm front.

As a warm front approaches, cirrus cloud appears, and this cloud gradually lowers and thickens into nimbo-stratus or strato-cumulus; the wind "backs" – that is, swings anti-clockwise, and strengthens. As the front passes the rain slackens. Cloudbase rises and the wind "veers" (swings clockwise from south-west to west, for example).

A cold front is marked by active cloud and (often heavy) rain, perhaps even thunder with cumulo-nimbus clouds if the front is an active one. There may be a "gust front" extending well ahead of cunimb clouds, making flying in their vicinity very dangerous. As the front arrives, the wind increases and veers. After the passage of a cold front the cloudbase rises again and the cold air may give a sharp temperature gradient. This leads to active convection and the formation of cumulus clouds in the cold sector behind the front.

There are differing varieties of front de-

Warm Front

and, therefore, there are likely to be strong convection currents (thermals). This means good weather for altitude and distance flying.

A pilot noticing cirrus clouds building in the west, sometimes noticeable as a "halo" around the sun, can deduce that a warm front is approaching and that the weather will soon deteriorate.

Fronts are shown as lines on a weather map. These lines indicate the position of the front on the ground. In reality, the gradient of a warm front is around 1° or 2° , so a frontal zone can easily be 150 miles wide. The illustrations have an exaggerated vertical scale so that they will fit on the page!

Remember Buy's Ballots Law – this is a simple rule to help you remember your position relative to a depression. In the northern hemisphere, if you stand with your back to the wind, the centre of the low will be on your left.

pending on the character of the aimasses involved, their temperatures and relative humidity.

A katacold front for example is a term describing a situation where the cold airmass is descending and there is therefore less convection and cloud. If you are interested in finding out more about the weather patterns that affect our flying, a list of books is given in the appendix.

Paraglider pilots do not need to understand how the weather develops in order to fly, but the more we understand, the easier it is to make accurate predictions of what is coming next. This obviously offers benefits both in safety and in saving wasted journeys. Take the potential cross-country pilot: by studying a synoptic chart (one showing depressions with isobars, and fronts represented by broad lines) the pilot can see that there is (say) a north westerly breeze and cold front expected to pass quickly overhead on Friday. This means that by Saturday afternoon he can expect a good temperature gradient (temperature falling rapidly with altitude gain) in the cold sector

High-pressure systems

These are the opposite of depressions. Because the pressure is high there is little rising air. The sky is often cloudless and there is little wind. If the pressure remains high for some time, dust and dirt in the atmosphere may not be circulated and so the air at low level (often trapped beneath a temperature "inversion", see below) becomes hazy and visibility diminishes. If there is sufficient wind to fly, the conditions are often very smooth, but the lack of any convection means that cross country flying is virtually impossible as all the air is gradually sinking. The airflow around a high-pressure system is in a clockwise direction in the northern hemisphere.

Thermals

The radiation given out by the sun covers a wide spectrum of wavelengths. The heat radiation, however, has very little effect on the atmosphere (unless it happens to be very wet or dirty) and most of it is reflected or reaches the ground. Some surfaces, such as water or green grass, reflect much of the heat and are slow to warm up. Other surfaces, such as dry sand, Tarmac or rocks, absorb heat and may warm quite quickly. This difference in warming is also compounded by uneven ground or aspect (a south facing slope is warmer than a north face, a west face is warmer in the evening and so on), and by other factors.

A result of this differential warming is that the hot surfaces then warm the air above and around them. Like most other substances, when air is heated its molecules become excited and bounce around more vigorously. The warm air expands and, in doing so, it becomes less dense. If the sun is still shining and the warming process continues, the "bubble" of warm air will grow larger and larger and become lighter and lighter as its pressure drops.

Eventually, it will break away from the surface and float up through the denser and cooler air around it, gradually cooling as it goes. Ultimately, it reaches a level where the surrounding air is at a similar temperature and pressure, and there it stops.

The warm air very often contains more moisture than the surrounding cooler air, and as the thermal rises it may reach the condensation level (dew point), and a cloud is formed. The condensation level occurs when the parcel of air is cooled to the point of saturation and the moisture it contains condenses as a cloud – air holds less moisture at lower temperatures. The process of condensation is a heat producing reaction, so the thermal receives a final boost, which is why cumulus clouds are heaped up and not just flat.

A thermal may be stopped at a low altitude if there is a layer of warmer air.

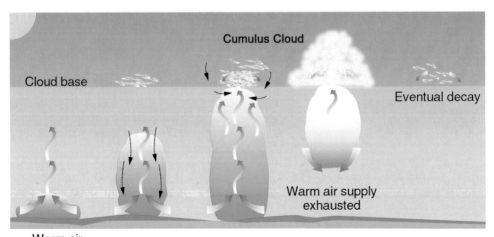

Fig 25.5: The birth and growth of a thermal to form a cumulus cloud.

These layers are known as inversions (because they are inverse to the usual gradient of temperature reducing with height). Very often the temperature does not reduce uniformly as you climb, so the thermal may be rising strongly then slow down, or vice-versa, as it passes through these layers. It is possible to plot the progress of a thermal if you know the temperature gradient. *Fig 25.6* shows a temperature trace for a particular day. As you can see, it generally becomes cooler as you gain altitude. This cooling is known as the lapse rate, and various factors affect this rate.

Dry air has a specific rate of cooling with altitude. This is known as the Dry Adiabatic Lapse Rate (DALR). The DALR is approximately a cooling of 1°C with every 100 metres of altitude (3°C with every 1,000 ft).

Armed with this knowledge, a temperature trace (or a thermometer and an al-timeter) you can predict the climb rate of thermals and the height of the cloudbase.

Pressure also decreases with height. On most weather forecasts the pressure is shown in millibars (mb) or hectopascals (hPa). Both units have identical values and are interchangeable. For our purposes we can assume, pressure drops by one millibar every 30ft or 9.8 metres. In fact it is slightly less than that at sea level and slightly more at 5,000ft.

There is also a Saturated Adiabatic Lapse Rate (SALR), which is approximately half the dry rate, at 0.5°C per 100 metres (or 1.5°C per 1,000 feet). The saturated lapse rate is the cooling rate of air saturated with condensing water droplets, that is, cloud.

In practice the lapse rates vary enormously, due to all kinds of outside factors, and the environmental or ambient air lapse rate actually varies around the

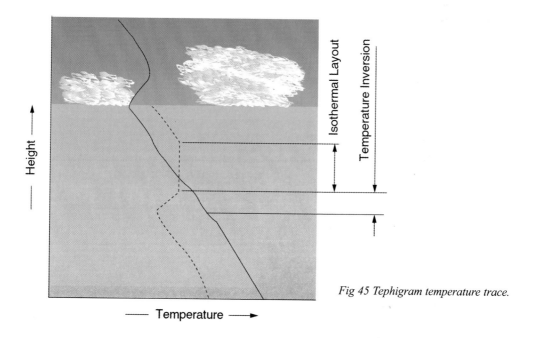

Fig 45 Tephigram temperature trace.

2°C per 1,000ft mark.

The solid line on the temperature graph or tephigram (*Fig 25.6*) shows a temperature trace that is realistic for an "unstable" day with some useful thermals. The broken line is included to illustrate two other features that may occur.

The first is an isothermal layer. This is simply a layer of air that does not change temperature. The second is an inversion - a layer of air that actually increases in temperature with height. This generally occurs in a region of high pressure – the air has been descending and this process compresses and warms the airmass. Thermals will, of course, be slowed or stopped by such features (depending on the strength and temperature of the thermal relative to the warm layer). This explains why a thermal can suddenly stop or can climb in bursts, or why only one or two thermals from particularly hot sources can penetrate to form clouds. The inversion may be quite high, so thermals can still be felt, even though they never reach high enough to form clouds. Note that the temperature increases again slightly at dewpoint. This is because inside a cloud the process of condensation releases heat and drives the further vertical development of the cloud.

Because the dry and saturated lapse rates are linked, you can determine the strength of a thermal from its vertical development. Towering cumulus clouds mean powerful lift, wispy ones (unless just forming) mean weaker lift.

Wave

Wave, also know as 'mountain' or 'lee' wave is a phenomenon usually caused when the wind is blowing over a series of hills. As we have seen in the section on ridge soaring, the air is accelerated as it is squeezed over the brow of a hill. This process adds energy to the flow. If the hill is solitary, the energy is usually dissipated as airflow downwind of the hill gradually flattens out again into a horizontal flow. If there is a line of hills, the energy has no time to dissipate before it is being reinforced by another injection of faster, vertically moving air.

The result of this happening several times is that each fresh input pushes the wave of lifting air higher than the last. (*Fig 25.7*) If there is a layer of stable air above the hills, the process is strengthened as it sinks back quickly after being pushed up by the rising air. The oscillation can

Lenticular cloud over the Yorkshire Dales, UK.

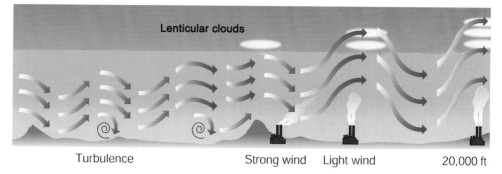

Lenticular clouds

Turbulence   Strong wind   Light wind   20,000 ft

Fig 25.7: Formation of a lee-wave system and lenticular clouds

then build up a powerful system. It is not unusual for a line of hills perhaps only a few hundred feet high to set up wave lift extending to 10,000 or 20,000 feet. When the moist low-level air is pushed up to these heights, the moisture condenses and clouds are formed. These lenticular clouds are arranged along the crest of the wave of air, so are at 90° to the wind direction. Because they are being formed at the front by rising air but then dissipating as the air descends again, they remain stationary. These clouds can cause charcteristic lines or 'bars' in the sky.

The crest of the wave may occur some way downwind of the hill that is causing it, hence the term "lee wave". At the bottom of the wave the wind – which may have considerable velocity – may have to make a sudden change in direction. The result is the same as when there is an obstruction on the ground – the air "tumbles" and forms a rotor. This can result in very severe turbulence. As the windspeed changes the wave position can move very quickly and may suddenly disappear altogether as the hills become "out of phase" for that strength. A spot that was enjoying good lift can be transformed fairly quickly into one that has

descending air or even rotor.

Wave may be identified by the changes of windspeed on the ground. It is not unusual to pass trees blowing in a good wind and a few miles further on to see smoke drifting slowly. If you are on a hill and the wind is light but it seems to be strong at altitude or nearby, exercise caution as it is likely that you are in a localised "out of phase" sector.

Once you are actually flying within the rising wave, the lift tends to be very smooth indeed and the greatest heights achieved by hang gliders and paragliders in the UK have been in this form of lift. *Fig 25.7* shows the ideal conditions for wave production: increasing wind strength with height and a suitable set of hills or mountains in phase with the wave length.

Certain conditions seem to favour wave production, in west-south-westerly winds in the north of England for example the wave systems can be seen by satellite photos to sometimes extend as far as the Czech republic! On other days wave has been reported on the western coast of Scotland where the nearest upwind hills are in North America.

149

In the mountains, as the sun rises, it heats the rock faces and any morning cloud is quickly burnt off.

Sea-breeze fronts

One other phenomenon that can give excellent flying conditions is a sea-breeze front. On hot, light wind days, the land is much warmer than the sea. As the warmer air over the land gradually reduces in density and pressure, the cooler air from the sea pushes in below it to form an on-shore breeze (*Fig 25.8*). These breezes may be soarable on coastal sites but the interesting thing is when this onshore breeze contacts a basically offshore wind.

The conflict between these airmasses is resolved exactly like a "normal" weather front, with the lighter warm air flowing up over the wedge of cool dense air. If the coastline is steep or the gradient of the incoming maritime air is sufficient, an invisible ridge is formed which can create sufficient lift to be soarable. When there is no significant obstacle on the ground, the sea breeze can penetrate many miles inland.

Fig 25.8: Sea breeze formation

Cross Country

To soar over the open countryside having to navigate and find lift as you go is one of the greatest challenges and most memorable experiences of paragliding. It is scarcely believable that pilots have crossed mountain ranges and deserts and maintained altitudes of thousands of metres using an aircraft that they can carry in a rucksack. Having once experienced it, pilots always fly in the hope of being able to go even further next time. Cross-country flights can be achieved using any of the lift sources detailed previously in this book, but typically rely on thermals. The potential XC pilot must first be able to recognise, and be prepared for, the right day.

A stunning view over Buttermere in the Lake District on a perfect cross-country day. (Photo: Patrick Holmes, UK Airsports)

Preparation

Good preparation is essential. First check the forecast. If it is possible that you may fly a long way, you may need to arrange how to get back home afterwards. Plan your likely route. At the current level of performance, pilots flying on a day with any significant wind will be obliged to travel in a predominantly downwind direction. You will need a suitable map on which any airspace or other hazards should be accurately marked.

Check your variometer and altimeter (there is nothing worse than the batteries dying just as you have left the hill behind you). Make sure you are properly clothed. It is far colder at altitude than on the ground. Assuming a standard dry adiabatic lapse rate, the temperature will drop about 3°C with every 1,000 feet. If the day does prove to have good thermals, you should try to choose the best time of day to leave the hill.

If it is very hot and thermals are growing quickly, it is best to get away early as the growing cloud cover may overdevelop and result in either cumulo-nimbus clouds or in so much ground shadow that thermals cease to be produced. For this reason, most of the best cross-country days are in spring and autumn, when the air is relatively cold and the thermal cycle can last much longer than in mid summer. On the other hand, if the thermals are far apart, or if the sky down wind is too blue, your chances of a reasonable distance are reduced. However, as the cloudbase usually lifts during the day, the radius in which you can search for new lift does increase.

When actually circling in a thermal, try to centre on the "core" – the lift may be only temporary and the thermal will be going up faster than you are, so it is quite easy to get left behind! Do not change the direction of your circling, but open out the pattern as the lift weakens and tighten as it strengthens. You may find that it is possible to fly at a slightly slower speed than usual if the lift is strong but be prepared to compensate quickly should you fly out of the lift.

Once at cloudbase there is a definite temptation to go speeding off and explore. At a good altitude your groundspeed seems negligible and many pilots compensate by speeding up. The golden rule with an aircraft as slow and inefficient as a paraglider is to never leave lift unless you can see another source within gliding range that will give some advantage.

To fly cross-country in any but no-wind conditions or in certain timed competitions, the trick is to stay off the ground for as long as possible. Allow the drift of the wind to provide your distance for you. Another reason never to leave lift is that it is very often surrounded by sinking air, and you could lose altitude faster than you have gained it.

After circling for a few miles your cloud finally ceases to lift. Look around for an active cloud to fly towards. With luck, the sink will only be gentle at this stage and your glide performance will take you to the next thermal where you can climb again. If no clouds are obviously waiting for you, study the ground. Is there an area that has been in sunshine for a while? Is there a likely thermal trigger point (a quarry or small town or perhaps a windward ridge)?

Always try to be aware of the position of the sun – the sheltered lee side of a hill that is angled into the sun, for instance,

The view from (just above) cloudbase.

is a better bet than an area where the suns rays are striking at a shallow angle. Needless to say, if you see a real giveaway – such as circling birds or other gliders – that is where to go. It is worth mentioning at this point that on your first XC flights it is far easier if you do not go alone; another paraglider, hang-glider or even a sailplane will give a wealth of information about the whereabouts of lifting or sinking air. If you should elect to go crosswind to a thermal or likely spot, your ground speed will naturally drop. However, it does not make any difference to your performance through the air. It is air distance that is important. If there

are no clues as to where to go next, then fly straight down wind. In this way your chances are as good as in any other direction and you will be covering ground at a better pace.

If the lift is strong, look up. If the cloud is large and solid looking, or if those around you have a good vertical development, it is always worth flying in a straight line for a while to determine the edge of the lift: you may wish to fly on the edge of the thermal so that you can "escape" if the lift becomes too severe. Do not allow yourself to be sucked into cloud. Apart from the possibility of turbulence in powerful clouds, they are also very wet, which will not do your canopy's performance any good. You will become disorientated in a matter of seconds and the chances of a mid-air collision increase dramatically. If you are very lucky you may find one of those clouds where it is possible to circle up the side without going right into it. Climbing above cloud on a paraglider is a rare and amazing experience. Do not forget that you are in uncontrolled airspace – or you certainly should be – and there may well be other traffic around. The visual flight rules are see and avoid. Do not let your eyes become glued to the variometer.

Flying with others

You already know about circling in the same direction as other pilots in a thermal. It is equally important to give those below you plenty of room as they cannot see you very well. If you wish to take any action, such as flying away from the thermal core and coming back, make sure you do it in such a way that the others can see you and do not have to disrupt their patterns. Never tuck in di-

Looking down from the top of the stack. (Photo: UK Airsports)

rectly behind another pilot: he cannot see you very well and you will be flying in his vortices, which will reduce your control. Always try to remain on the opposite side of the thermal from someone at the same altitude. If you have a good pattern established you may get the illusion that you are remaining stationary while he whizzes around you in huge circles – don't worry, it looks just the same to him.

Landing

Never, ever, fly cross-country over terrain where you are not always within range of a suitable landing field. You may get away with it once or even twice, but you can bet that eventually you will end up in a tree/water/gorge, etc. A height of 3,000ft will give you a search radius of about two miles for a suitable field. This area will be displaced downwind, of course. You require a large, flat field if possible, with no stock or crops and without any power lines – these are difficult to see from the air, so check for poles or pylons. Check the wind direction – there may be smoke or similar indicators but it can be surprisingly difficult to judge. The best way is to get a rough idea by watching your drift, or the drift of cloud shadows, and fine-tuning as you make your approach. After landing, try to make a point of thanking the farmer and you may even be offered a cup of tea and the use of a phone. If it is a sparsely populated area, try to land near a road.

If landing near a village and/or small settlement, do a quick aerial survey as you lose height to ensure you can give your retrieve driver accurate directions. Now all you have to do is get home.

Out and return flights

In the sailplane world, defined XC flights have been the norm for several years. They generally take the form of an out-and-return or triangle flight. The benefits of a long flight where you end up back at launch are obvious, and as distances steadily increase, hang-gliders too are using this option in more and more instances. As yet, paragliders are unable to make any significant progress into wind and so defined XC flights are confined to flights across wind and return, often along a mountain range, or those undertaken in nil-wind conditions (usually from winch or Alpine launch). Turn points are generally recorded with a photograph. The progress of our sport has always mirrored that of hang-gliding, and defined XC is sure to become one of the major areas of progress in the future. If you are entering flights of this type in a league you need to carry a camera to obtain photographic evidence of your turn points. More information on turn points and camera sectors is given in the section on competition flying.

Navigation

When flying cross-country it is vital to know where you are. Flying with a map is a necessity and on long flights to a specific goal, or in unfamiliar terrain, you may need to navigate using compass bearings. Navigation falls into two categories: planning and map reading.

Planning is done before take-off and will consist of drawing your intended track on a map, ensuring you have marked and planned for any hazards, and worked out any compass bearings you may require. A very useful exercise is to mark a point perhaps twenty percent of the distance to your goal, or 10km from the start, and time yourself to this point. In this way, you can easily calculate your ground speed and, therefore, your remaining time or your likely distance in a certain time.

Compass bearings are complicated by the fact that the compass will point to magnetic north whereas the grid squares on your map will refer to true north. The difference is known as VARIATION. If you look at the map key it will tell you the amount of variation when that particular map was printed (Yes, it does change with time!)

Map reading in the air is vital to paraglider pilots. Unlike a powered aircraft, we cannot simply stick to our intended track; we tend to go where the lift takes us. If you have done the ground speed

This 'photo of a superb XC sky was taken by a pilot in the Autralian outback shortly after landing. He was still walking and trying to tell his retrieve driver where he was several hours after dark! (Photo: Neil Cruickshank)

exercise, then one hour into your flight you should know how far you are from launch and, together with your compass reading and ground features, should be able to plot your position. These functions can all be performed for you by a Global positioning system (GPS) and more details of these can be found in the section on instruments.

Needless to say, if you are flying over desert or mountains then your compass bearings need to be accurate and up-to-date. Some years ago a well-known American hang glider pilot scored a zero flying in an Alpine competition for landing in the wrong country!

Measuring and recording your flight

After you get home you may wish to log your flight and distance. Some flight instruments offer the facility to upload the data to your PC and allow you to print out a trace. These are interesting to refer back to for yourself (but are just a squiggly line to anyone else).

A GPS can also give you a recording of the flight time, maximum height gain and actual distance flown (as opposed to straight line distance).

Many pilots still rely on the old (2,500yrs old) technology for calculating their exact flight distance.

Pythagoras, the ancient Greek philosopher and mathematician, hit on the theorem that can give us an accurate straight line distance between any two points on a map.

(Note: virtually all European maps use kilometre measurements.)

1. Log your 6 figure take-off map reference. (Say 123 456)

2. Log your 6 figure landing point reference (Say 133 499)

3. Subtract the first three digits of these references from each other.

   i.e. 133minus 123 =10

4. Subtract the last three figure of the references in the same way.

   i.e. 499minus 456 = 43.

5. Square each calculated figure (multiply it by itself).

   i.e. 10 x 10 = 100   43 x 43 = 1849

6. Add these two results together.

   1949 in our example

7. The distance travelled is the square root of this number: <u>44.147km</u>

NB. You may need to make an adjustment if your take-off and landing fall in different 100km OS grid squares.

What you are doing is making a right-angled triangle with the flight distance as the hypotenuse (longest side) – then using the grid references to plot the length of the other two sides. Pythagoras's theorem *(The square of the hypotenuse equals the sum of the squares of the other two sides)* then allows us to calculate the distance of the third side.

Thus proving that maths classes at school do come in handy in everyday life after all. (Along with pocket calculators).

Alternatively in the UK you can log onto the National XC league web site (see reference setion) and enter your co-ordinates. A simple bit of software will calculate your distance for you.

The Polar Curve

When we talk of the performance of a paraglider, it is sometimes difficult to visualise how to obtain the best from it in various situations. It is possible to gather various bits of information from tests that confirm that this model sinks at a rate of 1.4 metres per second at 17 mph and so on. When we have sufficient data we can plot them on a graph and the result is a performance "map" of the craft. This graph is known as a polar diagram (*Fig 27.1*).

The polar curve of a craft is time-consuming and painstaking to produce, but once drawn, it allows us to predict the glider's performance and so helps both designers and pilots.

If we wish to know our sink rate at 20kph we can simply read off the figure where the sink rate axis corresponds to 20kph. Our best (*i.e* lowest) sink rate is at the highest point on the graph, and our best glide ratio in nil wind is at the point where a straight line drawn from 0mph on the axis just intersects the curve (*Fig 27.1*).

We can also discover the performance in different situations. For example, if the canopy sinks at 1.2m/sec at 19kph, but we have a headwind of 13kph, how fast should we fly to achieve our best gliding (ie distance over the ground) performance? We can plot this by drawing another straight line that just touches the

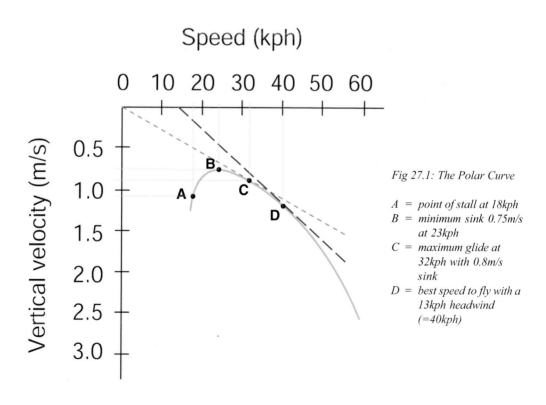

Fig 27.1: The Polar Curve

A = *point of stall at 18kph*
B = *minimum sink 0.75m/s at 23kph*
C = *maximum glide at 32kph with 0.8m/s sink*
D = *best speed to fly with a 13kph headwind (=40kph)*

curve but is drawn from the 13kph point on the horizontal speed axis (*Fig 27.1*). You can now apply the same technique to assess the performance of the craft in any combination of lifting or sinking air, headwind or tailwind. The fact is that the useful speed range on a paraglider is very small and a slight variation in your airspeed is not very significant compared to the options available to a hang-glider or a sailplane, for example.

However, scrutinising a typical paraglider polar diagram, it soon becomes apparent that in sinking air or a headwind, adding speed is a good idea if you wish to make progress over the ground, but in lifting air or a tailwind it is usually better to fly at trim speed or minimum sink.

In practical terms, the polar tells us that, in sinking air (of say 300ft/min), you should be using your speed bar for best results.

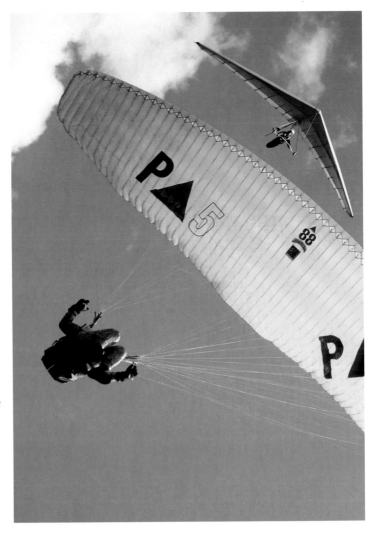

The minimum sink rate performance of hang-gliders and paragliders is very similar. However, a paraglider benefits from a lower minimum airspeed whereas a hang-glider has much better high speed performance.
(Photo: DW Photography)

Instability & Recovery

A canopy is virtually unique among aircraft in that it relies upon the weight of the pilot to maintain its shape and, therefore, the structural integrity of the wing. If the weight is reduced, removed or disturbed wrongly, the wing may collapse. In addition, the aerofoil shape is maintained by internal air pressure. If this pressure is reduced or lost, the wing is once again prone to distortion and collapse. This is in addition to the usual unstable behaviour of any aerofoil when stalled. It is therefore vital that the pilot understands his craft's behaviour and is able to help prevent, or anticipate, any problems. The pilot must also be capable of recovering promptly should he find himself in an unstable situation.

Dealing with turbulence

Prevention is better than cure. Before discussing how to recover from unstable situations, it is worth trying to understand how they can occur and how to prevent them. Gusts, thermals and turbulent air are invisible: the only way you have of detecting them (apart from basic site and weather assessment, of course) is by feel. Flying in rough air is all about feeling the canopy and reacting very quickly to the feedback it is giving you. The first rule is to maintain some pressure on the controls all the time in rough air. This gives you the option to speed up or slow down and also seems to pressurise the canopy to some extent, helping to minimise wing tip tucks, etc.

The second rule is to try to keep the canopy directly above your head! This requires active input from you and is known as active flying.

The most common situation is that the wing suddenly surges forward over your head. The reason could be a gust from behind or a lull in the air in front of you, but your reaction must be to apply instantly the correct amount of brake to arrest the surge. A head-on gust or thermal will try to push the canopy back.

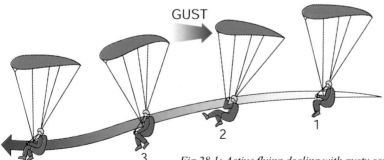

GUST

Fig 28.1: Active flying dealing with gusty conditions:
1. *Flying around mid-brake position.*
2. *Encounters gust – canopy pitches back – brakes high to provide speed.*
3. *Flying into lull behind gust – canopy pitches forward – brakes applied to slow canopy down.*
4. *Return to normal level flight.*

React to this by adding speed, but be careful – where there is a gust there is usually a lull behind it and you do not want to hit that at full speed just as gravity is swinging you back under the canopy. So be ready to brake again the moment the canopy starts coming back.

Thirdly, maintain your course. Do not allow turbulence (or a tuck) to turn you without countering it with the opposite brake. It is not always easy to identify what is causing you to turn. However, apart from the change in direction, you may find that you lose pressure on just one control if a thermal or gust has begun to deflate one side of your canopy

If is has collapsed, then use the opposite control to hold course, depress the brake deeply and smoothly on the collapsed side until you feel contact with the wing again and then let it back up again.

It may take more than one of these "pumps" to clear the tuck.

If you begin to lose pressure on both controls when braking deeply, let up smoothly as you may be approaching the stall.

If the canopy surges upwards and for-

Large assymetric collapse during glider testing. (Photo: Swing Gliders)

wards then you have encountered a thermal. If it surges upwards and backwards it is probably a gust. If you do not feel in control of the situation do not hesitate to land and fly again another day – don't forget you are doing this for fun!

> **CAUTION – WHILE IT IS DESIRABLE TO BE PRACTICED AND COMPETENT AT RECOVERY FROM STALLS, SPINS AND TUCKS, IT IS RECOMMENDED THAT BEFORE UNDERTAKING ANY OF THESE MANOEUVRES YOU RECEIVE ON-SITE BRIEFING FROM AN EXPERIENCED PILOT OR INSTRUCTOR. PRACTICE THEM OVER WATER, CARRY A RESERVE PARACHUTE SYSTEM AND ALLOW A ONE HUNDRED PER CENT MARGIN FOR ERROR WHEN ESTIMATING THE HEIGHT AND SPACE REQUIRED FOR RECOVERY.**

Asymmetric tuck

This is perhaps the most common situation. One end of the canopy collapses while the other side is still flying.

Recovery

If the canopy is turning towards the collapsed side and there is a danger of collision with the hill or with another pilot, carefully apply some opposite control to arrest or slow the turn. Give a long, firm pull on the control on the collapsed side and it will re-inflate. This forces air forwards and opens the cell entries to the airflow. If the collapsed area is 70 per cent or more of the wing, treat as a font tuck (pump both sides). In this case, the controls on the collapsed side may have little air to move and the pumping action

forces air through the internal vents.

Full front tuck

This occurs when the load on the front lines is substantially reduced – when the canopy overflies the pilot, for example, or in turbulence. The front "rolls" underneath.

Recovery

Give a firm pull on the controls; the canopy will re-inflate almost instantly. This forces air in the canopy forwards and unrolls it.

Full (dynamic) stall

This occurs when the canopy loses virtually all forward airspeed and, consequently, internal pressure. It can only be induced by "flaring", that is by applying full brake on both sides, or by extreme turbulence. The canopy produces no lift but a large amount of drag and it falls behind the pilot, usually in a "horseshoe" shape.

Recovery

Firstly wait – you are much heavier than the canopy and you will swing back to a relatively normal position below it. If you have induced the stall, keep the controls depressed. If you let up too soon, the sudden reduction of drag just as the canopy is swinging forwards anyway may cause he canopy to dive down in front of you and tuck. Once stabilised smoothly, let up the controls to about 25 per cent. Be prepared to brake a little more if the canopy tries to overfly you. Do not let up suddenly or all the way.

A dynamic, full-stall. (Photo: Swing Gliders)

Caution: Some canopies "dislike" being in the horseshoe mode and thrash about above you, so care must be taken as they may recover unevenly and enter a spin.

Deep (parachutal) stall

A small number of canopies can be stabilised in a deep stall. This is the state in which the canopy has little forward motion and the airflow over it is predominantly turbulent, creating no lift. However, the wing retains its shape and does not collapse. Its sink rate is very fast and normal control inputs are ineffective as there is little airflow over the controls. Some canopies can be deep stalled through gradually increasing braking. Others can only reach this state through the rear risers or poor recovery from B lining or big ears.

If you experience a deep stall, it is worth having your glider checked for line shrinkage or porosity.

Recovery

Some models can be recovered by vigorously depressing one brake. The canopy enters a turn, gains airspeed and resumes normal flight. The other recovery technique is to brake with both controls and cause the glider to rock back, then release, allowing the glider to surge forward into normal flight.

Spins

A spin is an unstable state where half the wing is stalled and half is flying. This causes the canopy to rotate violently, often on its own axis. There is a risk of the canopy collapsing (half of it may be flying backwards) and it is possible for the lines to become twisted between the canopy and the pilot. A spin is induced when the paraglider is flown at a high angle of attack (ie with deep brake) and then the controls are simultaneously raised on one side and depressed on the other.

Recovery: Let up both controls to gain speed. As the wing regains flying speed, steer out of the turn.

Caution: It is possible to gain considerable airspeed in a spin and on recovery you must be prepared to damp out any tendency for the canopy to surge forwards as this can result in a tuck.

In a severe spin, or one with a tuck, your lines may become twisted. While this may be recoverable given time and altitude, the best course of action is to deploy your reserve.

Other manoeuvres

360° turns

This is simply flying around in a circle. 360's are worth noting because they involve flying on a downwind leg (if there is any wind). Therefore, some planning is required – how far downwind will the

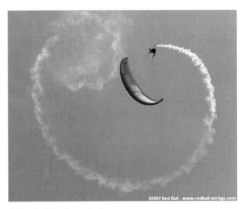

Spiral dive from below.

drift be, etc. A 360 is particularly useful for approaching some landing areas, and for thermalling, where you can drift at the same speed as the thermal and so stay with it as it moves.

Spiral dives

A spiral dive is simply a series of tight 360° turns. It is very inefficient and so the canopy can lose height very rapidly – very useful for getting down quickly or combatting strong lift. A spiral dive is induced by strongly depressing one control and raising the other, gradually steepening the turn until the pilot is swung out from the canopy which can eventually be at almost 90° to the ground.

Caution: when recovering from a spiral dive you may have excessive airspeed. A canopy that may have a top speed of say 45kph without accelerator in normal flight may reach 65kph-plus in a 2g spiral) The canopy must be " damped" if it converts this energy into a climb, or you may either stall at the top of the climb-out or the canopy may tuck as the load on the front risers is momentarily reduced. The safest way to do this is to gradually back off the spiral into a more gentle turn before levelling up. For these reasons a spiral dive should always be aborted with plenty of altitude remaining.

"Big ears"

This is the common name given to the practice of deliberately collapsing the calls at the tips. This has the effect of reducing the flying surface and so increasing the sink rate. It can be very useful indeed for combating strong lift (unlike a spiral dive it can be done at lower altitudes and without involving drifting downwind). Modern canopies are "big eared" by grasping the outermost one or two A lines on each side and pulling them out and down to induce the outermost cells to tuck.

Many modern designs feature a separate "mini" riser or split A risers that give a convenient handhold for performing big ears.

Big Ears

Be particularly careful if you have short arms– it is easy to pull the whole thing when trying to affect just a couple of lines and thereby inducing a front tuck.

Always pull slowly and smoothly and, always close one side at a time. To re-

inflate the tip cells simply release the risers or lines. If the ears do not clear themselves, pump the controls as you would for a minor tuck. Again it is wise to do this on one side at a time.

Note : When in "big ears" mode the wing loading of the canopy is increased and therefore the stalling angle is lower. To add additional drag by pumping the controls in this situation can quickly induce a stall. For this reason it is recommended that ears are not cleared by pumping the controls, or, if this is unavoidable, you should clear one side at a time and in a gentle way.

For the same reason, do not use big ears when flying though turbulence or wind shears or in close proximity to the ground.

"B" line stall

Some canopies can also be made to sink very quickly in a stable state by pulling down the centre (B) risers and "breaking the back" of the canopy. This disrupts the airflow and destroys the aerofoil

"B" lining is a useful manoeuvre to lose height quickly. However, there are some potential problems. Some canopies will remain deep stalled, particularly if the pilot lets up very slowly. During a B line stall, all the weight is through as little as six lines: that can put terrific strain on the lines and the attachment points. Know your canopy: always release smoothly but quickly and in the case of being stuck in a deep stall use a dab of deep brake and then let up to allow the wing to surge forward. This will re-establish a correct airflow and the canopy will recover. If you pull very hard on the B lines the tips may come forward, forming a horseshoe shape, and descent will be very rapid. Before attempting this, check the canopy's suitability with your instructor, dealer or manufacturer. If the canopy starts to turn during this manoeuvre the pilot may be tempted to try and turn by letting up one riser more than the other. Do not do it. The canopy may enter a spin in this way. If the wing is turning you, you must recover to normal flight before attempting to steer.

Front centre line stall

Like the B line stall, this breaks the back of the canopy, but fore and aft rather than across the span. This places a great strain on the centre lines. This manoeuvre is rarely performed, as it has no useful purpose. The same provisos apply as for B lining.

Wing-overs

By reversing the controls and using radical weight shift a paraglider can be speeded up to the point where there is sufficient energy to make a past vertical turn (ie with more than 90 degrees of bank) and still remain fully inflated and flying normally. This is a wing-over.

Pilots who are skilled at performing wing-overs can achieve angles of bank of 130 degrees or more

It can be very dangerous to combine manoeuvres - spirals with ears in, for example. The exception is combining big-ears with speed system, which is an effective way to deal with a strong wind on a ridge. NB: You must always apply ears, then speed - not the other way round.

Wing-over

Emergency Procedures

These fall into two distinct categories – equipment failure and "sticky situations". Both can almost invariably be prevented by pre-flight checks and good flight planning. The piece of equipment most likely to let a pilot down is between his ears!

Equipment failure

Broken or lost control line

A limited form of steering is available by adding pressure to the rear riser. All canopies can be well controlled by weight shift. As it is difficult to flare with the rear risers alone you should be prepared for a fast landing which may mean running or a PLF.

Other damaged lines

Generally, a paraglider will fly quite well with only a couple of lines missing (though it may have a tendency to turn). Land as soon as possible and have them replaced. If a lot are broken, after a mid air collision, for example, throw your reserve.

Major damage to the canopy, harness or connections

If you have any control, it is best to fly down as best you can. The only other option is to throw your reserve, which, of course, can neither be steered nor flared.

Canopy inextricably twisted or tangled due to spin, severe turbulence or mid air collision

Deploy your reserve, subject to the provisos above.

Deploying a reserve

Once you have decided you are in trouble do not hesitate. Grab your reserve handle and pull hard; the reserve in its deployment bag should be hanging from the strap in your hand. Fling it away from your body; this will certainly be a weak throw as your body swings away in reaction, so the reserve will drop away until the lines reach full stretch and the deployment bag opens. If it does not open for some reason grab the bridle and tug it hard, this should shake the bag off the canopy itself. As the air channel fills the reserve will snap open with tremendous force and you will feel yourself pulled hard by the shoulders. The main canopy will tend to dive forward and may well go

Reserve deployment. (Photo: Sup'Air)

below you. If you can grab a bit of leading edge or trailing edge, do so, as it will minimise the paraglider re-inflating or thrashing around.

If you do have to deploy the reserve during a spin, always try to throw it in the direction of the spin, as it is less likely to get twisted up. Avoid throwing it between your legs. If you have time, you may be able to collapse the main canopy even if you missed the fabric, by pulling in the lines until the canopy itself can be grabbed. When approaching the ground, assume the position for a PLF.

Sticky situations

Being blown back over a hill

First check that any trim devices are fully off and that the controls are at maximum speed (against the keepers). Apply your speed-bar. If your speed-bar does not provide sufficient penetration alone, let it off, apply your ears, then apply the speed-bar again, with your ears in. Your forward speed will increase slightly and your descent rate markedly. If these ploys do not work, you are committed to top land.

Look back over your shoulder. Can you land safely in the area where you will end up? If so, wait until the touch-down and the turn and run after the canopy, collapsing it as you go. If the area looks unsuitable, try to track to the most suitable spot within range.

Flying right off the end of a ridge might be an option. If the area behind you is really diabolical, such as a cliff top or a spine backed ridge, and you have any significant height, continue to soar the ridge at minimum sink speed, trying to

gain as much height as possible. You may find that the lift extends to way behind the crest. When you are as high and as far back as possible, turn downwind and make a run for it, retaining a little brake and being prepared for turbulence as you fly through any rotor.

Note: if you have any control as you approach the ground, try to establish the wind direction. If you are in rotor, it may be from any direction. Be prepared to PLF.

Remember that the above situation need never occur if you assess conditions properly, treat ridges with poor top landings with respect and leave a greater margin for error. Be aware of changing weather. If penetration does seem to be reducing, land quickly or at least track to one end of the ridge where flying out of the lift is possible if required.

Water landings

Once again, the emphasis here is on prevention through good flight planning, rather than cure. However, if you should find yourself in a situation where a water landing is inevitable, try to prepare before you touch down

1. Take off your gloves if you are wearing them.

2. Undo your chest strap(s) – the harness will feel strange as the risers are now further apart but you will not fall out unless you lean right forwards.

3. If you have time you can also slacken or undo your leg straps.

4. Land as normal, but ensure that the canopy does not end up on top of you. This is best achieved in light winds by flaring very little. If there is a good

breeze, land cross or downwind and allow the canopy to fall in front of you. It will then stay full of air.

5. Wriggle out of, or unbuckle the leg straps. Try to avoid the lines.

6. If you are well away from land, you can use the canopy as a float by trapping air in the cells. It also acts as an efficient marker for any rescue attempt.

If you habitually fly near water, carry a hook knife. These can slice through your lines or risers in seconds and free you if necessary. Avoid surf; it is probably better to land hard and PLF downwind on a

Water landing.

beach than get caught in moderate surf as you could be tangled up and pulled around quite easily.

Tree landings

If you hit a tree, hit it hard and hang on. The main danger is falling out of it or getting pulled out of it by a gust of wind. Keep your legs together. Try to protect your eyes; turn your head or use one forearm. Gather in the canopy quickly if you are able to, or release yourself from it.

Nesting season comes early at the Dune de Pyla, France!

Power lines

Do not hit power lines. It is worth taking virtually any avoiding action including stalling at low level or crashing downwind to ensure that you do not contact power lines. Two broken legs are preferable to 40% burns or death, both of which have been the results of pilots tangling with power lines in recent years. If "hung-up" or assisting another pilot, it is essential to wait for the power to be properly cut off by the authorities before attempting to get down or start helping. Many power lines have an automated system that switches the power back on to attempt to "blow" branches off the lines. Even a broken cable on the ground

Power lines can KILL

can kill you if you approach too closely by transmitting the voltage through the earth.

Even Low Tension power lines (the type mounted on poles rather than pylons) carry a current sufficient to kill you 100 time over.

Snow and heavy rain

Should it begin to snow or rain heavily while you are flying, lose height and land as quickly as possible. A weight of snow or water building up inside the trailing edge of the canopy can affect its flying characteristics and possibly cause an unrecoverable stall.

Flying in cloud

If you should find that a powerful cloud is sucking you upwards, the preferred method of losing height is a B line stall or a spiral dive. If these are ineffective, the cloud must be a cu-nimb or strong wave. The up-currents and turbulence within clouds of this type can be severe. Induce a full stall and hold it until you have lost sufficient altitude.

Accidents

The best thing to do about accidents is avoid them! Most accidents are recorded and the statistics are published. Here is a summary of how to hugely reduce the chances of having an accident.

● Do not fly in strong or rough conditions.

● Get proper instruction.

● Buy equipment the right size and skill level for you.

● Only buy equipment with a Certificate of Airworthiness.

Clouds such as this giant Cumulonimbus are capable of sucking a paraglider pilot to unsurvivable altitudes. (Photo: f8 Photography)

- Don't show off "hot dogging" near others on the ground.
- Wear decent boots and a helmet (a back protector is also recommended).
- Do not attempt instability manoeuvres over land.
- Do not take delivery of your new wing just before a trip to a new area or a competition. Get used to it on familiar territory.
- Never take off from lower down on a hill because it is too strong on top.
- Be very cautious of flying slowly close to a hill when the wind is "off".
- Take local advice.
- Never fly to impress others (or yourself).
- Always pre-flight check and take good care of your equipment.

Accidents do sometimes occur (often for one of the reasons above). If you suffer, or witness an accident (or an "incident"), it is essential that you report it. The reasons are self evident: if the national safety committee discovers that a large number of a certain type of canopy are involved in similar accidents or close shaves, then it can take some action to prevent a repetition. If each incident is considered unimportant and ignored, then obviously the problem will persist for much longer before coming to light.

The same applies to tightening up some aspect of training, etc. An accident that is not reported promptly may also jeopardise any subsequent insurance claim. Your club safety officer or instructor will have report forms for this purpose.

Incidents that should be reported

- Those involving any injury, either to pilot or third party.
- Those involving any damage.
- Those in which an insurance or legal claim may arise.
- Those in which any equipment failed to function.
- Those involving use of non standard procedures or training.
- Anything that may highlight safety points or was unusual.

Actions after an injury or fatality

- Administer first aid.
- Call an ambulance / rescue services (mountain rescue can be reached through the usual emergency services number).
- Call police (essential if fatal).
- Do not disturb equipment.
- Photograph any equipment in the area.
- Take names and addresses of witnesses or bystanders. Inform the next of kin, or (in the case of fatalities) ensure that the police do so
- Inform the national association without delay

The numbers of the BHPA Safety and Development Officer and the Chairman of the Safety and Training Committee are published in the monthly magazine, Skywings, or your instructor or club committee will have them.

Administering first aid

It is beyond the scope of this manual to cover all but the most basic first aid, but there are some practical points that are worth noting. Injuries generally fall into three categories:

Slight injuries

That is to say that the injured person is not in any great danger. If there is any doubt at all, these people should still be referred to hospital. Very often, the shock of an injury and the wish to be OK makes the person belittle or not appreciate the damage. Many "sprained" ankles and "badly bruised" arms turn out to be fractured. Someone should always stay with the patient until they are passed into someone else's care.

Major injuries

Major fractures or a combination of injuries are dangerous, not only in themselves, but because shock can kill (particularly out on a cold hillside for long periods). Administer first aid as soon as possible. **DO NOT** attempt to move the patient and make sure that the emergency services are told about the location and injuries. If you need a helicopter, ask for one. Do not wait for the emergency services to arrive before informing them that you are up on a mountain miles from the road. If you are in a remote location, station people at the road/track junction to help direct the ambulance to you. A canopy offers insulation and excellent protection from the elements. If a helicopter is called for, make sure that the area is cleared of unpacked canopies etc. A canopy left out, well weighted down with stones is a useful marker.

Extremely serious/fatal injuries

In addition to the steps above, you must contact the police and BHPA straight away. Do try to take photos of the site and the equipment. Do not disturb any of the equipment if possible. The police will want to see it "in situ". Make sure that the names and addresses of witnesses are taken (this includes bystanders as well as other pilots).

Important basics

A.B.C. This stands for **A**irway, **B**reathing and **C**irculation which are your priorities.

A. Make sure an unconscious casualty's airway is clear (head back, neck extended and chin lifted), and obstructions – teeth etc – are removed

B. Check for breathing: if they are not, do it for them (mouth to mouth). Pinch the nose, seal the mouth with yours and blow smoothly; the chest should inflate. Wait for it to go down and repeat. Do it slowly. One inflation every four seconds is about right.

C. Check carefully for a pulse in the neck. If you cannot detect one, try to assist the heart with CPR. Place the heel if your hand about 2cm above the point the ribs join the breastbone and lean on the heart five times. Check again for a pulse. If you still cannot detect one, do two more inflations of the lungs (to get some oxygen in) then 15 more heart compressions (to pump it round to the brain). Compressions should be about 80 per minute.*

If a casualty is bleeding badly, then apply direct pressure by gripping the wound firmly. Elevate the wound as high above the heart as you can and get plenty of padding to try and stop the bleeding. Fluid loss is the prime cause of shock. If the casualty is lying on a hill or mountainside, or is obviously badly injured, do not attempt to move him unless it is necessary to keep him breathing, as he may have spinal injuries. Do not remove helmets (unless required to do mouth to mouth). If the casualty is breathing, but unconscious, and you do not suspect spinal injuries, place him in the recovery position.

Keep him warm and if he is conscious, try to keep him that way. Keep a note of his condition (level of consciousness, pulse etc) – it may help the medical services.

Many clubs run first aid courses. It is always useful to try and make an effort to attend one: there are few feelings worse than helplessness in a situation such as this.

Once a casualty's heart has stopped completely it cannot be re-started except by a defibrillator. Statistics complied by the paramedic services in Scotland show that CPR can move enough blood to keep the brain functioning longer than if CPR is not given, by several minutes.

However, without a defibrillation shock being applied within about 15 minutes of the heart stopping, the fatality rate is virtually 100%. (The rare exceptions are people who have been "frozen" by drowning in freezing water.)

This means that if a casualty is (say) 20 minutes or more from a paramedic unit and their heart has stopped completely then there is little point in continuing CPR for prolonged periods.

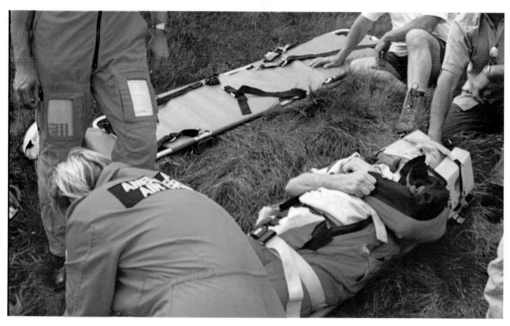

A pilot with a broken pelvis is prepared for airlift to hospital.

Photography

As the many pictures in this book illustrate, paragliding itself (unlike many of the pilots!) is very photogenic. Almost all pilots choose at some point in their flying careers to snap a few pictures with which to bore their family and friends.

Whilst it is presumptuous to advise those who are already competent photographers, there are a few helpful guidelines that may be helpful to the new "paraphotographer".

Firstly and most importantly, safety is paramount. There are numerous incidents of cameramen and women being trampled over during a launch. One tourist from Germany, videotaping a hang-glider launch in Yorkshire a few years ago, suddenly stood up as the glider came

Photoshop magic! (Photo: John Brettoner)

down the slope towards him, and was caught across the stomach by a wing wire (presumably invisible in his viewfinder). He found himself airborne over a 200ft hillside (briefly!) with the pilot, before completing a near perfect 360degree turn and arriving back at his start point. Sadly we never got to see the tape (which I keep expecting to turn up on TV.)

The moral is pretty clear - getting the shot comes second to getting out of the way. On cliff or ramp-type launches there is a very serious risk to the photographer, either of being struck or of simply walking backwards over the edge.

When training, cameras are also implicated in a number of situations where concentration is lost when the photographer shouts "look at me" at the pilot, usually just whilst the instructor is saying "look where you are going". Pilots are just as guilty as photographers of initiating this divided attention situation. It is better to have pic-

ture of yourself in profile looking grim and determined, than a grin and a wave with the next shot being of you getting some first aid!

For "training course" snaps the best re-

Photo: FreeX.

sults are always of the pilots preparing and launching in a full frame: a paraglider from behind and moving away quickly is usually a poor subject.

Shooting upwards into the sky is a problem for many autofocus and autoexposure cameras. Very many flying pictures and videos feature a distant and rather dark and underexposed wing as the camera compensates for a bright sky. The best option when shooting upward is (if your camera has the facility) to use manual exposure and focus settings.

Many digital video cameras boast a huge digital zoom facility. This is basically useless; only the optical zoom gives watchable results. For this reason some videos that may appear to have a smaller range in fact have a bigger useable range in practice. For any serious telephoto work you will need a tripod.

If shooting paragliding from the ground you really require a reasonable telephoto to get a well composed shot (except of take offs and landings, of course).

If you are shooting from the air, you do not want a heavy or expensive camera with you, but to take "self-portrait" type shots from arm's length you do need a fairly wide angle lens (of 22mm or less if possible). See picture on previous page.

Several of the pictures in this book are shot from a point a metre or two away from the pilot. This takes some preparation, and you will need a device such as a pole to mount your camera on. An effective and easy-to-use tool for this is a modern adjustable crutch, which is perfectly designed to give you a secure point of contact at elbow level and a good grip. Some pilots who regularly take in-flight shots have even wired up a shutter re-

lease that can be operated by your thumb. At the business end of any extension you need an adjustable camera mount, which is available at most photography stores. Whenever you carry a camera or any other item of equipment with you, always ensure a safety line attaches it. This is not only to save you from losing it, but also to protect others if you should drop it. Needless to say this takes a good launch technique to keep out of the way while you take off.

The low-resolution picture below is an image "grabbed" from a video of the author soaring a row of hotels in Israel. The distortion of the fish-eye lens is very clear and you can just see the pole that is fixed to the harness seat.

It is also possible to mount a camera or video on your helmet to give "point of view" pictures. This is difficult to do securely without drilling a hole in the helmet, which of course compromises the integrity of the shell. If mounting a camera this way always use a "spare" helmet and do not use it at any other time. It is very interesting to watch video shot this way as it is immediately noticeable that experienced pilots "scan" the sky all the time as they fly. Of course this is a good thing normally, but you need to learn to keep your head motions smooth and slow if you do not want the resulting tape to make your viewers feel sick.

Never fly with your eyes locked onto a viewfinder: your distance perception is distorted and it can cause potential conflict with other pilots. Most modern digital video cameras have a rotatable or even a detachable screen and this is a huge advantage - you can even monitor the screen as the camera is shooting backwards at someone flying behind you, which can make for some great footage.

If you do carry a camera, ensure it has

fresh batteries, has film in it, is accessible in flight, and stays with you all the time. Otherwise that classic day when you reach 8,000ft in wave and can clearly see both the east and west coast of England, or when you and your mate climb up the side of a cumulus cloud will remain unrecorded!

One final tip: make sure your camera gear is well insured. And when they ask you what happened to it confine your explanation to " I was just sitting down when I dropped it and it just broke"

A pilot's-eye view of the Alps.
(Photo: Sup'Air)

Tow Launching & Skis

Tow launching

Tow launching is generally done using a boat, vehicle or winch to provide the motive power, and launches to over more than 1000ft are commonplace. In the UK, the tow-launching of both round and ram air canopies has been well established for several years, usually using a Land Rover or similar vehicle and a fixed line over land, or a boat with a fixed line over water.

With the advent of soaring flight and lighter, better performing and less forgiving canopies, procedures have been altered somewhat to reflect the changes. Weak links are now commonly used to prevent overstressing (125 kg is about correct for a tow pressure of around 100kg). Payout systems are often used to maximise height, and powered winches that work by exerting a constant pull towards them enabling the pilot to climb as they approach the winch. These latter can be easily used without the need for a long smooth runway.

By adding another element to the flying (in this case a pull of about one "g"), you do alter the dynamics and stresses on the wing. Towing places twice as much stress on the canopy and because there are more variables there are more things that can go wrong. For example, if the canopy drifts to one side, it could reach a situation where the towing force is actually pulling it sideways into the ground, rather like a kite that is poorly controlled. This is known as "lockout".

The consequences of a partial collapse or a stall while under tow may also be more serious than in free flight. Finally, there are also more people and more items of equipment that could malfunction. For all these reasons, tow launching must only take place with tested and approved equipment and, most of all, with an experienced and qualified instructor/operator.

There are a range of checks that must be learned, including the release mechanism, signals to the driver or operator and so on. Typically, there is a release mechanism at the pilot's end and an emergency release at the operator's end. The tension of the towline is kept constant, either through a tensiometer or by an automatic process like a clutch.

A typical tow launch in the UK usually follows a set pattern:

1. The canopy and the winch are pre-flight checked.

2. The line is attached to the pilots quick release.

3. The pilot tries a test release to check everything is OK.

4. Reattach.

5. The signaller tells the operator to "take up slack" (either by radio or by under-arm swings of a bat).

6. When the line is straight and some tension is established, the pilot launches the canopy. When inflated and checked the pilot gives the command to go (usually "all out" or "push"). This is passed on by the signaller (overhead swings of the bat). If the pilot (or anyone else) wishes to

abort the launch, he shouts "Stop" and the signal is a stationary vertical bat.

7 The tension comes on and after a couple of steps the pilot is lifted into the sky. When he is well clear of the ground, the operator may increase the power slightly to give a better climb rate.

8 During the climb, the pilot uses small control inputs to keep in line with the tow line. He can signal for more or less power to be released should he wish. At any point, the operator can cut the power and, when the line goes slack, the pilot releases and flies down (or up if he can find lift!).

9 As the line falls (supported by a small drogue 'chute), it is rewound by the operator ready to be laid out for the next launch.

People have, in the past, attempted to launch by tying a rope to a fixed object and allowing the wind to "kite" them up. This is unbelievably dangerous and is a banned practice. The last person who tried it was discovered by the BHPA when the safety officer was asked to attend the inquest.

If you are a foot launch pilot thinking of towing for the first time, there are a few points that are worth checking. Ensure the canopy is fully inflated and flying straight before requesting the tow to commence at normal power. Keep glancing up to check the canopy as you launch. Be very careful not to use lots of brake at launch as you could stall or deep stall the canopy as it takes off, which is a very difficult situation for both the pilot and winch operator to deal with. Remember that the control pressure will be increased while you are under tow. Do not forget to

A low performance paraglider descending after a tow launch and a payout winch (inset) fixed to the stern of a boat.
(Photos: DW Photography, Northern Paragliding)

check that the line has gone when you have operated the release.

Air law also extends to tow launching – it could be a disaster if pilots started towing up to a couple of thousand feet from their local fields all over the country. It would only be a matter of time before low-flying aircraft flew into invisible and unmarked lines. The Civil Aviation Authority has granted permission for towing activities at various locations throughout the UK (almost always airfields) to qualified groups. These groups or clubs may tow to the height stated on the permit, (usually a maximum of 2,000ft). Any towing from a site without CAA permission must still be by qualified personnel and is limited to 200ft AGL (60m). Towing activities are marked on air charts.

Because it is easy to gain substantial altitude while having no hill behind you, towing is an excellent way to practice instability exercises. Over water is recommended until you have established some expertise.

Launching from skis

Paragliding was really born in the Alpine ski resorts and, naturally, some of the first pilots were skiers. On snowy mountainsides with little wind, it is often not possible to run anyway, so skis allow a fast and effective way to become airborne. The technique is the same as for an Alpine launch, but great care must be taken not to ski over the lines. It is very easy to damage them with the edge of a ski, particularly if there are rocks beneath the snow or if it is icy. It is difficult to get any traction, so in order to pull the canopy up you require a reasonably steep slope – your body weight should then provide the forward force. A steep slope with snow and skis may make stopping difficult once you are committed, so be meticulous in laying out your canopy and in your checks. Be careful when moving the canopy about to keep the snow out as far as possible. If much snow gets inside, it can make the launch more difficult and, at worst, even affect the flying characteristics of the paraglider.

The landing area may well be without snow; think about it before you take off!

An early paraglider is ski-launched in the Alps.
(Photo: L. Moore)

Tandem Flying

Tandem flying is great fun and an excellent way to teach certain disciplines such as soaring and thermalling. For the experienced pilot it is a good way to share the sport and it really adds to your own enjoyment to share the air, especially on smooth "boring soaring" days. Many pilots and instructors who have seen tandem operating have shown great interest in doing it themselves. Most manufacturers have a tandem wing in their range, and canopies carrying two people are a routine sight.

How do you become a tandem pilot?

You must be a very experienced and careful pilot and you will need to pass a tandem assessment.

The assessment criteria include practical demonstration of skills discussed below, correct briefings and a good understanding of the ramifications (practical, legal and political!) of flying two people on one wing.

There are some preconditions to applying for a UK tandem assessment:

- You must be a full annual member of the BHPA.

- You must be a very experienced and capable pilot with a minimum 100 hours logged. (or 100 tows for tow pilots).

- You must hold the "pilot" rating.

- You must have flown a minimum of 12 tandem flights with an existing tandem rated pilot (or under the supervision of a tandem instructor). Two of these flights must be in the student position. *(The BHPA, or any centre offering a tandem course, can provide details of precisely what is required).* ·

Note 1: In the case of instructors, the exam shall include assessment of the candidate's understanding of the use of tandem as an instructional tool.

Note 2: The candidate is required to provide his own equipment for the examination.

Each candidate is assessed by a tandem instructor who will demand a very high degree of competence to award the rating.

This qualification is VITAL, otherwise your insurance (BHPA or otherwise) will not be valid, and if you have an accident flying tandem, consequences both for yourself and for the whole sport could be catastrophic.

The law in the UK states that there must be no commercial gain or payment of any kind unless the P2 (passenger) is on a proper course of instruction (i.e. on a course and flying with a qualified instructor).

The pilot in command is often referred to as the P1 and the passenger as P2.

The Equipment

To fly tandem you need specialised equipment.

- A purpose-made tandem wing. Only paragliders certified by SHV, Afnor/CEN or DHV for tandem operations may be used. They must be used with proper regard to the manufacturers stated weight range and other recommendations.

- Both P1 and P2 require a properly fitting harness and CEN certified helmet (see below).

- A spreader bar system that places the P2 slightly lower and in front of the pilot to prevent them being squashed together is recommended. (A good tandem canopy should come with these fitted.)

- A full-face helmet is highly recommended for the P1 – your chin will be perhaps 25cm above and behind the P2's helmet and even a good landing could easily result in contact. Passengers may look up sharply on take off and a crack on the chin is easy to come by.

- A tandem reserve sufficiently large to give a safe sink rate at the maximum payload is a mandatory requirement.

- A spine protector of some description is a good idea for the pilot, as even a gentle stumble backwards will mean the other person's weight can fall on you as well.

- A log book of tandem flights must be raised and maintained.

Points to consider before launch

Personnel

Obviously you must be a qualified tandem pilot (or be under training with a tandem instructor) to fly as the P1. But there are also some considerations when considering your passengers.

If you wish to fly children, make sure you are still within the canopy's specified weight range. Ensure that you also get written parental consent for under 18's, and exercise extreme caution.

If the flight is part of a course, the pilot must be an instructor and the P2 must be a member of the BHPA and enrolled on the rating system. *(This is the ONLY way a tandem flight can take place if any money or other "valuable con-sideration" is involved. Flying for hire or reward is not allowed in the UK).*

A word of caution

It is not unknown for people to claim to wish to fly with you when actually they are very nervous about the idea.(This includes your own wife/husband/girl-friend/children and mother!)

Before launching, do take a minute to look them in the eyes and ask them (alone) whether they are happy about it. This is especially true with groups, as peer pressure can be a hazard. If you have some doubts, make an excuse and don't do it. (It's no fun when the passen-ger stops dead when you get close to cliff edge, or is sick on you in flight!!)

Whilst you do not want to frighten your passenger, it is important that the brief-ing includes explaining the possible risks. Passengers should not be under the in-fluence of drugs, including alcohol.

It is vital for safe operation that another experienced pilot is present to act as an-chor-man, helper and to pre-flight check the P2's equipment. For both practical and insurance reasons, this should be a BHPA member.

P2's should usually be fit enough to be able to cope with flight themselves. If you wish to fly a disabled person, you should first contact the BHPA office for advice.

There are some technical considerations too. A very light P2 will tend to move up and may obscure the pilot's vision. This change in relative positions may also mean that you cannot reach the "ears " either. Very tall P2's may make launch-ing difficult: if in doubt, try a small hop first.

Because of the P2's lower position, a tan-dem wing set up for the P1 to fly will mean that the P2 (if a pupil under in-struction) must fly with the brakes up near their ears; a "normal" brake posi-tion may induce a stall. (This is particu-larly true when landing). If your tandem flying is usually as an instructor, it may be worth setting up the canopy for nor-mal brake position when flown by the P2 and using "wraps" when flying yourself and landing.

The site and conditions

Flying tandem does impose a few restric-tions on your choice of take-off and land-ing site. Co-ordinating 2 pairs of legs over flat or uphill ground makes it very diffi-cult to move forwards. A sharp edge in light winds is also a problem, as the P2's weight leaving the ground first will pull you and the wing forwards. If you haven't sufficient pressure in the wing at this stage the launch could be dangerous.

Ideally, you need a shallow slope falling away to a steeper one. This also helps with the actual inflation technique and if you are flying multiple P2's, helps to speed up your turnaround time.

The conditions you can fly tandem in are much the same as usual. With a good technique it is easy to launch and land in nil wind even with a 190kg payload. If you are top landing, you need to be cer-tain you are not drifting backwards at all, as with four legs to co-ordinate, a quick twist and run is not practical. Tur-bulence is, of course, worrying to a non-flying P2, but certainly with almost all tandem wings, the extra wing loading makes the wing feel more solid than a solo canopy.

Launch technique

The P2 must be properly briefed about what to expect. His equipment must be pre-flight checked by an experienced helper. He must know how long the flight is expected to last, where you are expecting to land and that he must not fully depress the brakes or make violent inputs if he has control.

Above all, he must know not to sit down or stop running during launch until he is told to do so by the pilot.

It is quite possible for the P2 to face forwards while the pilot does a cross-brake reverse launch. This is perhaps the most useful method in the UK, where you are likely to be launching in gentle soarable winds. But if the canopy does not come up straight, this can be problematic, as you cannot easily sidestep to make a correction. In stronger soarable winds, where you may come off the ground as you reverse launch, an assisted alpine launch can be used, but you do need a competent helper for this.

Tandem launch.
(Photo: f8
Photography)

The cross-brake reverse launch technique is identical to a solo launch except that, because of the position of the passenger, one riser is much further away from you than the other. You must compensate for this as you pull the wing up. It is easy to do provided you are already fluent with this launch technique solo. Takeoff and landing are the fun parts. In a breeze you may need an anchor-man to hold you or your passenger's waist strap while you get the canopy up.

Your cross-brake and Alpine launch techniques must be to a very high standard, as "blowing it" on a tandem may mean an ignominious tumble over your passenger.

In very light winds the Alpine is the preferred system, though if there is sufficient wind to support the wing a cross-brake reverse is appropriate. In a good wind the safest system is to revert back to high wind Alpine launches with a skilled helper. Zero-wind launches can be interesting. The preferred technique is to run side by side with your passenger using a flexible spreader system. If you are running behind them and they slow down or stop you are in trouble!

A very useful launch technique for tandem is to "de-power" the wing as it climbs. The easiest way to do this is to launch from well off-centre of the canopy and pull it up with the A riser from just one side, whilst controlling it with the brake from the same side. This avoids pulling the wing through the "power band" in the dead-downwind position.

Flying Technique

Flying tandem is pretty much like flying alone, with the pleasure of some company, but there are some differences. You may have to deal with a nervous or enthusiastic passenger and this can affect concentration. The actual canopy is larger and will be travelling slightly faster than a solo wing; this means you need more room for manoeuvres as the turn radius is bigger, and you may well be constantly catching up with solo pilots on a ridge.

The tandem wing, being more heavily laden, leaves a more powerful wake vortex as it travels, and this can disrupt other pilots who fly near you. It is the tandem pilot's responsibility therefore to avoid other traffic by a good margin. The controls are also heavier and it can be quite tiring on a long flight.

On the plus side you will have a good glide at speed and can cover a lot of sky, and the resistance to slightly turbulent air is slightly better than a solo wing.

During flight, all movements should be progressive, and the pilot should tell the P2 everything that he is doing and why. If all is well when they have plenty of room, an instructor may hand over control to the P2, keeping his own hands just above the risers so that he can guide or restrain any inputs if necessary. Within five minutes, most people can fly around with no trouble. (The term "instructor" is used here because to hand over control introduces an element of instruction). If the pilot is not an instructor, any incident or problem while the P2 has control would probably put them on very shaky legal ground.

If you are not an instructor, do not let a passenger take the controls.

Training Tandem

If training tandem it is useful to use the aviation terminology "I have control" or "You have control" to prevent any confusion. Do not let the pilot under instruction try spiral dives or any similar manoeuvre, and BE CAREFUL – because of the P2's lower position, a tandem set up for the pilot to fly will mean that the P2 may need to fly with the brakes near their ears. Talk with your P2 all the time. It is very reassuring and you can tell by

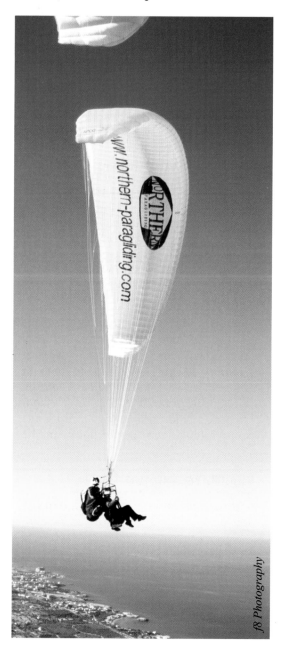

f8 Photography

the way that they talk back (or not) if they are happy or tense. Warn them in plenty of time of impending glider wash or any manoeuvre you are doing and always make sure they are sitting forwards in their seat in time for landing.

If you are top landing in a good breeze you must have your helper ready to grab you and help dump the canopy, as it is easier to fall over with, and much harder to stop a 40m+ canopy dragging you. When teaching, it is usually advisable to keep the flights to not more than 15 minutes.

If the site and conditions allow, it is helpful to aim to land on a slight slope so that you can launch again without moving. For best results with teaching, the brakes should be long enough for the student to use normally, which means you will often have to launch and fly with a wrap. You will find that the control pressures are greater than usual (particularly with flaring), so be prepared to take a couple of wraps to land and give yourself a rest every three flights or so.

A key skill when flying any passengers and making them comfortable is to keep talking to them.

This relaxes them and lets them know what is happening; to suddenly turn without warning is frightening, but to say "we will be turning in a moment at the end of this ridge" is helpful.

Landing is straightforward until you touch down. Once on the deck it requires good technique to dump the wing safely without falling over your passenger whose legs may well have "gone" after 15 minutes airborne!

If top landing in fresh winds you should be confident of landing right on your chosen spot so that you can hand-off your controls to your (qualified) helper, who can "shock stall" the wing for you by stepping sharply backwards with them.

Clearly all these techniques require practice and a good level of expertise to master, and it is no coincidence that most tandem pilots are professional instructors.

Renewing your rating

In the UK a CFI's support is required for both registration and annual renewal of a tandem rating. An annual fee is payable to maintain your rating and your insurance cover.

Tandem pilots and candidates are reminded that they must remain in current practice and on-going training is necessary should they fly in differing conditions, fly a different model of tandem wing, or use a different harness arrangement.

In the current litigious climate an accident involving a member of the public on a tandem wing is almost certain to result in a claim against the pilot. For this reason it is foolhardy to attempt to fly tandem without suitable qualifications or insurance. It is even more foolhardy to fly as a passenger with an unqualified pilot!

Mountain Flying & Flying Abroad

Before setting out to fly in completely unfamiliar territory, it is always worth-while seeking information from your fellow club members or from the local pilots when you arrive. The more you know about the site and the region, the safer and more enjoyable the flying will be.

Do not be in a hurry to be the first to launch – always wait and see what the local flyers are doing. Always ask before flying – they may be a local school, or the club may have specific rules about who can fly. A little courtesy costs nothing and could pay dividends in advice and help later on.

All these points apply equally to flying nearer home, of course. Before flying abroad, always take out medical and repatriation insurance – the cost of a helicopter rescue and treatment in many parts of the world are chargeable and expensive!

If you are going up in a cable-car or similar, always take your flying licence or membership card as some operators will not let you up the mountain without them. Do not take anything you cannot easily fly down with. A mountain is nothing but a large hill – some are ridge-soarable but others are simply used as launch points to contact thermals rising from the valley floor or sides. Because of

Terrain doesn't come more extreme than this! Eddi Colfox on Bubeli Peak in the Pakistan Karakorum. (Photo: John Silvester, www.flyskyhigh.net)

their scale, mountains create their own "micro-meteorology" – that is to say that the wind and thermal development may be influenced as much by the mountain itself as by the prevailing conditions.

An important example of this is the air-flow patterns throughout the day (*Fig 33.1*).

In the morning there may well be a gentle katabatic flow (downhill) as the cool air sinks from the mountain-top into the valley bottom. There is no point in rushing over to the other side of the mountain, as the flow will be the same there.

It is not unusual to find cloud in the valley bottoms in the morning. As the sun climbs and the valley sides warm up (rocky areas facing the sun first), the air will start to rise up the mountain-sides (anabatic flow) out of the valley and may become soarable *(see Fig 33.1)*. As the rocks and slopes warm up, the thermals grow more and more powerful and turbulent. In summer it is not advisable to fly at all in some regions when activity

is strongest. As the sun sinks, the convection gradually decreases and large weak thermals are found. This is a good time for the inexperienced pilot to get used to the site. As the day ends, the air becomes calm and the lift dies. This scenario is fairly typical of Alpine flying conditions.

Large mountains have several effects on the airflow and it is not unusual to find an apparent wind blowing up both sides of a large ridge. This can give a convergence effect that can be usefully employed to fly many kilometres along the ridge crest. The same effect means that mountains facing in different directions can often be soarable simultaneously.

Valley winds

If there is a wind blowing it may only be felt at the tops of the mountains as a light breeze.

In deep V-shaped valleys, the mountains can have the effect of compressing and

Dawn / Dusk

Noon

Fig 33.1 Shows the effect of daytime heating and night time cooling on airflow in valleys.

Be cautious of wind in the high mountains. In this shot, you can see spindrift blowing from the crest of the ridge behind the pilot.
(Photo: www.flyskyhigh.net)

accelerating the flow (the venturi effect), giving strong winds in the valley bottom – a kind of inverse wind gradient. This effect means that the valley bottom may well be the most turbulent area. Ask the local pilots, who will probably be going home. An approaching weather front will also tend to push up the valleys before it is noticeable at launch.

Foehn

Foehn is a term used to describe a wind condition that is found in the Alps. The Foehn is, typically, a wind blowing across, or out from, the mountain range. The airmass may lose moisture as cloud often forms on the upwind side of the peaks where the altitude causes the vapour to reach dew point and where it may sometimes fall as snow. This moving air-mass can cause rotor effects in the valleys and wave formations above the peaks. It is generally considered dangerous to fly in these conditions - something similar occurs in mountainous areas throughout the world. Telltale signs are dry wind blowing in the morning and poor visibility at low level.

Flight planning from mountains

If there is a large drop, there is a chance that the wind in the landing area will be different in speed and direction from that at launch. Always allow a large margin for error and approach your field with spare altitude. Approach by circling over the field to establish the strength and direction (by noting your drift). Air density reduces with height, so do not forget that your stall will occur at a higher speed and therefore launching in no wind at high altitude will require a faster run than normal.

Very high mountains where the air density is markedly lower means that you may need a fast or long run for launch, so a shallow slope or one covered in deep snow may not be practical. High altitude launches also mean that the dewpoint and therefore the cloudbase level may be below you. This can mean that you will have smooth air to launch, but as you lose height you may be faced with a developing cloud layer below you. This can have implications for visibility and for turbulent air.

If you are going for a long fly-down it may be wise to launch early to avoid the cloud cover closing before you get there.

Different conditions and different terrain can have other implications for the unwary pilot. Flying in hot regions even at

low level you may find that wind creates less lift than expected due to the low density of the warm airmass. Conversely in very cold conditions what might be an acceptable wind strength at home may cause you penetration problems.

Eu023opean pilots are used to generally friendly launching and landing areas. In many parts of the world the hazards posed by thorny trees and bushes and even by rocky terrain can be serious. If flying away from recognised landing fields always give yourself plenty of space to manoeuvre by setting up an approach with spare height.

If flying cross-country it is important that your communications and plan for a pick up are well organised. More than one pilot has found himself down in an unknown area with a phone that will not work and without speaking any of the local language.

Until you have plenty of experience it is well worth flying in a new environment with an experienced guide or on an organised tour. A good guide with local knowledge can make all the difference between an enjoyable trip and a disaster, not to mention the knowledge that if something does go wrong someone is there to help you.

View from high above the Kyreni Mountains, North Cyprus. (Photo: f8 Photography)

Competitions

Many pilots enjoy flying competitively and there is a range of events, from club level up to world championships, that are hotly contested.

A typical task might be to fly cross-country as far as possible or around a number of turn points and landing at a "goal".

Tasks like these test the pilots' skill and judgement in the most comprehensive way. Competition flying does carry a slightly increased risk, as the pilots often push themselves further than they might otherwise, and many pilots may be competing for a small area of lift.

Competitions may take the form of one versus all or, in large events, several groups. In the latter case there is a "cut" after the first few tasks so that only, say, 30 per cent of the pilots go through to the final contest. There may be tasks that are timed from take-off to landing, but these are hard to marshal, so the usual method is a launch "window". This means that any competitor is free to launch at any time during the preset time window and the fastest, or the furthest, wins.

Judging exactly when to launch becomes a major part of the competition. The technique for winning tasks where you are flying with a group is to select the thermal that has the biggest (or best) group of pilots and stick with it. All you have to do is fly better than anyone else in your "gaggle"

and you are assured of a reasonable placing. Of course, someone unexpected may score better than you but if you keep winning the "A" team gaggle, eventually you will come out on top or very near it.

Hints

Good equipment is vital, not only a canopy but a reliable camera (used to prove that you have reached the turn points), instruments and a reserve. Know the rules! Competitions have been won (and lost) because only a few pilots real-

Former world champion, John Pendry, in full competition garb. (Photo: DW Photography)

Launch can get very crowded! This is the scene before the window opened at the anual spring meet at Bassano in Italy. (Photo: Neil Cruickshank)

ised that the rules biased points in favour of speed over distance or a target landing over speed, etc. Do not rush – inexperienced competition pilots often fly too early. You must know the weather forecast to decide whether it will improve or not. You must also keep tabs on how you are doing in the competition – if you are not aware of everyone else's position as the competition progresses, you will not know who you should "target" in the tasks. Should you play safe? Or should

you go for it if you have nothing to lose?

But don't forget, you are doing it for fun!

Increasingly, competition tasks are judged on photo evidence of turn points rounded or by GPS flight logs. For photo evidence it is important that you understand the rules, particularly the FAI photo sector regulation (see *Fig 34.1*). For GPS logs only certain models are acceptable. Check with the organisers for details.

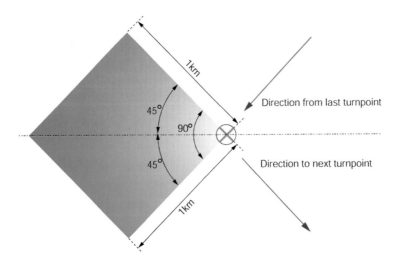

Fig 34.1: An FAI sector. To be judged to have passed the turnpoint correctly, the pilot must take a photo from any point position within the green area.

Another hotly contested area of competition is accuracy landing. This has grown from paracending and tow field operations and the skilled accuracy pilot can measure their deviation from the dead centre of the target in centimetres. The wings used for this type of competition are usually of lower performance and so have a steeper glide path than most free-flight wings but the skill involved is undeniable, and it is a great spectator event!

Many pilots do not enjoy fighting for thermals, but they do enjoy cross-country flying and measuring their acheivements against themselves and others. For this reason the BHPA have a Cross-country league, and pilots can log and enter their best flights, which are published on the web and in Skywings magazine.

When you look at the distances covered by pilots in a single good day in the UK, it is astounding how much skilled flying is being done.

XC flight is often done alone and so it is not quite competition in the true sense, but it is an excellent way to measure your skills, and the tables also allow club rivalry to be given an outlet and consistently high scoring pilots in the XC leagues (which are open to any qualified pilot) are invited to join the national competition circuit.

Like many countries the UK has a busy competiton calendar. This is a great benefit to the competing pilots in driving improvements in skills, and to other pilots in that the manufacturers can measure, compare and improve their products in this way.

The top few pilots in each country are

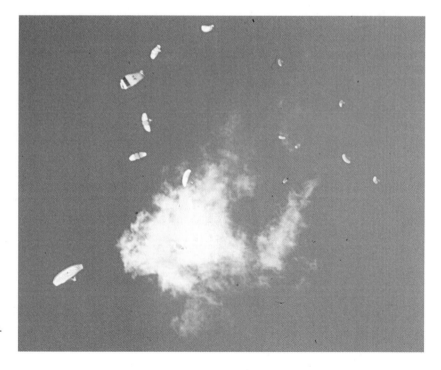

Spot the thermal!
Try to be at the top
of a gaggle like this.
(Photo: Sup'Air)

invited to join a national team for international meets; these are generally run on a team basis with an aggregate score for each country's team. With several teams in each major comp it can get a bit frenetic but the safety record is surprisingly good!

There are slightly differing competition circuits. As well as club and National level competitions, there is also a European championship.

There are of course other international competitions as well, from friendly "flyins" to Acro competitons.

Perhaps the best known is the PWC (Paragliding World Cup) which is a series of comps that is based on individual merit rather than national selection. These are held at venues thoughout the world.

Finally there is a world championship, which again is a national team event although as it is a totting up of individual scores there is of course a world champion at the end!

Everyone loves a winner! (Photo: Sup'Air)

Instructor Ratings

In Britain, most of the responsibility for selecting, training and using instructors lies with the Chief Flying Instructor (CFI) of a training centre. If you are interested in teaching you first need to approach a CFI and convince him that you have the right stuff to make an instructor. If he agrees you will be signed on as a Trainee Instructor (TI) and begin to help at the school. At this stage, you cannot take charge of students and must be under the supervision of a senior instructor, though after some time and if he thinks you are capable enough, he may decide to take a larger group than usual. At this point (usually after a week or two) it is usual for the school to pay a nominal rate.

Whilst doing your practical training you will also need to attend a trainee instructor course. These are intensive two-day courses and cover all aspects of administration and instructional theory. After a period of working in the school and gaining some experience, you will need to attend a further coaching course to polish your skills.

If your flying, instructing and first-aid qualifications are suitable, and you have successfully completed the BHPA courses, your CFI may put you forward for an examination. An exam takes all day and is conducted by an experienced instructor. You will be asked to do some hands on training, demonstrate your flying skills, pass a theory exam and have an interview. You will be informed as to whether you have passed or failed on the same day. If you have failed you and your CFI will be told why. You may be advised to reapply when any weak points are resolved..

When you have amassed considerable experience as an instructor, including

Sometimes being an instructor can be very nice indeed! Instructor Paul Farley hard at work.
(Photo: Pete Gallagher)

training new instructors, etc, you may apply for the senior instructor rating. You will need to attend and pass another two-day course, which sets a high standard not only in instructing skills but also in the administration of a training centre. After a further examination day you may achieve senior rating, which is a requirement for appointment as a CFI.

That is the bare bones of the BHPA system. However, the most important element is the on-the-job experience and practice. The courses and exams are really only a confirmation that you have learned the requisite skills at the school.

The standard required has increased a great deal in recent years and is particularly high for Senior level.

Making a living from paragliding is not easy. The work is seasonal in nature and involves a lot of weekends. The days themselves start early with obtaining forecasts, etc at 7.30am and often end with completing admin. records at 9pm!

However, there is tremendous satisfaction in seeing your pupils progress to a good standard, and plenty of opportunity for flying, travel and meeting new people.

Demonstration is one of the key tools at an instructor's disposal. (Photo: www.sunsoar-paragliding.com)

Paramotoring

In the 1980s as the sport progressed, a number of paraglider pilots who loved the freedom their sport gave them, but lived far from the hills or were often frustrated by the weather, sought the freedom to go where they wanted rather than where the wind dictated. Although paragliders were initially designed for un-powered soaring flight, it was inevitable that as hang gliding gave birth to microlighting, so paragliding would eventually lead to paramotoring.

The attraction of being able to fly from almost anywhere at any time is very appealing to many modern pilots.

There are two main paths that have been developed. Reinvention of the microlight trike configuration with a ram-air wing has been one method. Using specific wing configurations more akin to a parachute for easier ground control, they can often seat two people. This has some operating advantages, although their larger size and weight has generally meant that they demand considerable de-rigging or a trailer for transportation.

These machines are popular in the USA and some other countries, and had a big boost from their appearance in a James Bond movie a few years ago.

Unfortunately, they are not legal in the UK without expensive certification as a microlight wing which no-one (presently) is prepared to obtain.

The second is the backpack (paramotor),

Michel Carnet of Sky Systems flies hi Adventure paramotor in Indonesia. (Photo: Sky Systems)

which appeals very strongly to paraglider pilots because of its simplicity, small size and weight, and because it can often be used with their existing paraglider wing. As with a paraglider, a disadvantage is that you usually need to train solo, although much of the additional motor control can be demonstrated on the ground. The additional skills for ground handling and launching a PPG demand a reasonable degree of fitness and co-ordination.

For pilots who want to enjoy free flying, a paramotor provides a very flexible alternative to towing or long drives to the hill to get airborne. Paramotors can be used both for powered flight and free flight. Those with an air-start capability offer a distinct advantage to those pilots who may then choose to switch off and thermal in the usual way. These are the most popular variant and this section is principally concerned with this type.

An introduction to the equipment

The paramotor consists of a lightweight engine (usually a two stroke) driving a pusher propeller. This is mounted in a rigid frame of steel or aluminium. A fuel tank (up to a legal maximum of 10 litres) is also incorporated in the frame, while the propeller is shielded by a "cage" covered in a mesh . This allows a free flow of air whilst protecting dangling lines and flung back arms from the spinning propeller, rather like a giant household fan!

Some smaller units use direct drive but

Lightweight paramotor made by RAD Aviation.
(Photo: RAD Aviation)

most feature a reduction drive of some sort to efficiently match the rpm of the engine to the propeller. A long flexible throttle boom with a hand grip provides the pilot with engine controls. The pilot's side of the frame has connection points for attaching the harness so that the whole unit can be worn as a backpack. Typical weight is around 14–35kg, depending on type.

The engines are chosen for lightness, good fuel consumption, reliability and suitable power output. The result is that the same few models are incorporated into many different paramotors. Typically, they are from 80cc up to around 300cc. A usable power output for a pilot who wishes to be able to launch comfortably from flat ground is around 15bhp, although some smaller units designed principally for sustaining flight may generate as little as 7bhp.

More important than engine size is the thrust generated by a paramotor, and this is dependent on matching the correct propeller type to the power of the engine at the right rpm. The prop choice is one of the major design factors in manufacturing a paramotor.

Designers typically test many props before settling on a final design. But thrust is only one consideration. It may be easy to increase it with a larger propeller, but this also has implications for the torque effect applied to the pilot and the noise level generated. If the propeller tips become supersonic the resulting increase in noise levels can be significant.

Many paramotors use a wooden propeller with a diameter of between 90 and 130cm. Depending on the diameter, rpm, and tip speed, two, three or four blades may be used in the quest to reduce noise or increase thrust.

Blades are commonly made of wood, with a variety of replacements being readily available at relatively cheap prices. Against this, one must accept that a wooden blade is going to suffer more easily from stone chips and will, by the nature of wood, be harder to maintain and keep in balance. Also, to maintain their strength, they have a thicker profile than composite blades. This produces more drag when spun through the air and higher levels of torque effect. Increasingly more popular, composite blades are inherently stronger, and can be manufactured in thinner and more radical swept shapes beneficial to thrust and noise reduction. They will tolerate more abuse and can overcome many of the problems of wooden blades, BUT at a price. Most paramotor pilots will at some point be guilty of some propeller damage, so it's worth remembering that if replacement is necessary, a wooden prop is typically going to cost about half the price of a composite blade.

The frame and cage are frequently made from aluminum alloys, although stainless steel and steel alloys are just as suitable. Fibreglass or carbon fibre rod has also been used for the outer rim of the cage. The great advantage of being bendable is that it can be disassembled and packed into a small place. It may be less likely to sustain damage from being dropped than a metal rim, but being flexible the cage may not offer so much protection to a spinning propeller.

Most manufacturers offer a choice of size. The larger units with bigger engines and props give more thrust, but need a much larger and heavier cage. These may then have to be disassembled for transportation. The tiny ones may not be designed to get the heavier pilot off flat ground but are, of course, lighter and more compact.

Most paramotors are started with a recoil starter (pull handle), in the same way as a lawn mower or chainsaw. Because the compression is relatively high it is important that the engine has a decompressor fitted, otherwise restarting in the air can be very difficult, if not impossible. A very useful feature on any unit (particularly for the soaring or fuel conscious pilot) is an air restart system. This can be a hand or kick start with an automatic de-compressor to allow an easier pull, or an electric start of some type.

The throttle control is typically a "squeeze for power" hand unit. These are initially rather awkward whilst ground handling, as the same hand is simultaneously controlling a brake, but with good training and practice pilots soon master this technique. The throttle incorporates a kill switch so that the engine can be stopped at any time during the launch or flight if a problem occurs. A slip or stumble on landing can result in considerable damage if a rotating prop contacts the ground or the wing collapses onto the spinning prop. Landings are typically made "dead stick" with the engine off to avoid this risk.

At least one design features a centrifugal clutch, which means the engine is

Paramotor with J-Bar connection points.
(Photo: Northern Paragliding)

Paramotor with 'mid-point' connection points.
(Photo: Northern Paragliding)

disengaged from the propeller whilst the pilot is ground handling, landing, or even just putting the paramotor on his back. Once the wing is fully inflated and overhead, the throttle is applied, engaging the clutch and spinning the prop for launch.

Another important design factor is the connection of the harness to the risers of the wing. A well designed harness should allow the wing to relieve the pilot's shoulders of the additional weight.

There are three usual alternatives described here which all have their pros and cons.

The first method, using relatively high hang points at about head height, is the J bar. This is a curved metal extension of the paramotor frame which looks like an upside down letter "J". This extends up and over the pilot's shoulders. The risers are then physically attached to the

Paramotor with spreader bars to allow low hang-points. (Photo: PAP Paramotors)

top of J bar, while the harness is supported from the protruding ends. This type of set-up provides an excellent, if not almost remote, sense of stability. The inherent stability means the torque effect is less apparent but ability to steer by weight shift is significantly reduced. Another important consideration is that the controls will now be considerably higher up for the pilot to reach. In fact the operation of big ears may be impossible.

With higher than normal attachment points the pilot might not be able to reach the brakes at the keepers if they are released, hence lengthening of the brakes is sometimes necessary. This set-up is best suited to dedicated paramotoring use, particularly with powerful motors or larger propellers.

Another method uses 'mid' hang points incorporated in the harness webbing, to which the risers are attached directly. These are similar to a paraglider harness, but with the hang points typically about 20cm higher, closer to shoulder-chest height to achieve the correct centre of gravity. To ensure the pilot's comfort and to provide the correct angle of thrust, the position of the hang points is adjustable. This type of harness requires no additional frame work to attach it to the motor. This set-up is simple; however, it still requires some lengthening of the brake lines, and it can make getting comfortably into the harness after launch a bit of a struggle. It is not very suitable for use with heavy machines.

The third method uses a lower hang point at a similar height to a paraglider harness. Due to the extra weight of the motor trying to tip the pilot backwards, it is necessary to provide some additional method of moving the C of G backwards or forwards to provide the correct motor angle. To do this, one end of a pair of metal spreader bars is fixed to each side of the frame to support the motor's weight. The other end of the spreader bars protrudes forward below the pilot's arms to support the harness. The wing risers are then attached at an appropriate position along the spreader bar until the correct balance between motor and pilot is achieved. This solution has one particular advantage in that the position of the risers, brakes and big ears will be very similar to that of a paraglider harness. However, because there is less pendular stability than a high hang-point set up, the torque of the prop, especially at high revs, is much more noticeable.

The effects of torque are covered in more detail later in this section.

Aerodynamic considerations

Weight

A paramotor full of fuel can add anything between 20-45kg to the payload carried by the wing. This raises a common question asked by pilots venturing into PPG: what weight is acceptable on their wing or what size wing should they consider using?

To answer that question we need first to understand how the recommended PG loadings are arrived at originally. Most manufacturers agree that the wing loadings for free flight are chosen to offer a reasonable range of pilot weights, while still providing the best sink-rate performance possible without sacrificing stability and recovery characteristics.

If you intend to use your paramotor sim-

ply as a means to "get up there" to thermal and free fly, then clearly it is an advantage if you can keep the total payload within the optimum free flight range to get the 'best performance'.

If, however, the intention is principally as a powered platform for taking off and cruising around the sky, then sink-rate becomes less important and a smaller wing may be a better choice by offering enhanced handling, speed and stability. As a rough guideline, a pilot who is placed in the top 30% of a wings weight range for PG will find that the addition of a motor provides a total weight that is usually well suited to the aerodynamic requirements for PPG flight.

Unfortunately, particularly for heavier motors, this total weight may exceed the recommended PG weight range. While it is current opinion that flying at an increased wing loading on a wing for paramotoring is advantageous, it is clearly a reasonable argument that disregarding the certified maximum is unwise.

This leaves many pilots in an awkward position; fortunately the growing interest in powered flight means more and more wings are now being tested with a certified weight range for each discipline.

Most wings will accept power without too much problem, but there are a few models that have proven less suitable for this discipline. If you are considering powered flight, it is important that you seek expert, impartial advice from someone with broad experience. If you already own a free-flight wing and are considering adding a paramotor, it is well worth investigating whether the particular combination you are considering has already been tried (most have!).

Using the same wing for powered and un-powered flight requires some subtle variations in the application of brake input. Aside from the different safety considerations, you will often be launching and landing your PPG in a flat field with little or no wind. With the added weight and propeller effects to contend with, your techniques must be specifically tailored to the job in hand. Many "have a go" self taught pilots have tried and failed, resulting in broken props, damaged wings and a dented pride to boot. Powered paragliding requires additional skills, and to achieve these, dedicated instruction is vital.

Most of these techniques will be taught during your training or conversion, and in time you will develop skills that will suit your particular PPG setup.

Powered flight practicalities

The main effect of flying with power is, of course, the ability to climb when there is no lift; but it is also important to understand that thrust also alters the behaviour of the wing in certain circumstances.

To understand the effect of thrust on a paramotor it is first necessary to cover a few practicalities.

Power to weight ratios

Wing-loading is an important consideration; powered paragliders are very slow aircraft, and in an effort to maximize speed, many dedicated power pilots may choose a small fast wing. This has a number of effects; the most immediately apparent is that a long hard run may be required in calm conditions and the climb

rate may be relatively poor. Conversely, on landing the approach will be fast and require a good technique to land gently.

Some wings designed with powered use in mind, are fitted with trim devices that allow the wing to be flown at a range of angles of attack, (i.e trimmed back for T/O and landing and trimmed for speed for cruising).

Flying fast and with a higher wing-loading requires more thrust to maintain level flight.

This increases fuel consumption, and reduces flight duration.

A PPG pilot sitting upright with a big round cage on his back and with a significantly higher payload adds considerably more drag, reducing the glide and sink rate performance very noticeably. Quite a few paraglider pilots imagine that they can power up to altitude and then thermal as usual. This is certainly possible, but some are quite disappointed to find that the wing feels rather sluggish and unresponsive when the fan is switched off!

Your final choice of wing and motor size depends on the importance you give to speed, manoeuverability, response, and resistance to collapse from flying heavily loaded on a smaller wing, as opposed to a good power-off sink rate, easy launches and landings in light winds from flying on a more lightly loaded wing.

Understanding the aerodynamic effects of Thrust on PPG flight

The Paramotor throttle effectively governs both thrust and pitch (elevator) at the same time. This is because, unlike any other aircraft, the thrust line is far below the wing. The result is that, as thrust is applied, the pilot is "pushed" forward and the angle of attack increases, generating a climb. Due to the aerodynamic geometry of a PPG, this dual action is always present: you cannot add thrust without also producing the elevator force. (Although the addition of trimmers can slightly offset the effect).

The result: adding power increases the angle of attack and reduces airspeed.

The maximum speed of a powered paraglider is when the engine is switched off.

Typically, the increase in angle of attack experienced by a PPG in level flight is normally not enough to cause anything more dramatic than a small drop in airspeed . However, a very large amount of thrust from a powerful motor, or a sudden burst of power applied by the pilot can affect the aircraft's stability.

At any stage under power this increase in angle of attack must be taken into consideration when applying brake input. There will occasionally be circumstances where the amount of brake the pilot uses when gliding could be too much when under power. Brake input, when the wing is at a higher angle of attack than the PG pilot is used to, can cause instability, where parts of the wing may approach or experience a stall. This must be taken into consideration, particularly when making tight turns and adding power.

This is particularly important for the pilot who switches from powered to unpowered flight and back on the same wing to bear in mind.

With proper training and the correct

equipment these variations in flying techniques will be taught to you when learning from an experienced and qualified instructor.

Torque

Sir Isaac Newton was the first person we know to state the "equal and opposite reaction" law of motion. Unfortunately for him, he never had the opportunity to try it out on a paramotor. While the propeller spins one way, the rest of the aircraft will try and spin the other. Of course it cannot, because of the far greater mass of the pilot, but the effect is still felt as a tendency for the aircraft to turn in flight in the opposite direction to the propeller.

Large props, turning at high revs, can produce quite a noticeable effect. This problem can be reduced in a number of ways.

Wings that can utilize specially designed power risers with trimmers help enormously. These adjustable trimmers can be used to ensure dead straight flight or to adjust the wings rate of climb and speed at a particular throttle setting. If you do not have the luxury of the above, a simple alternative is to attach a diagonal torque strap across the front of your harness. This system is useful as it may allow you to alter the strap in flight. (A harness set for straight flight under power, will, of course, drift off track when the power is cut!) A little time spent adjusting your own setup on static hang points will often pay dividends in flight.

Piloting considerations

Backpack paramotors are great fun to use and are certainly the most compact and portable powered aircraft on earth.

However, like almost all designs, they are a compromise of many design criteria, and in addition to the complications of adding power to the aerodynamic equation we should also consider the effect on the piloting requirements.

Launch

A paramotor can be launched in the same two basic ways as an un-powered canopy - forward and reverse. It is generally done with the engine already warmed and running on tick-over.

If there is a little wind, then the reverse launch is a better bet, as the rotating prop and lines are kept away from each other until you are happy to turn round for take off. You also have a far better view and control of the canopy prior to commiting yourself to takeoff. With heavier motors, a snatched launch in too strong a breeze can result in the pilot falling backwards, resulting in the aptly named "turtle" position. An expensive and embarrassing situation to be avoided. When reversing, 'cross brake' technique should be used, so that your brakes remain firmly in each hand for the entire launch. The alternative method of letting go of a brake while turning runs the real risk of a brake line being sucked into the prop. Scrabbling overhead for handles while trying to run and control your throttle is a recipe for failure.

For nil wind conditions a forward (alpine) launch must be executed. Careful preparation of the wing in clean crescent, with all the lines untangled and free is critical. A poorly prepared launch, where the wing comes up asymmetrically, usually results in an aborted takeoff. This then requires the pilot to unclip, stop the motor, and often take it off in order to lay out the wing again. It will only take a few failed attempts like this to lead to exhaustion and frustration.

Take your time, do not let yourself be rushed. If necessary, stop for a few seconds and compose your self before continuing.

In a forward launch the arms must be held out at the 10 to 2 position to hold the lines clear of the propeller cage. On larger machines this can often require a concerted amount of arm work. If you are not used to launching on flat ground, be aware that a paraglider may need a more committed pull to get it all the way overhead, as the tendency to drop back if you let off the pressure can be more marked. If your wing has speed trimmers, always check that they are correctly set for takeoff. Once again your choice of wing is important here, as some wings are distinctly better at flat field launching than others. The higher the hang-points, the more effort is required to get the wing to rotate up.

Once the pilot is running forward and satisfied with the wing's overhead flying position, full power can be applied to commit to the takeoff. To avoid any sudden torque effects care must be taken not to "blip" the throttle; power must be introduced swiftly but smoothly. You must be able to run fast enough to keep the wing solidly inflated and in control until it is flying at its required takeoff speed. This part of the launch is the most energetic and the correct posture is important. The natural inclination is to lean forward, but if the position is too exaggerated the thrust will drive you down rather than along.

When you can feel the wing starting to provide lift, you must move to an upright running position with your shoulders back. This allows the propeller's thrust to take over and to push at the correct angle. In the next few paces the thrust should provide enough airspeed for the wing to lift you cleanly off the ground. On some wings a small dab of brakes at the critical moment of 'rotation' will help promote a swift departure from the ground. Use of techniques like these will depend on your wing and will be advised in your training. Do not retract your undercarriage until well clear of the ground. During the launch procedure the thumb should be poised over the kill switch to stop the prop spinning if anything goes wrong. Once fully airborne sit back into the harness and make a few post takeoff checks. Look and listen for anything that may indicate a problem.

For motors that produce torque steer, you may immediately feel the wing starting to fly slightly off the desired line. Whilst you can compensate to some degree with the brakes, it may not be possible to hold the wing perfectly straight. For this reason your launch "runway" should have adequate space to allow some deviation. Once you are happy that everything is as it should be, tuck in and make yourself comfortable for your flight.

In flight

Flying a paramotor is virtually the same as a canopy in free-flight, but with the distinct advantage that you will be able to explore your horizon in any direction almost immediately

With a paramotor, every flight can be a cross-country flight. (Photo: RAD Aviation)

New paramotor pilots may find they have a tendency to treat the motor as something that might pack up at any moment, which is perhaps not a bad thing. You may witness experienced pilots turning downwind at almost zero altitude and then climbing away. However, this is not advised; always climb to a safe altitude before turning dowwind, so that if you suffer an engine failure you have the option to turn into wind to land.

Flying under power does require a slightly different mindset, but the advantage of being able to fly more regularly in smaller windows of opportune weather makes using power to get up into the sky a very worthwhile skill to master.

Instability situations

A paramotor is really a light wind machine. Any paraglider is hard pressed to make much headway into wind, and a powered wing is no exception. For this reason they are not generally flown in strong wind conditions. However, it is perfectly possible to use the motor to put yourself above previously unreachable terrain: flying up a narrow valley, for example, or contacting high altitude wave, or viewing cloudbase from above! Of course turbulence may still be encountered and occasionally cause closures of the wing.

Because the motorised wing is likely to be more heavily loaded than in free flight it will retain a higher degree of stability. However, the additional weight, and the complication of thrust, may work against you in some situations, such as a spin. The best advice if conditions become rough is to escape the area as soon as possible, which may well mean a landing out. In the event of non-critical asym-

metric closures it is preferable to keep the power on whilst you clear the tuck if at all practical. In serious instability situations, however, it is better to cut the power. This is primarily to reduce the effects of thrust and torque. Tucks, etc should be dealt with in the same way as for free flight, by maintaining course and pumping out the collapse. But above all enjoy the flight and put faith in the mechanics on your back.

Allow it to take you places and experience views that very few people will have had the opportunity to experience.

Noise

Because the groundspeed of a canopy is so slow, the noise from the motor lingers for some time. Though not noisy by aircraft or even microlight standards, because of its slow speed, the paramotor does have a very large "acoustic footprint". At the time of writing the Ministry of Transport has yet to impose a maximum noise level on these machines, but it is likely, (as is already the case with microlight aircraft in the UK) that a level will eventually be set. To minimise the noise for residents of your launch area it is important to vary your flight patterns and to avoid high revs for long periods at low altitudes. Research has shown that people are more annoyed by noise if they can see the aircraft! The very portability of the machine should make using a selection of different launch sites feasible. Noise affects the pilots too. If a radio and headset is not used then ear defenders are certainly a good idea for prolonged flights. Maintaining altitude at minimum revs is the most comfortable way to fly!

Landings

As a general rule landings should be made "dead stick" – with the power off. As you land, the weight of the unit being transferred to your shoulders can make keeping your footing more difficult. In the event of a slip or stumble, a dead stick landing avoids the obvious hazard of a spinning propeller. Good landings are essential, so ensure your landing area is suitable and that your approach is accurate. There is no excuse for losing the wind direction with a paramotor as you have the facility to examine the area and fly a complete circuit to establish drift before entering your final leg.

Flying a heavily loaded wing requires a committed and well-timed flare. Unlike a paraglider it is not restricted to one approach for landing. So remember your final circuit checks, if you feel unsure, keep the power on and go around again. With practice you will be able to execute a perfect final approach with a paramotor into a flat field and achieve consistent landings.

Learning to fly a paramotor

What will a paramotoring training course consist of? The proposed syllabus below has been arrived at by the BHPA development and training panels, with some input from the British Micro-light Aircraft Association (BMAA).

Whist it is being continuously refined, it is very likely to reflect the content of UK training courses for those with some paragliding background. The ab-initio (complete beginner) student who wishes to learn paramotoring will at present need to undertake a short period of un-powered paragliding training and it is likely to remain the case.

If this is your situation, it is recommended that your paragliding tuition is tow (winch) based, as this is much more akin to the situations and effects that you will experience when you strap on a motor. Much hill flying is concerned with using lift and the peculiarities of flying in proximity to a slope; and useful skills like 360° turns and circuits are not a feature of early hill training, for example.

Theory

Show an appropriate understanding of the following topics;

1. The power unit

1.1.1. Configuration, including two stroke operation

1.1.2. Mixing fuel

1.1.3. Safety

1.1.4. Starting procedures

1.1.5. Power generated torque effects

1.1.6. Running in

1.1.7. Hang-points (effects of altering)

1.1.8. Weight checks

2. Power checks

1.2.1. Clearing the fuel supply of bubbles

1.2.2. Clear prop

1.2.3. Cut-off switch

1.2.4. Power on

3. Theory of flight

1.3.1. Thrust and drag

1.3.2. Forces in turns

1.3.3.   Climbing and diving turns

1.3.4.   Reduction drives

1.3.5.   Propellor theory

4.   Taking off

1.4.1.   Choice of safe field including climb out clearance, ground conditions and turbulence generators

1.4.2   Assessment of conditions

1.4.3.   Safe areas for onlookers

1.4.4   Noise nuisance

1.4.5   Torque effects

1.4.6   Methods of inflation

1.4.7.   The run. Use of brakes

1.4.8.   Emergency stopping (launch abort)

5.   Flight

1.5.1   Torque effects

1.5.2   The micrometeorology likely to be found in XC situations. Valley winds, rotors etc.

1.5.3   Speed systems. The effects on a powered paraglider. Power on and power off situations.

1.5.4   Techniques for avoiding and recovering from tucks, stalls and spins.

1.5.5   Navigation exercise. The student will plan a 30km (total) flight either as an out and return with a pre-declared turn-point or as a flight to a declared goal.

6.   Flying rules

1.6.1   Congested areas

1.6.2   Noise nuisance

1.6.3   Flying over water

7.   Air law

1.7.1   Aeronautical charts.

1.7.2   Restricted and prohibited airspace

1.7.3   Line features, quadrangle rule.

1.7.4   VMC minima

1.7.5   CANP system

1.7.6   Radio considerations

8.   Landing

1.8.1   Power on/off

1.8.2   Kill switch management

1.8.3   Light wind/high wind situations

1.8.4   Effects of weight on flying speed. Stall speed and flare.

Practical

Demonstrate the following in an effective/competent manner

1.   Pre-flight

2.1.1   Perform an effective PLF (not wearing a back-pack)

2.1.2   Canopy ground handling

2.1.3   Launch assisting

2.1.4   Pre take-off control of the paramotor

2.1.5   Post landing control of the paramotor

2.1.6   Parking the paramotor

2.   Flight

The student will perform the following tasks to the satisfaction of the instructor:

2.2.1 Three consecutive powered flights from a flat site with at least 100ft ground clearance with unassisted take off runs, smooth 90° turns to left and right and stand up landings.

2.2.2 Demonstrate a short field landing by landing within 40m of an imaginary 5m high construction.

2.2.3 Complete three landing within 10m of a defined spot in winds of less than 5mph.

2.2.4 Complete three landings within 10m of a defined spot in winds of more than 10mph.

2.2.5 Minimum of 10 paramotor flights logged including full deflation and inflation of wing between flights.

2.2.6 Demonstrate safe and effective use of rapid descent technique (not B riser stall)

2.2.7 Maintain directional control and show recovery from tucks of between 20 per cent and 30 per cent.

2.2.8 Carry out power-off landings to the satisfaction of the instructor from various heights some of which are over 500ft.

2.2.9 Show knowledge of forward and reverse launches and demonstrate them.

2.2.10 Complete a 30km (total) flight with a pre-declared goal.

Competence and experience

1. Competence

The student will demonstrate competence of the following topics to the satisfaction of the instructor:

3.1.1 Consistently demonstrate safe airspeed control

3.1.2 Safely demonstrate slow flight awareness and discuss symptoms and dangers (deliberate stalls must be avoided)

3.1.3 Demonstrate an ability to fly co-ordinated 3600 turns in both directions

3.1.4 Display the ability to fly safely with others maintaining a good look out complying with the Rules of the Air and exhibiting good airmanship. Demonstrate an ability to manoeuvre the paramotor safely, considerately and in accordance with air traffic rules.

2. Experience

Prior to being certified as a paramotor pilot and/or flying outside direct visual range of the training field other than to execute specific training tasks, the student must satisfy the instructor regarding the following and, where required, furnish the appropriate evidence.

3.2.1 Passed the BHPA PPG exam

3.2.2 Must have successfully flown paramotors or paragliders or hang gliders or micro-lights on at least eight separate days within the previous nine months

3.2.3 Must have a minimum of five hours logged airtime on paragliders, hang gliders or micro-lights of which at least three hours must be on paramotors.

3.2.4 Satisfy the instructor that the pilot has correct attitude to continue a flying career both safely and competently

Training course

An actual training course is likely to conform to the following basic pattern.

At ground school you will be introduced to the actual equipment and learn about safety checks and procedures and watch the instructor demonstrate what a paramotor is capable of. This will include

RAD Aviation

airfield discipline, the importance of correct clothing, (even simple things like long hair or a drawstring on a jacket can be drawn into a rotating prop), mechanical checks and dealing with spectators etc. If the school has a static simulator you may then have the opportunity to hang up in a paramotor and try it out, learning to respond to radio commands and just get the feel of the unit on your back. Launch is the critical phase of flying one of these machines and some time will be given over to practicing forward (alpine) launches. If the school is using a winch for pre-motorised flights you will then have an opportunity for low un-powered flights to get used to basic control of the wing, working up over a coupe of days to towing up to a reasonable height and flying a good circuit with a dummy motor on your back. This stage can be reached almost straight away if you have some free-flying experience.

Mixed in with these exercises will be a fair bit of theory, covering much of the same ground as a free flight club pilot course with additional sections on air law and, of course, the use of power.

Very soon it will be time for your first paramotor flights and you will soon be buzzing around the field practising coordinated turns, dead stick (power off) landings, maintaining level flight etc. you will also cove subjects such as reducing noise nuisance, rapid descents (big ears), dealing with small trucks, reverse launching and be able to demonstrate accurate landings. Once your instructor is satisfied that you have absorbed sufficient information and expertise, it is time for your 30km cross-country navigation exercise.

The "Navex" will mean you must decide

on the suitability of the weather, calculate your approximate ground speed and fuel consumption and be able to navigate either by compass bearing, ground features or even GPS to a prearranged goal. Very often this will mean flying an out and return pattern or perhaps a triangular course. It may mean avoiding airspace of some type. Your instructor may or may not follow you depending on his or her level of confidence!! If you can successfully manage this task and convince your instructor that you are suitably competent and have a good safe attitude, it remains only to pass the theory exam paper, for which you should now be well prepared.

A non-pilot will take around nine days to achieve this level. Beware of anyone who seems keen to sell you a paramotor and tells you that you can be trained in much less time!!

For a pilot with experience in a related discipline – especially paragliding, this time could be as little as two or three days.

Foot launched powered aircraft (FLPA) Code of Practice

Preamble

This code of practice was written in mid 1996 as FLPA were being de-regulated. There has been some justified concern by other flyers that the unrestrained use of FLPA may jeopardise other free flyers which is why this document was drafted.

Scope and authority

The Code of Practice is intended to give general guidance and unless stated its contents are not mandatory. However, it should be noted that where disputes arise which lead to legal action, non-compliance may be detrimental.

Mandatory requirement

All FLPA pilots should comply with the spirit and the letter of the General Exemption and all relevant Air Law.

Association requirements

In addition to mandatory requirements the BHPA and BMAA may introduce regulations from time to time. Pilots should maintain their membership of one of the Associations and keep up to date with existing and new regulations and guidance. If you are not a member of BMAA or BHPA you should join and obtain a pilot rating and acquire insurance. If you become involved in legal action in the future, proof of your skills, knowledge and pilot rating obtained via a recognised organisation will be an obvious advantage.

Taking off – general

Wherever possible FLPA should take off from a recognised and/or secure area. The ideal situation is an existing microlight airfield that has the appropriate Local Authority permissions.

When pilots take off from existing microlight areas they should familiarise themselves with and comply with local rules.

If the FLPA takes off from other areas, the following procedures should be taken

- The area should be secure from the possibility of animals and/or spectators being in an area of damage (note: a shattered propellor can scatter sharp shards of wood at high speed).
- Any spectators should be properly marshalled and any dogs should be firmly attached to a lead (they have been know to chase the FLPA when it starts to move).
- The take off are should be closely inspected for possible trips and holes.
- Proper permission should be obtained from the owner of the land.
- Any neighbours should be warned of your future activities.

Taking off – planning approval

Unless the land is in a special zone such as a conservation area you can usually fly from a temporary take-off area on 28 days in any 12 months. If you fly on more than 28 days without Planning Approval the owner of the land may be served with an enforcement by the local authority and could be subject to a fine. Local authorities will generally include all of the land in one ownership in an enforcement order so don't try to argue that you are taking off from different fields and they each have a 28 day dispensation. The local authority may also have local byelaws that should not be contravened.

Taking off – nuisance

Even if you comply with the planning regulations you may fall foul of the law of nuisance. For a prosecution to take place, there must be evidence that the nuisance has occurred on a regular basis. A video of you taking off ten days in succession at 6am very close to a house could result in a large fine and the confiscation of your aircraft.

Taking off – hang gliding and paragliding sites

Don't - unless you have permission from the club.

Flying – general

If you take off from one place, vary your flight path to avoid annoying the general public.

In particular, powered paragliders flying against the wind will remain in view for a long period of time. If they fly higher to make less noise they will fly slower due to the wind gradient. If you are not making much headway it may be safer to land and get a lift back to base.

It should be noted that German research has shown that an aircraft is a greater source of annoyance if it can be seen.

Flying – hang gliding and paragliding sites

It will be very tempting to buzz your mates who are grounded on a nil wind day. Don't.

A number of hang glider and paraglider clubs have introduced rules that generally exclude FLPA and in at least one case there is a self-declared exclusion zone round each site. FLPA pilots from BHPA and BMAA cannot be expected to be conversant with every rule introduced by clubs participating in other types of flying. However, where such a rule is known to exist it should be respected.

The general rule to be followed is "use your common sense and stay away".

Flying – livestock

Adherence to the General Exemption should mean that livestock is not disturbed. However, you should particularly avoid bird sanctuaries and riding stables. If you are taking off from a field you should check that there are no riders in the vicinity. If there are – wait.

Landing

For a variety of reasons you may decide to "land out". If you are landing on private land you should always find the landowner and tell him/her of your arrival. Courtesy takes five minutes of your time and invariably results in a pleasant experience. One pilot always carries a miniature bottle of scotch with him to offer to the landowner that is always accepted with amusement and gratitude (it's the thought that counts!).

It is worth noting that a forced landing due to exhausted fuel supplies is not generally accepted as a good reason to land where you like. In fact for aeroplanes it is considered a CAA offence.

Display flying

Display flying should be undertaken only after seeking and being granted permission by a Display Evaluator appointed by the CAA. BMAA or BHPA head office will be able to give you the names of Display Evaluators.

Conclusion

Any breach of common sense or good manners is a breach of this code of practice. Please remember that the General Exemption has been issued on a temporary basis.

Above all enjoy your sport, respect regulations, and maintain our freedom to fly.

Passing Your Exams

Most countries require their pilots to pass some form of written theory exam before qualifying as a pilot. There are several reasons for this – the most obvious to ensure that each pilot has sufficient knowledge to fly safely at the chosen level. Exams, when properly debriefed, also educate the pilot, allow the instructors to check their own thoroughness, strengths and weaknesses and, when collated by the national association, help pinpoint areas that require particular attention.

Preparation

It need not be a struggle to absorb the information that you need. Paragliding is something we do for fun and have an interest in and so the theoretical aspects can be related to real events or experiences. It may be hard to recall what cloud type occurs where, but recalling how the sky looked the day you first found yourself thousands of feet off the ground should not be too hard. Be aware of the level you are aiming at. It is not much use answering an advanced pilot question about the development of a thermal by saying "hot air rises". Equally, a student pilot level question about stability will not require a critique of design factors. Your instructor should brief you about what level to expect.

Taking the exam

- If you are not ready don't take it. Ask your instructor to ask a few similar questions first if you are not sure you are prepared. If it is a long exam, particularly for one of the higher levels, make sure that you are not tired, wet or hungry before you start. In other words, do not sit the exam straight after getting in from a day's flying.

- Make sure you have the correct equipment; some exams may require a calculator or a ruler.

- Read the instructions! In a multiple choice exam set recently the instructions clearly stated that one or more answers may be correct, but the majority of pilots still failed to tick more than one box, even though it transpired that they knew two options were right!

- Allow plenty of time. Make sure you have sufficient time to do the exam in the longest period allowed and some spare to go over it afterwards with your invigilator.

If the invigilator is a club volunteer or an instructor is staying on late to help you out, don't forget to buy them a beer!

In the UK the exams are set by the BHPA and are all multiple-choice papers. The topics you will need to know are:

Elementary Pilot (EP) level

- Rules of the air.
- CAA restrictions on when and where you can fly.
- How an aerofoil works.
- The stall.

● Airspeed groundspeed and windspeed.

● Identifying areas of lift and turbulence.

● Dealing with problems in flight.

● Basic weather and forecasts.

Sample questions for a student level exam:

1. A hang glider is circling in a thermal, you wish to use the same thermal. What rules apply?

   A. You must circle in the same direction as him?

   B. You have right of way as he is faster and more manoeuvrable than you?

   C. The lower pilot has the right of way?

   D. You must both circle to the left to reduce the risk of a collision?

2. You are flying downwind with an airspeed of 17mph, the wind is 18mph. What is your groundspeed?

   A. 35mph

   B. 1mph

   C. 18mph

   D. 17mph

Club Pilot (CP) level

All the topics for student pilot plus:

● Cloud types (including ground level).

● Basic air law.

● Principles of flight, lift/drag etc.

● Restrictions on other types of parag-

liding activity (eg power/towing/dual etc).

● Unstable situations, spins, stalls, tucks, etc.

Sample questions for a club pilot level exam

1. Define VMC when flying in Type G airspace at 5,000ft AMSL.

   A. 5 nautical miles visibility, 1000ft clear of cloud vertically and horizontally.

   B. Clear of cloud and in sight of the surface.

   C. 1,000ft clear of cloud vertically and 1,500m horizontally with visibility of at least 5km.

   D. Clear of cloud and in sight of the surface with visibility of at least 8km

2. A deep or parachutal stall can be caused:

   A. By braking too deeply

   B. When recovering from "B lining"

   C. By pulling on both rear risers

   D. By any of the above

Pilot (P) level

All the topics for club pilot plus:

● Reading an air chart (including abbreviations, symbols, scales, magnetic variations, etc).

● Temperature and pressure gradients and rates

● Aerodynamics and performance of a

paraglider

● Instruments

Sample questions for pilot level exam

1. What meteorological conditions could give rise to an inversion?

   A. A high pressure area with extensive cloud cover during the night to trap convective heat

   B. A prolonged period of high pressure when the air has become dirty with trapped dust and smoke particles

   C. Warm air at altitude being pushed over colder air at ground level by an occluded front

   D. An airmass being warmed as it is compressed by sinking in the centre of a high pressure area

2. The following symbol taken from an air chart shows:

   A. A disused airfield with gliding activity.

   B. A civil airfield with parachuting and winch cable activity

   C. A civil airfield with microlight and paragliding activity.

   D. A military airfield with winch cable and parachuting activity.

Advanced Pilot (AP) level

The topics for the advanced pilot paper are beyond the scope of this book, but it deals essentially with cross-country navigation skills.

How a Paraglider is Designed, Built & Tested

Manufacturers try to target the market with canopies they hope will sell a lot of units, and in order to do this they must first identify their customers. In Europe the instructors demand very forgiving DHV1 type wings for their students' first buy, especially when they will be coping with thermals early in their career. In the windier areas with smaller hills, like Britain, speed is important, and easy launching in windy conditions.

Some markets like Japan have been very performance driven; a long queue for a launch slot means you want to get the maximum out of every flight. The manufacturer will look at these requirements, see what his dealers have said (good and bad) about his last model and set to making improvements.

Most paragliders these days are evolved versions of earlier models. Only rarely does an innovation make a dramatic change.

All the major manufacturers now use CAD-CAM programmes to design and plot their fabric patterns and line lengths on a computer. It takes a matter of hours to plot, cut and sew together the first prototype.

After that the development is in the hands of the pilots. How does it handle? Is it likely to pass the certification at the right level? Will it go faster without becoming too prone to collapse? There are a hundred questions that must be asked and answered by the pilots and designers. By contrast this can be a very lengthy process.

This procedure must be repeated to some extent with each size in the range, and eventually, when the design team is satisfied, a few dealers may be allowed to try the wings to get some feedback from the market.

If all is well (and everyone likes the name and the colour scheme!) the wing is sent for testing and the production line is geared up to produce them.

After being laser plotted, templates of the individual panels cut from some inert material such as mylar. The line lengths are also transferred onto a marking jig of some type, the materials are sourced and the paraglider is ready to go into production.

Panels from as many as 40 gliders may be cut at once, and each piece must be accounted for and put in the right place for sewing together. Stitching a paraglider is a skilled job, demanding great accuracy; catching just one stitch of a rib onto a top surface can ruin a glider.

A laser plotter.

Once the envelope itself is assembled, complete with line hook-up points and reinforcement, the lines are attached, starting from the canopy and working down, until they are linked to the risers.

Some manufacturers simply pack the wings into the bag for the dealers to inspect; others inflate each wing individually; the majority check sample wings from each batch.

Quality control throughout the industry is very good as a rule, but it is worth noting that many gliders are built by sub-contract companies in the Far east, Eastern Europe or Sri-Lanka and the person sewing it is not known to the designers or dealers selling it. Mistakes can (and have) been made, and for this reason it is always advisable to inflate and check every new wing before taking to the air.

Before any reputable dealer will sell a new paraglider, it will have passed an independent airworthiness test. This test is designed to ensure that the wing has no hidden vices, will react correctly to proper control inputs and is sufficiently strong.

Buying any paraglider without certification is not only likely to invalidate any insurance cover you may hold (including BHPA 3rd party cover) but it will also be virtually impossible to resell and could be bad for your health.

There are two main bodies awarding airworthiness certificates. The German DHV (manufacturers association) which awards the Guteseigel standard, and the AFNOR/ SHV (French and Swiss) system that is recognised in the rest of Europe. Both standards are acceptable in the UK and worldwide.

CEN is the European standards institute, and it is expected that this body will almost certainly accept the latest proposed amalgamated tests as a Pan –European (and therefore effectively worldwide) standard, though agreement and acceptance of each others' systems by the two testing bodies has been very slow in coming.

Some older wings may still carry ACPUL certification placards. This was the original system that later evolved into the identical French AFNOR and Swiss SHV test criteria.

As the CEN standards are not yet completed, this section gives details of the current AFNOR / SHV test programme.

During the last few years, the AFNOR certification has been based upon a strength test and a number of flying tests. These flight tests are filmed and, depending on the behaviour of the wing, awarded a grade for each manoeuvre. Whilst the tests are far from perfect, as they only simulate what might happen to a wing in various attitudes, and cannot take account of turbulent air, for example, they do offer a reasonable guide to the relative stability of the canopy

Since October 1994, the tests are basically as outlined below. A manufacturer puts forward his product to be tested at one of the following levels: (The equivalent levels in the DHV system and the proposed CEN system are outlined in chapter 18).

Standard (STD):

Those that have a combination of handling and stability to make them suitable for use by student and recreational pilots.

Performance (PERF):

Those that have a combination of handling performance and stability intended to make them suitable for use by regular weekend/club competition level pilots. Such pilots can be expected to have some skill at avoiding and recovering from departures from normal flight.

Competition (COMP):

Those that have a combination of handling, performance and stability intended to make them suitable for experienced national competition level pilots. Such pilots can be expected to be highly skilled at avoiding and recovering from departures from normal flight.

Dual:

Suitable for tandem (2 person) flight.

Load test

The paraglider must successfully pass a load test with a payload equating to eight times the maximum placarded payload i.e. on a wing with a weight range of 80-100kg will need to withstand a load of 800kg without showing any structural damage. There is also a shock load test where the wing is suddenly loaded to 6G. This is done by "snatch" launching it with a tow line with a 6g weak link.

This is done by pulling the wing at speed,

Launching for a test flight, fully equipped with buoyancy aid, just in case! (Photo: Swing Gliders)

using a truck fitted with the appropriate load cells and monitoring equipment.

Flight tests

Note: "trimmers" are referred to in almost every test. These are devices that alter and fix the wing's angle of attack. They are not commonly found, except on wings being tested at the higher levels and tandems. If your wing has trimmers fitted you must be aware of their effect on the flying characteristics and how to use them.

1. Launch

5 launches to be made. 3 out of 5 to show no abnormal characteristics.

- STD – if trimmer fitted then 5 with slowest setting and 5 with fastest.

- PERF/COMP/DUAL – trimmers set as per users manual.

2. Landing

The pilot must be able to land on his feet without the use of extraordinary skill

- STD/DUAL – trimmers set to slowest and to fastest.

- PERF/COMP – trimmers as per manual.

3. Speed range

Slowest maintainable speed to highest maintainable speed.

- STD/PERF/COMP – range must be at least 10kph.

- DUAL – range must be at least 12kph.

4. Effects of trimmers and secondary speed controls (accelerators)

- STD/PERF/COMP/DUAL – 10 seconds at minimum settable speed with no adverse behaviour and 10 seconds at maximum speed (trimmers and accelerators at max) with no adverse behaviour.

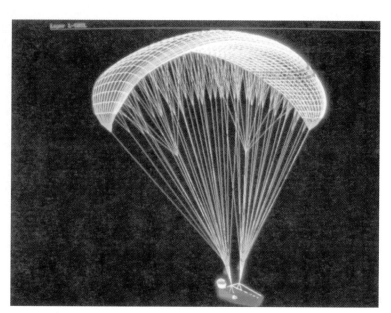

Computer programs are used to model gliders and the information from them generates each panel for manufacture.
(Nova gliders)

5. Pitch stability

Slowed to stall point and controls released.

● STD – trimmers full on and full off. The wing must not dive more than 45 degrees and if it tucks may not alter course and must recover spontaneously.

● PERF– trimmers full off. The leading edge shall not dive below 90 degrees; if it tucks it should not alter course by more than 90 degrees and spontaneously recover to normal flight.

● COMP/DUAL – not tested.

6. Recovery from deep stall

With trimmers set to slowest speed the wing is slowed to stall point, then the controls are slowly and smoothly released.

● STD – with no input the wing must recover to normal flight within 4 seconds and shall not dive to more than 45 degrees above the horizon. Must not alter course by more than 45 degrees.

● PERF – with no input the wing must recover normal flight within 4 seconds. The leading edge must not dive below the horizon.

● COMP - with no input the wing shall recover within 4 seconds or, if it remains in deep stall, the pilot shall use the procedure given in the manual. In this case the wing must recover within a further 4 seconds. In either case

the leading edge must not dive below the horizon. The wing may tuck, but shall not alter course by more than 90 degrees.

● DUAL – with trimmers on and off. The wing must recover within 4 seconds and must not dive below the horizon. The wing shall not alter course by more than 90 degrees.

7. Recovery from B line or similar deep stall (slow release)

Trimmers on, B lined until near vertical flight is achieved. Slow and smooth release.

● STD – (also done with trimmers off) – with no input the wing must resume normal flight within 4 seconds. The leading edge shall not dive to more than 45 degrees above the horizon. The wing shall not alter course by more than 90 degrees.

● PERF – with no input the wing must resume normal flight within 4 seconds. If the wing remains in deep stall the pilot shall use the procedure given in the manual to exit the stall. In the latter case the wing shall recover within a further 4 seconds with no tucks. In either case the leading edge shall not dive below the horizon.

● DUAL – as PERF but also tested with trimmers off.

● COMP – not tested.

8. Recovery from B line stall or similar (fast release)

Trimmers off. Fast smooth release.

- STD – (also with trimmers on) – with no pilot input the wing must recover normal flight within 4 seconds. The leading edge shall not dive more than 45 degrees above the horizon. The wing may tuck but may not alter course.

- PERF/COMP – with no input the wing must recover normal flight within 4 seconds and not dive below the horizon. If not recovered within 4 seconds the pilot must act in accordance with the manual and normal flight must be resumed within a further 4 seconds. The wing may tuck, but may not alter course by more than 90 degrees.

9. Turning ability

Trimmers set to slowest. 360 degree turns one way then reverse direction and 360 degrees the other way, in normal flight and with no spins.

- STD (also with trimmers off) – manoeuvre completed within 18 seconds.

- PERF – manoeuvre completed within 20 seconds.

- COMP – manoeuvre completed within 23 seconds.

- DUAL (also with trimmers off) manoeuvre completed within 23 seconds.

10. Spin tendency

Trimmers set to slowest. From no control instantly apply full control on one side (weight shift may also be used). When turned 90 degrees control is released. Tested on both the left and the right side.

- STD (also with trimmers off) – the wing must remain under full control throughout.

- PERF – the wing must remain under full control throughout.

- COMP – the wing must not depart from pilotable flight.

- DUAL (also with trimmers off) – the wing must not depart from pilotable flight.

11. Turn reversal

Trimmers at slowest and at fastest. Rhythmic turns to obtain at least 45 degrees of bank.

- STD/DUAL – no tucks shall occur.

- PERF – tucks may occur, but the wing shall spontaneously recover normal flight within 90 degrees.

- COMP – tucks may occur but the wing must spontaneously recover to pilotable flight within 90 degrees.

12. Asymmetric tuck recovery (immediate release)

Trimmers on fast. Quick 55 per cent tuck. Immediate release,

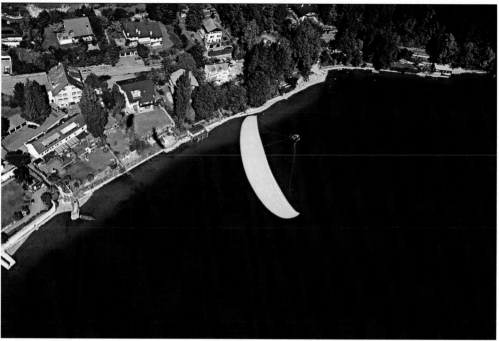

Glider testing is allways carried out over water with the correct safety equipment. (Photo: Swing gliders)

weight transfer to tucked side.

- STD (also with trimmers at slow) – the wing shall spontaneously recover to pilotable flight within 4 seconds and 180 degrees.

- PERF – the wing shall spontaneously recover to pilotable flight within 4 seconds and 360 degrees.

- COMP – if spontaneous recovery has not occurred within 4 seconds or 360 degrees (whichever is sooner), the pilot shall intervene as per the manual and the wing shall regain pilotable flight within 4 seconds or 90 degrees.

- DUAL – as COMP but also tested with trimmers at slow.

13. Recovery from maintained asymmetric tuck

Trimmer set at fastest. Tuck of 55 per cent of wing. Weight to tucked side. Held in for 720 degrees and then released.

- STD/DUAL (also with trimmers at slowest) – the wing shall spontaneously recover to pilotable flight within 360 degrees.

- PERF – if spontaneous recovery has not occurred within 360 degrees of 4 seconds, then it must be possible to regain pilotable flight using actions from the manual within a further 4 seconds or 90 degrees.

● COMP – if spontaneous recovery has not occurred within 4 seconds or 360 degrees then it must be possible to regain pilotable flight using recommended actions within a further 4 seconds or 360 degrees.

14. Spin recovery

Trimmers at fastest. From minimum speed, one control off and the other on far enough to induce a spin. Hold for 360 degrees and release quickly.

● STD (also with trimmers set at slowest) – the wing shall spontaneously return to normal flight, it may continue to turn in the direction of the spin for up to 360 degrees.

● PERF – the wing may continue to spin for a maximum of a further 360 degrees before spontaneous recovery to pilotable flight, which shall occur within a further 90 degrees.

● COMP – not tested.

● DUAL (also trimmers at slowest) – the wing shall return to

A tandem glider being put through its paces. (Photo: Neil Cruickshank)

pilotable flight in les than 720
degrees in the same direction.

15. Asymmetric stall recovery

Trimmers set at fastest. Slowed to
minimum speed. One control
depressed further to induce
asymmetric stall. Immediate
release of both controls.

- STD (also with trimmers on
  slowest) – the wing shall
  spontaneously recover normal
  flight without changing course
  more than 90 degrees.

- PERF – if spontaneous recovery
  has not occurred within 180
  degrees the pilot shall intervene
  as per the manual and the wing
  shall regain normal flight within
  a further 90 degrees.

- COMP – not tested.

- DUAL (also with trimmers on
  slowest) – as PERF

16. Symmetric tuck recovery

Trimmers set at fastest. A full front
tuck and immediate release.

- STD (also with trimmers on
  slowest) – with no input the
  wing shall recover pilotable
  flight within 4 seconds without
  changing course. The leading
  edge shall not dive more than 45
  degrees above the horizon.

- PERF – if spontaneous recovery
  ha not occurred within 4 seconds
  the pilot shall intervene as per
  the users manual. The wing
  shall regain pilotable flight

within a further 4 seconds and
without changing course by
more than 90 degrees. The
leading edge shall not dive below
the horizon.

- COMP/DUAL - not tested.

17. Spiral dive recovery

Trimmers at slowest. A tight spiral
is induced and held for 720 degrees,
the pilot slowly and smoothly allows
the controls to return to the
released position.

- STD – the wing shall
  spontaneously recover and shall
  remain in the turn for less than
  360 degrees.

- PERF – the wing shall return to
  pilotable flight and shall show no
  tendency to tighten the turn.

- COMP – if the wing has not
  recovered to pilotable flight
  within 360 degrees, the pilot
  may intervene as per the
  manual and the wing shall
  regain pilotable flight within 360
  degrees.

- DUAL – the wing shall
  spontaneously recover to normal
  flight within 720 degrees.

There is a terrific amount of information
available in these tests, but even knowing this is only part of the story. Some
wings, for example, have a tendency to
enter a spin more easily than others, and
this is not measured in the tests. Also,
the tests themselves, while thorough, are
conducted in smooth air by very experi-

enced pilots, and this is no guarantee that the wing will behave the same way in turbulence.

The DHV system comprises very similar manoeuvres, but the results are slightly more subjective in nature. If a DHV pilot evaluating a glider for, say, spin recovery feels that it is a bit unstable, he will explore this element further to see if the wing's behaviour is consistent. The pilot may add a note to the test report making further comments.

The test pilot gives each element a score ranging from 1 for very quick and easy self recovery up to 3 for needing decisive and expert pilot input to prevent deterioration.

Though initially just 3 levels existed, this was felt to leave too broad a range of possibilities in each category (a criticism still valid for the AFNOR system today) . Intermediate categories were introduced at 1 /2 and 2 /3 to give a total of 5 classes. The final grade of a glider refers to the worst score that it obtains. A wing with mostly "2" grades and just one 2/3 grade is categorised as a 2/3.

You can check the scores of your glider (or the glider you are thinking of buying) by logging on to the DHV website at http://www.dhv.de/english/testberichte/index.html

There is a tendency by some pilots (and glider sellers) to try and read between the lines and say things like "it would be DHV 1 without the accelerator". This means that the wing is actually a DHV 1/2, and should be judged on that grade given by the test pilot.

Occasionally the test bodies may appear to disagree. An AFNOR test may find a recovery within 4 seconds on a manoeuvre and award a Standard rating where the DHV pilot may think the same wing is a bit too easy to collapse, for example, and award a DHV 2...

There are, of course, pros and cons to the Objective versus Subjective methodology, and whilst most gliders score broadly similar grades, there have been STD rated wings that have scored a DHV 2 and DHV 1/ 2 wings that have scored a PERF rating. It is hoped that the Proposed CEN tests will take the best of both systems and will not take too long to come into operation. In the meantime, the best advice is to always treat the "worst" rating as the most accurate.

You may hear the term "Serial class" with reference to competitions. This is not a precisely defined term, but indicates a competition class that is only open to gliders that are rated no higher than DHV 2/3 or PERF level. This was introduced by some competition organisers to try and improve safety, and to give a more level playing field to "regular" pilots who did not want to have to buy out and out racing machines to be competitive.

Pushing the Limits

or ...

Licking the sticky bit of the flight envelope!

(Or other exciting things you can do with your paraglider).

SIV

Many pilots are, very wisely, a little concerned about how they will react if their canopy should suffer a major collapse, or if they should find themselves in a spin or deep stall situation. Undertaking more radical manoeuvres like spirals, B lines, or wingovers can also be quite a daunting prospect, but these are skills that may one day be required to get out of trouble.

Pilots may have read the test pilot's reports on their wings, but there is really no substitute for trying it yourself, to discover the true limits of your paraglider's flight envelope.

SIV (Simulation d'Incidents de Vol) courses have been designed to allow pilots to become better acquainted with these situations in a (relatively) controlled environment, and hopefully, in doing so, making them safer and more confident pilots.

Typically such courses are run by highly experienced instructors. They take place at venues where there is plenty of altitude to play with and where manoeuvres can be practised with radio communication over water with a rescue boat on hand.

Pilots are unlikely to benefit much from an SIV course until they have a pretty good level of familiarity with their equipment. For this reason it is not ideal to do a course like this if you have less than 10 hours or so airtime, or have just changed glider. Nervous pilots are unlikely to get the best out of this kind of course.

Photo: Neil Cruickshank

SIV courses offer an opportunity to explore the limits of your canopy in a safe environment. (Photo: Neil Cruickshank)

Synopsis of a typical SIV course

Initial briefing: This will cover the theory of the manoeuvres to be attempted and why they are important. *(If your instructor cannot give a convincing reason why you need to know something, then it probably is not worth doing- this applies to all courses).*

The briefing should also include a discussion of your own experience, why you wish to do this course and the option to quit the manoeuvre programme if you are uncomfortable.

Introduction to the equipment and procedures:

1   How to deal with water landings and getting into the boat.

2   The radio protocols that will be used, including commands, what to do if communication is lost and supplying waterproof containers for radios, etc.

3   Checking your reserve deployment system, and ensuring you know how and when to use it.

Flying

A good SIV course will start gently, and a briefing will precede each manoeuvre. A typical programme will include:

1   Asymmetric tucks of steadily increasing degrees of severity. Both sides should be collapsed and recovery technique.

2   As above, but with the speed system applied.

3   Exploring the glider's envelope. Turn reversal and gentle wingovers. Exploring the edge of the speed range. Recovery from incipient stall.

4   "Get down quick" manoeuvres like spirals and B lines, and appropriate recovery.

5   Searching for, identifying, and recovering from the onset of a spin. This is done by making steadily more radical turns from a steadily decreasing airspeed. It will also cover what to do next if it all goes horribly wrong... how to deal with a full spin, when to deploy a reserve, etc.

6   Other manoeuvres, such as symmetrical tucks and searching for deep stall with rear risers and recovery.

7   Reserve deployment (see below).

You should be cautioned against "cascading" manoeuvres into one another, as this can cause unexpected behaviour of the wing.

Each manoeuvre will be watched by the instructor, who will coach you on the radio and after completion you will receive a de-briefing on how it went, and points to help you next time.

In the past some pilots (and instructors) have amused themselves by advocating manoeuvres that have no real value other than looking radical, such as holding in spins or repeated dynamic full stalls. As these situations never happen in reality, their only use is in training for Acro display flying.

For most pilots the additional risks involved in attempting them are unnecessary and unwise. Even on an SIV course with a boat, etc, falling into your canopy and getting gift-wrapped is likely to seriously injure you.

One radical situation that some feel is useful, (and others an unnecessary risk) is a practice deployment of your reserve. You do not learn much except how it feels, but as many pilots are reluctant to chuck it out, even when things do look bad, on balance a practice deployment that teaches you to trust your system is probably a good thing.

During the course you will learn to "feel" "the onset of a stall or spin, to react calmly and correctly to collapses, and be secure in your ability to lose height quickly.

There is little point in doing a manoeuvre just once.

The primary object of SIV training is to learn to prevent and recover from unstable situations, and to do this you must be reasonably familiar with them. To go on a course like this and have "done" a spin for example is almost worthless. Far better to have identified an incipient spin and successfully recovered from it several times. Repetitive practice is the key to all these tasks.

A real eye-opener to many pilots is the difference between a typical first time buyer's wing and higher rated wings. The high aspect ratio and faster wings are, interestingly, often easier to control during less severe asymmetric tucks, and will usually wingover much better, due to improved energy retention, but the behaviour in a spin, or if most of the wing is lost in a severe asymmetric, can be much more radical.

The first time wings tend to self-recover in smooth conditions if the pilot is not sure what to do and does nothing. With some higher-level wings, the situation can deteriorate very quickly if the pilot is not quick and decisive in his actions.

It follows that if you have ambitions to fly a glider which requires pilot input to recover from unstable situations (DHV 2 or equivalent), then an SIV course is probably the best way to acquire these skills.

When your SIV course is completed, you should be more confident in your ability to deal with unexpected situations, and should be a better pilot for it.

Bernard Kane after his practice reserve deployment.

Expedition and Safari Flying

The beauty of a paraglider is its portability. Moving a sailplane, a microlight or even a hang-glider to a remote location can be a major logistical challenge.

Taking a paraglider with you on holiday is as simple as carrying it to the airport.

Some pilots have been quick to capitalise on this aspect of the sport, and paragliders have been flown in Antarctica, from mountains on every continent, in deserts and over jungles.

Of course flying the Himalayas, or the Great Rift valley requires a little more planning than your local hill, and all the advice given in "Flying Abroad" is even more applicable.

You may need to carry spares such as line material and repair tape. For long trips you will need food and bivouac gear like tents or stoves, and of course you will need maps and probably a GPS.

Naturally you will need a harness and wing capable of carrying all this.

In recent years some manufacturers and pilots have come up with wings and harnesses that are specifically tailored to portability and ease of use in extreme situations.

Very lightweight expedition paragliders are available that can be packed very small for climbing and long carry-ups. Harnesses are also available in a huge variety of styles that include those with no seat plank at all for fly-down use only, and those with massive storage space for all your kit. The French harness company Sup-air (whose founder Pierre Bouilloux is one of the original bivouac flyers) even produce a purpose-built tent that fits in your pocket and weighs in at less than 1kg.

There is a kind of sub culture of ultra-light gear users that is steadily becoming more popular as pilots venture further afield and as the mainstream equip-

The essence of travel with a paraglider. One of Pierre Bouilloux's bivouac sites during his 'vol bivouac' traverse of the Pyranees. (Photo: Sup'Air)

You are nearly allways given a warm welcome when you drop in on your paraglider! Children from a small Himalayan village near Manali, India. (Photo: Neil Cruickshank)

ment gradually gets more sophisticated, but also heavier and bulkier.

Innovations from outside the sport like satellite phones, lightweight digital movie cameras, solar powered battery chargers and of course GPs systems, have all made flying in remote parts of the world just a bit easier and more accessible.

Expedition flying does require a different mindset, as, despite all these toys, essentially you will be cutting yourself off from the infrastructure of prepared launch areas and help from others. This is a big step, and you will be pioneering in the true sense. Clearly it carries increased risks, but

The Karakorum range, Pakistan. (Photo: John Silvester, www.flyskyhigh.net)

Flying over the desert near the Red Sea, Israel.
(Photo: Apco Aviation Ltd)

this is an element of the sport that encapsulates the feeling that attracts many into flying in the first place: total self-reliance and complete freedom.

Whether you are flying dunes in the Sahara or glaciers in Siberia, flying in unknown territory is an experience that you never forget. The look of incredulity on the faces of the local people who have probably never seen anything like a paraglider is an experience in itself.

Expedition flyers are unanimous in their discovery that some of the world's poorest and most isolated people are among the most generous of spirit and welcoming of strangers. Paragliding certainly gives you a talking point when you drop in.

Acro Flying

One of the reasons that we fly is that we enjoy testing our own limits. Another strong reason is that we all have an exhibitionist tendency to a greater or lesser degree. Certainly we all enjoy the praise and approval of our flying colleagues. To some with competitive instincts this is manifested in a desire to enter competitions, and this has been a driving force in the improving standards of our equipment.

For a few pilots, the most interesting area of flight is in aerobatic flying. Paragliders are quite possibly the least conventionally aerobatic of all aircraft, in the sense that they can be collapsed and alter shape in mid air in difficult-to-predict ways. But for aerobatic pilots this is simply another challenge, and the discipline of Acro flying has steadily attracted more pilots over the years. Acro flying is a mixture of the technical and the artistic and is - to pilots and the public alike - fascinating to watch.

Acro competitions are held in various locations which have similar requirements to SIV courses, as the chance of a catastrophic failure and the need to deploy a reserve is reasonably high compared to most flying situations. They are typically flown from mountain sites overlooking lakes, but can also be winch launched (though this will give limited altitude), and there are even plans to drop the pilots from a helicopter for future competitions.

Big wing-over. (Photo: Swing Gliders)

A typical Acro sequence will involve a number of manoeuvres, which are linked into one another to give a display sequence. This is marked in competitions by a panel of judges who give points for difficulty and presentation.

Elements of an Acro display may include:

Spins

Where the canopy is rotating horizontally through a vertical axis. If the centre of rotation is outside the wing, the canopy can be kept fully inflated.

Photo: Neil Cruickshank

Helicopters

A variation of the spin, where the axis of rotation is inside the wing-span, so that effectively part of the wing is flying backwards. Depending on the internal pressure in the wing this can cause the portion flying backwards to collapse and fold under (rather like a big-ear in reverse). This can further tighten the spin.

MC Twist

Invented by Raul Rodriguez, the Mc Twist is an advanced figure that even he cannot explain…

Misty Flip

A variation that has evolved from the McTwist. (That's clear then).

SAT

Invented by the flyers of the interestingly named Safety Acro Team, this figure takes its name from their team initials. It is hard, to describe accurately, even

after having watched it done in slow motion! The glider is descending in a spiral somewhat like a regular spiral dive, but with the centre of rotation between the pilot and wing. The pilot is therefore rotating in the opposite direction to the glider. This manoeuvre is unlike anything found in any other form of aerobatic aviation!

Spirals

Linked 360 degree turns where the centrifugal force throws the pilot out at 90degrees to the wing. The nose-down attitude of the wing and fast rotation mean that height is lost very rapidly (the flight path is similar to the thread on a drill bit). This manoeuvre generates massive speed and therefore energy, which can then be converted into a wingover or other figure.

When continued to ground level (when a wing tip or hand touches the ground), this is known as a 'death spiral'.

Wingovers

When a glider has excess energy, either from a series of pitching movements, or from linked turns, a hard control input can generate a high banked turn. Turns of more than 90degrees are known as wingovers, and Acro pilots frequently link wingovers into one another, achieving angles of bank of 140degrees or more, where their bodies are completely above the wing, which remains fully inflated and flying normally.

Loops

The logical extension of the wingover is a loop, and given sufficient energy the pilot can achieve a positive loop (ie with lines tight all the way over). If there is not quite enough energy to pull a full "G" all the way over, the lines may go slack as the pilot free- falls for a moment until the loading is resumed.

Tumbles

The wing is no longer flying as an aircraft but is falling in an unstable manner rather like a leaf or paper bag in the wind.

Accuracy

The old favourite with the crowds is trying to land on a specific spot. This is a skill in itself, and in Acro comps the spot is frequently placed on a beach, or even on a floating pontoon, so that the pilots can make stylish approaches in relative safety. Spiralling until one wing-tip touches the water before levelling up on a final approach is a real crowd pleaser, and demands commitment and perfect timing.

©2002 Red Bull - www.redbull-vertigo.com

©2001 www.redbull-vertigo.com

Synchro

What could be more thrilling than watching a pilot doing a superb Acro routine? The answer is watching two or more pilots doing them in synchronisation. This is, of course, more of a display than a competition, and demands excellent communication and teamwork. Flying a manoeuvre like a spiral dive or wingover in close proximity to another pilot also demands a high degree of trust in each others abilities!

Stacks

It is a short step from Synchro to stacking, ie linking canopies and pilots together in some way. This is already a favourite activity among sport parachutists, and it is likely to become a feature of future Acro competitions.

Testing new wings.

If competitions and aerobatics are not exciting enough for you, there is always being a test pilot! (In fact several top Acro flyers and competitors are designers and test pilots by profession)

Testing new canopies falls into two categories. There are professional pilots who work for the

This page: Death spiral to landing (top). Perhaps not the most elegant landing Robbie Whitall has ever done, but on the pontoon nevertheless! (middle). Acro judges Alex Louw and Alain Zoller at the Extreme Sports event in Norway 2002.
(Photos: Neil Cruickshank)

237

testing authorities and whose job is to allocate ratings to production wings.

Each manufacturer also has development test pilots whose remit is to work with the other members of the design team to refine the prototype craft into saleable products. Tasks can vary from trying to remove creases from the leading edge by endless launching, landing and trimming the wing to checking the recovery characteristics in a stall and making modifications to the design. Much initial design work is now done with computer aided design programmes, but there is still no substitute for getting the craft into the air. The process of designing and testing a new wing is covered in Chapter 38.

The State of the Art, Innovations & the Future...

At the time of writing (July 2003), the top performance canopies are offering a sink rate of around 0.9m per second. This is similar to the wings of the last two or three years, but the real improvement has come at the top end of the speed range: 50kph + top speeds and glide performance of 8.5or 9:1 are now achievable and on these machines cross-country flights are becoming more and more commonplace. The world open distance record is currently 421km, and even more notably, the distance and average speed being achieved in international competition tasks is still climbing steadily. Perhaps the most important achievement, however, is that the wings aimed at the recreational pilots are now only a very small performance margin behind those of the top competition pilots, and the safety and security offered by them far superior to that available just a few years ago.

Interestingly, the price of paragliders and equipment has reduced steadily over the last few years as well; there has never been a better time to get involved!

Over the last few years prototypes have been flown that are swept forward, contain spanwise battens, have air intakes on the underside of the wing, valved entries, and ever more sealed cells. There is a trend for an ever-decreasing number of lines.

Perhaps the most enduring and notable changes in the last few years have not been in the wings themselves but the in

the harnesses and instruments we fly with.

Harnesses have evolved enormously, and the addition of air and foam spinal protection systems has been a major change. On the instrument side, the revolution in navigation caused by the handheld global positioning system has had a major impact.

What of the future? Prices will need to remain low, and the sport will become ever safer, and more accessible (as it has been doing) to keep growing and to remain attractive to a wide range of people.

It will never be a huge mass-appeal sport, as most people are not that keen on throwing themselves off mountains into space. But as we continue to buy sites and work with local communities and landowners it will become more firmly established.

The biggest threat to paragliding is the insurance situation. Insurers are worried by the prospect of big payouts to injured people, and are shunning many activities that involve risk. A few high profile claims could make us uninsurable.

In the UK the trend is no longer for the hardened enthusiast who racks up thousands of hours and spends almost every weekend out on the hills, but for pilots who enjoy their sport by flying on a few of the best days of the year at home, and taking two or three week's holiday a year flying in the Alps, or perhaps somewhere warm like the Canaries, Greece or Cyprus. Spring and autumn have become the favourite times for flying trips to destinations like this, or winter for combining skiing and flying or travelling to the southern hemisphere.

This is the same pattern for many sports, from scuba diving to windsurfing and of course has always been the norm for skiing. With our busy lives, our sports and hobbies have to fit in with a million other things.

Sports go in and out of fashion in our culture, and paragliding has certainly had its meteoric rise, but it has now set-tled to a more sustainable level of development, and with the explosion in TV channels and media available, and development of the new and visually appealing discipline of Acro flying, it has a bright future.

Flying is one of mankind's oldest dreams, yet sport flying just for fun has always been very inaccessible. You needed time, money and expertise to get airborne, making it impractical for many people. Paragliding makes flying accessible to a huge range of people; it is well established and still growing. After all, a flying machine you can carry with you wherever you travel, or store under your bed, is a dream come true for most of us.

FreeX Gliders

Information Section

Useful web addresses

National associations

British Hang- Gliding and Paragliding Association (BHPA)

The Old schoolroom
Loughborough rd
Leicester
LE 1 5PJ
UK

Tel : 0870 8706190

e-mail Elaine@ bhpa.co.uk

www.bhpa.co.uk

United States Hang-gliding & Paragliding Association.

www.ushga.org

FFVL (French Association)

www.ffvl.fr

DHV (German Association)

www.dhv.de

Australian Federation

www.hgfa.asn

New Zealand

www.nzhpa.org

Canada

www.hpac.co/pub

Korea

www.kpga.or.kr

Hong Kong

www.glink.net.hk

Israel

www.users.actcom.co.il

Italy

www.fivl.it

Denmark

www.danskdrageflyverunion.dk

Sweden

www.paragliding.se

Switzerland

www.shv-fsvl.ch

S Africa

www.paragliding.co.sa/sahpa

Weather Information.

UK weather forecasts

www.bbc.co.uk/weather.

www.met-office.gov.uk

Actual weather at launch sites: www.wendywindlblows.com

Weather Jack, gliding weather: www.itadvice.co.uk/weatherjack/wx.htm

Meteogram models using US prediction model: http://www.arl.noaa.gov/ready/cmet.html

Aviation weather, Europe: http://www.phd.nl/aviation/wx/

USA weather forecasts

www.windcall.com

European weather

http://www.phd.nl/aviation/wx/

Other Useful Information

FAI (Federation Aeronautique Internationale)

www.fai.org

Parapro rating information & record data

www.fai.org/hang_gliding/documents/parapro.asp

Paragliding world Cup data inc pilot rankings

www.pwca.org

UK Air chart updates

www.caa.co.uk/dap

AFNOR (Glider certification data)

www.afnor.fr

DHV (Glider certification data)

www.dhv.de

UK National Cross-country League

www.pottyplace.com/xcl.html

Further Reading

Skywings Magazine (BHPA publication)

Subscriptions : BHPA office.

Editor: Joe Schofield, skywings@bhpa.co

Pilot Handbook

Mark Dale

Paramotoring From the Ground Up

Noel Whittal

Meteorology and Flight

Tom Bradbury

Understanding Flying Weather

Derek Piggott

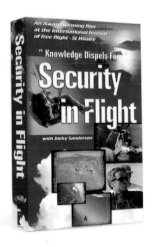
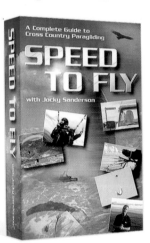

NORTHERN PARAGLIDING

Since 1988

Photo: Patrick Holmes

TUITION IN UK

Headed by Touching Cloudbase author, Ian Currer and based in the beautiful, uncrowded Yorkshire Dales, our team offer a full range of BHPA courses in the Dales and Lakes.

TUITION ABROAD

Beat the bad weather!! We offer beginner courses on the famous Dune de Pyla near Bordeaux, France and Club Pilot courses in Cyprus. We also have a range of holidays to many excellent locations.

MAIL ORDER

We are the mail order specialists, please ring for a copy of our 32 page, FREE catalogue, Paragliders Direct.

EQUIPMENT

We offer an unrivalled choice of new and used equipment. We have a massive ONLINE SHOP. We are importers for several major brands.

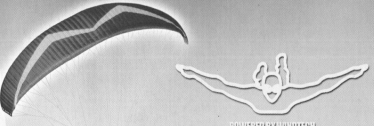

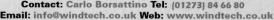

Glossary of Terms

"A" line

Line to the leading edge of the wing

ACPULS

Now defunct European airworthiness testing body

Aerodynamics

The study of moving air

Aerofoil

The shape of a section through a wing

AFNOR

Current European airworthiness body.

Airspeed

The speed of the aircraft through the air

Angle of attack

The angle at which the airflow meets the wing

Aspect ratio

The ratio of the span to the average chord (width) of the wing

ATZ

Aerodrome traffic zone

Brake

Control used to alter the speed or direction of the wing

"B" line stall

A manoeuvre to disrupt the smooth flow over a wing by pulling down the "B" lines

Chord

Straight line distance from the leading edge to the trailing edge at any given point on the span.

Cirrus

Very high ice clouds

Cumulus

A "heaped" cloud found above thermals

Drag ailerons

The correct term for the control system of the paraglider

Dyneema

A type of line material

Flare

Either the action of applying full brake hard to slow down on landing, or a triangular piece of cloth that helps to distribute evenly the load from a line

Glide ratio

Ratio of distance travelled horizontally to the height lost

GPS

(Global Positioning System) - a hand held navigational instrument

Groundspeed

The speed of the aircraft over the ground

Keeper

A ring or pulley sewn to the rear riser to retain the control line

Kevlar

A type of line material

Lift

Either the upward force created by the action of the aerofoil, or air that is rising faster than the wing is sinking

Lapse rate

The rate of temperature decrease with height

Maillon rapide

Trade name of the steel links used to connect the lines to the risers and sometimes the risers to the harness

MATZ

Military aerodrome traffic zone

Min(imum) sink rate

The canopy's slowest rate of descent

Pitch

Rotation of an aircraft through lateral axis (nose up or down)

PLF

Parachute landing fall

Polyester

Type of canopy fabric

Rip-stop nylon

Type of canopy fabric

Riser

Webbing connecting the harness to the lines

Roll

Rotation of an aircraft through its longitudinal axis (banking)

Sink

Descending air

Stall

Point at which the airflow over the wing breaks away an there is no longer sufficient lift to support the aircraft

Thermal

Bubble of a column of rising air

Wind gradient

Reduction in wind speed near the ground due to friction

Conversions

1 knot	=	1.15 mph
1mph	=	1.609 kph
1kph	=	0.622 mph
1kg	=	2.204 lbs
1,000ft	=	305 metres
1000 metres	=	3,280 ft

Index